P9-ELG-045

Universal Wisdom
A Philosophy for the Modern Age

Benoit Chartier

Copyright © 2019 by Benoit Chartier

Cover illustration by Curtis Tiegs, www.ninjatitan.com
Edited, and layout by Fiona Plunkett, Beyond The Realm
www.beyondtherealm.ca

All rights reserved. No part of this publication may be reproduced,
distributed, or transmitted in any form or by any means, including
photocopying, recording, or other electronic or mechanical methods,
without the prior written permission of the publisher, except in the
case of brief quotations embodied in critical reviews and certain other
non-commercial uses permitted by copyright law. For permission
requests, write to the publisher, addressed "Attention: Permissions
Coordinator," at the address below.

Trode Publications
www.trode.ca

Ordering Information:
Quantity sales. Special discounts are available on quantity purchases by
corporations, associations, and others. For details, contact the
publisher at the address above.

Orders by U.S. and Canadian trade bookstores and wholesalers. Please
contact Trode Publications at www.trode.ca

Printed in Canada

ISBN 978-1-989550-01-4
1. The main category of the book —History —Other category.
2. Another subject category —From one perspective. 3. More categories
—And their modifiers. I. Johnson, Ben. II. Title.

HF0000.A0 A00 2010
299.000 00–dc22 2010999999

First Edition

I'd like to thank my wife Mariko and my two boys: Kota and Zenji for being a wonderful family. I'd like to thank everyone on the human spectrum for *being*. I'd like to thank this Universe for having supported us as long as it has. It's not always easy.

Other Books by Benoit Chartier

The Calumnist Mafesto and Other Improbable Yarns
Red Nexus
Afterdeath

"This is my simple religion. There is no need for temples; no need for complicated philosophy. Our own brain, our own heart is our temple; the philosophy is kindness."

Dalai Lama

"The problem, often not discovered until late in life, is that when you look for things in life like love, meaning, motivation, it implies they are sitting behind a tree or under a rock. The most successful people in life recognize, that in life they create their own love, they manufacture their own meaning, they generate their own motivation. For me, I am driven by two main philosophies, know more today about the world than I knew yesterday. And lessen the suffering of others. You'd be surprised how far that gets you."

Neil deGrasse Tyson

Universal Wisdom
A Philosophy for the Modern Age

Table of Contents

Universal Wisdom

Preface

Q: What is this thing I'm holding/reading?

A: It's a toolbox.

Q: It doesn't look like a toolbox. Why does it look like a book?

A: Because it is. When you think of a toolbox, you might think of a red metal box filled with drill-bits and a hammer, measuring tape and a level, etc. But a tool can be all sorts of things. Some of the best tools we have are the tools in our heads. They are the tools we use to cope with the world around us. They help us navigate it, comprehend it, beat it into submission or live in harmony with it. It all depends on how we decide to treat the infinite universe as a construct.

Q: Why do I need to read this toolbox?

A: Short answer? You don't. You can put it down and forget about it. You can burn it. There is no pressure put upon you to keep going. All I do is provide a toolbox. It's up to you to decide whether you want to open it and peek inside. There's no click-baity tag line that will make you try to believe you can't live without it, however, you might find, simple tools you could apply to your life to make it easier. That's what I think I provide. Then again, you might not think so, and you'll put that tool down and look for a different one. Either way, you gain someone else's perspective, which is how we learn things and grow as people. It's win-win for you.

Q: Why is it called *Universal Wisdom*?

A: It went through many iterations. It started off as an idea I had with a friend a decade ago. We called it "Les Néo-Moralistes Globales Uni-fiés," or "Unified Global Neo-Moralists." Basically a name with nothing attached. I have to credit my friend Sébastien Lapointe for coming up with it. It was meant to signify a new global morality. Something for everyone. It was then that I started searching for global themes. It transformed into a thing called "Being Human," and then became "Universal Sentience," and is now *Universal Wisdom*.

Q: That's not an answer. That's a history. You're boring and I'm going to put the book down if you don't give me straight answers. Why is it called *Universal Wisdom*?

A: Sorry. Universal meaning the entire Universe, and Wisdom for the better use of our minds. The idea is that there are common themes that could be applied to all sentient beings in the Universe, if they wished to attain *wisdom*.

Q: The entire Universe? Aren't you reaching a bit?

A: Not really. There have been millions of galaxies counted. Each galaxy contains millions of stars. Each star could have dozens of planets circling them. The possibility of being alone in the Universe is infinitesimally small. The fact that we haven't met anyone from a different planet does not preclude their existence.

Q: You believe in aliens?

A: Undoubtedly. Whether or not they actually have come to visit is subject for debate, however, that's not why I flung the door wide open to this topic.

Q: Why is it, then?

A: Artificial constructs.

Q: Artificial *what*?

A: Constructs. The ability to create things that would not grow from nature – structures that we build, whether physical, societal, or metaphorical.

Q: How's that related to Universal Wisdom?

A: Because we live in artificial constructs. Right now. Societies, as we speak, are artificial constructs. Money is an artificial construct. Government is an artificial construct. They have specific rules and boundaries, laws and diktats, punishments and rewards. We don't ask questions about them because, well, most of us don't generally question. Each society has their own rules that help them cope with their internal struggles, and external pressures.

Q: Why do you call them *artificial constructs* though? They seem to be working just fine?

A: Ah, you seem to be confusing *artificial* with *fake*. No, societies, money and government are very real things, obviously. You won't find groups of people living in anything much bigger than a tribe, or extended family, unless you have internal pressure to make the group bigger.

Q: Why do you say that?

A: Because unless we develop mental tools to cope with inhabiting in extremely large groups, we tend to break down into smaller pockets of like-minded individuals. Think of people in your own family who might not get along. Now think of how much harder it might be for a group of thousands, or even millions of people to come together as a group, to move in the same direction, so to speak.

Q: So why did this happen in the first place?

A: Like a lot of things humans do and create, for survival. It's only a matter of time before another group, or several, come together to crush another. Whether for resources, living space, violent tendencies borne out of fear, etc. It's in our best interest to shape ideas that will make it so that we can continue to exist as a community. We've been doing it for thousands of years.

Q: Okay, so name me one *idea* that people have created to get along this way.

A: Love thy neighbor. Yes, religious thought. One of the first and most effective ways of promoting rapid growth in populations was religion. It is also an artificial construct. You won't see squirrels building altars to squirrel gods.

Q: Right, but that's pretty obvious. Everyone should, technically, love their neighbor. You're not turning religious on me, right? I was starting to enjoy this read.

A: Is it obvious, though? If you look around the planet, there are a lot of things that for the local populations look *obvious*. It's *obvious* to certain people that female genital mutilation is a *natural* thing. It's *obvious* to others that raising dogs to cook them while they're still alive is a *natural* thing to do. Just like there are a million examples of things that are *natural* and *obvious* to others, these things are weird and kind of gross to you. The same can be said of the things you do, from the point of view of other cultures.

Q: Sure, but what I do is the right thing, the natural thing. How does that relate to artificial constructs?

A: What you consider normal is a product of the length of time you have been doing it, and the amount of people around you who do it as well. It relates to artificial constructs because there are certain common themes inherent to almost everyone on the planet. The smallest natural construct was the family and tribe, and we endeavored to grow it to Nation States (Cities that were countries unto themselves. Think Babylon, Ur, Nineveh, and a few other cities from ancient times. Civilization was everything within the walls. Outside was chaos and banditry). Then we created religions, artificial thought constructs with their inherent logics. The largest and most vast artificial construct we've come to is Religion, followed by the Nation. A land-mass controlled and protected by a government.

Q: And?

A: It's no longer enough. We need a new paradigm.

Q: Why?

A: Because we are an ever-renewing population on a finite world with finite resources and we are drowning in garbage. Soon we will drown in internal and external wars to control what is left of our natural resources. That is, if the rising temperature doesn't kill oxygen-producing organisms first.

Q: That's pretty grim. How do you propose we solve this problem?

A: My father used to say: "We don't solve a problem. We displace it." Before you call me cryptic, let me give you an example: before the advent of the automobile, cities were drowning in horse shit. Thousands of horses went through every major city on Earth until the twentieth century. Problem. Someone invents a viable alternative, the automobile. Problem solved? Not quite. There may have been little to no horse poop to sully the streets and create a stink on a hot summer's day anymore, but there was now a whole lot of pollution created by cars. So, we got rid of a problem, and created another. What I'm proposing is that we displace our problem by heading out to the next frontier: space. Before we do so, however, I would like to see the planet returned to a more or less pristine

18

state, and the people living there still, getting along. This takes a different way of thinking about how we live. And if we are to go into space, I would like it to be with a different mindset. More explorer than conqueror. It would be nice if we learned from out past mistakes.

Q: You watch a lot of *Star Trek*, don't you?

A: Here's the thing: when you imagine the future, do you see *Mad Max*, or *Star Trek*? Do you see a handful of people scrabbling for what's left of the planet's resources, or do you see people who have grown a teensy bit wiser, and aimed for the stars?

Q: That sounds mighty Utopian. What makes you think you or anyone can achieve this?

A: Nothing tells me this. All I, or anyone else can do, is try. If you don't shoot for the moon, you can't fall among the stars. I don't want the human experiment to be over. As much as there is bad, there is good. There is, in fact, more good than bad.

Q: The world is crap, though! You can't tell me otherwise. You just have to look around you, on the news. All the raping, and killing, wars, injustice, all of it! Humans are garbage! Why do you think they're worth saving?

A: Because humanity has constant, renewable *potential*. In the grand scheme of things, we aren't much, to be sure. But look how far we've come, from a human-sized point of view, and a living, thinking being point of view. And to be fair, you're wrong about humans. Yes, a lot of humans are rapists and murderers, liars, cheaters, and worse, however, that's nowhere near the majority. If it were, none of us would have survived. Keep in mind that love whispers, and hatred screams. You can't hear the love for all the screaming sometimes, and the media is a screaming specialist. You don't get much airtime for raising a loving family, or being there for your kids, or helping older people in the day-to-day. No, you get it for the atrocities. The things that hurt, and scare, and bleed.

Q: And how is this related to artificial constructs again?

A: Because we've reached the limits of what we can achieve with Religion and Nations as binding agents for the planet and our species.

Q: "Binding agents" sounds creepy and New World Order-y. Are you trying to enslave the planet?

A: Well, if it was a cabal of secretive wealthy men and women pulling the strings in the shadows to shape societies and the planet to do their bidding, then it would be pretty New World Order-ish. What I'm proposing are a set of tools so that we all get along. As a planet, and a family of beings who all come from the same place.

Q: Kumbaya. I think you're bound to fail. Tell me again why you think this could work?

A: And again, there are no guarantees, except the ones that, if you try something, you might achieve something. If you try nothing, you achieve what?

Q: I ask the questions. But the answer is *nothing*. It just seems like expending a lot of energy working on something that simply will not work. Why even bother?

A: There are a slew of ways of dealing with reality as we perceive it. They boil down to: accept it, deny it, work to change it.

Q: Still not answering the question. What makes it worth working toward?

A: Right. It all has to do with the easy versus the difficult path. There are things that you can do in your life that make everything easy, or at least seem to. You can just coast along, and even though it might seem hard at times, the only other option is to work toward something else. If the effort is greater in change than in remaining the same, we often choose to keep the status quo.

Q: What do you mean by that?

A: For example: let's say you walk every day. Getting to where you want to go takes a lot of time, you have to plan around it, etc. The alternative is getting a driver's licence. But then you have to take courses, both practical and written, you have to take tests, you have to pay for all this… so in the end you might decide you don't want to go through all the trouble, and you just decide to keep walking.

Q: Why can't I take the bus?

A: Because it's a magical, bus-less world. It's just an example. There are a lot of these examples that you can think of. Studying is one of them. You need to study to learn, and learning is one of the most important things we can do to add to our tool box. The down-side is that learning mostly comes from the act of reading, which is hard for a lot of people. There are a million things we can do to entertain ourselves which require no effort. The hard things we do change us forever, in ways we can't even measure. But that's the crux of the matter: they're hard.

Q: Are you saying people are lazy?

A: You could put it that way, or you could say they don't have the proper motivation.

Q: Why is it so important to learn things anyway? I'm done school. I don't need to keep reading, or learning for that matter. I know enough.

A: A lot of people seem to think so. Personally, I can never know enough. Every new answer brings with it a new question. That's the thrill of living for me: never having all the answers. But to answer your question, I should ask you one of my own: is it better to go around in life unable to go through certain doors, or to be able to walk through them with ease?

Q: Depends on the door, I guess, but yeah, being able to go through the doors I want to is pretty important. What does that have to do with knowledge?

A: In this case, knowledge really is the key to unlocking doors. The more things you know how to unlock, the better locksmith you become. Until there are no secrets for you, unless you choose not to pursue them.

Q: I've got better things than knowledge, though. I have a car, a house, a stereo, and my computer. How is knowledge better than all that?

A: Oh, it's not, because we're comparing pineapples with chainsaws now. Knowledge is different, in that it is transportable with you at all times. Objects are important, of course, but can't give you the same satisfaction, no matter how hard people try to convince you otherwise.

Q: So, artificial constructs, *Universal Wisdom*, how does all that fit together.

A: Well, in analyzing what we are and what we do, as humans, I've come up with my own personal philosophy, which is A) A thought process to live in harmony with other people, B) A goal to strive for, and C) A system of living to help those in need.

Q: What makes you think we need any of that?

A: Well, I've been analyzing things, as I've said, and I see a lot of finger-pointing as to the causes of social disintegration, and have come up with my own conclusions.

Q: Are you better than a social scientist with a degree?

A: What? Me? No! Not by far. But I have *some* insights, and *maybe* they are true. They seem true to me anyhow. I'll leave it for others to gauge the validity of my claims.

Q: Why should I trust you?

A: Because I want to give you the tools to create a more just, more harmonious world?

Q: I'm not convinced. Seriously, why should I trust you?

A: As I've said before, I don't want to try and convince you of anything. All I have is a tool box, and I want to share the tools I've created. You don't have to take a single one if you don't want to. As a matter of fact, you should remain sceptical. That's probably one of the best attitudes to have: question everything.

Q: Fine. But I'm watching you!

A: …And I'm thankful for your presence.

Q: What kind of tools are we talking about, anyway? You said they were mental tools, but you didn't really elaborate.

A: Let me narrow it down. A lot. For me, there is the logical and the emotional. For some, that's the same thing. For me, the hardest part is pinpointing a beginning. That one moment from which everything can spring forth and branch out, making sense as much to the writer as to you, the reader.

The problem in this case, is that everything is interrelated, and there is no easy beginning from which we can take a simple stroll from, walking down a straight path from start to finish. This can be done when taking every single detail and unrolling them, but not when we consider something as complex as the human mind, which is what is at stake, in this case.

We constantly try to simplify things, but what I want to discuss is complex, because it has to do with our history, our sociology, and our philosophy. It has to do with body and mind. It can't be simply unraveled as a single, unwavering path, because one thing encompasses another, and all are interrelated. I'm not trying to be cryptic, only to prepare you mentally to a different kind of thought process.

So instead of picturing a straight road, put the image of a brain in front of you. Inside this brain are millions of paths, going from neuron to neuron, firing off and thinking a million different thoughts – faster than the world's quickest computers (well, maybe not for long, the way things are going). Electrical currents are the vehicles that shoot in every direction, making us act, react, think, ponder, and emote.

From a very young age, we are taught which of the paths inside our minds we are to use, and which we are not to. Remember, inside of us are all the possibilities in the world. It's just that our education has pointed us away from certain possibilities.

We learned to sit on a toilet to pee. We learned to eat with a fork and knife. Almost everything we do in society is conditioned by the education we received, either through parents, peers, or the unsupervised wildness of nature itself (think of someone who is afraid of dogs because they were bitten as a child. That is also a lesson.)

We are action and reaction, and much of that comes from our educations. Much of the strife that exists in the world is caused by our education as well. Parents teaching their kids not to like others of a different skin tone or sexuality, cause strife. Governments who teach their citizens that it is okay to kill, cause strife. Religions that tell their adherents that marginalizing certain people or harming them is okay, causes strife.

The thing is, every individual and every group has the possibility of causing harm. It is not because someone is Atheist, Christian, Muslim, Jewish, Gay, or Straight, or any of the myriad other groups that are more prone to harm than others.

It is their thought process.

It is their education.

It is what their brains have been taught to tell their hearts.

The basis of any group, large or small, is a system. A thought system. It is our thought systems which cause us to take action, or not, and which action is preferred. More basic than that, though, is a simple fact. At the core of our being, we are emotion, and then we are thought.

What do I mean by this?

I love my wife. I want to show her my love. So I buy her flowers. My thought process is that, if I love her, she will enjoy the flowers I get her. This is an example of love as a driving emotion. I put my love in the driver's seat, and my thought process brought me to the action of showing affection by buying my wife a gift. How sweet.

Or perhaps something a bit more sinister: My parents could have taught me that certain people in society are *untouchables*, or unworthy of equal treatment. Whether through a caste system, the colour of their skin, their religion, or perhaps even their sexuality.

Having been taught to hate is not done in a vacuum: if mine taught me this, there is a strong possibility that a lot of parents in my environment have as well, and I am simply perpetuating the ordinary evil that is prejudice and hatred.

But it works in all the possible ways you can imagine your emotions working. We are, sadly, not only made of love. We are made of all the other positive as well as negative emotions that an animal can have. Hate, anger, jealousy, greed, envy, and a whole lot more, as well as their positive counterparts, love, peace, satisfaction, generosity, patience, forgiveness, and all the rest. They work either for us, or against us.

They all have their place in our mental ecosystem, but many talk out of turn, and make for dangerous societies, when too much of one or more negative trait takes up all the space.

Because that's the point of this entire exercise: the desire to live in a better society. Before you step back, telling yourself: "Well, I've heard this proposition before, and it never ended well for a lot of people." ask yourself, do you feel safe in your community? Your country? Your entire planet? If you do, you are one of the lucky few. You know that there are reasons why your society gets along without going at each other's throat. If you don't, you may want to ask yourself: why?

Why is it that my society is so dangerous, or that I am marginalized, or beaten for who I am? Is it racism, sexism, homophobia? Is it because I belong to a different class, or tribe? It is all of those reasons, but the true basis for all this discrimination is education. Educate people to accept others for who they are and they will.

Educate the elite to stop oppressing and start working for better societies as a whole, and they will stop fearing those they consider below them and work with them. Educate the authorities to stop usurping their power and they will. They key is education, and the education must come from somewhere.

Q: What if you can't educate those people?

A: Then you replace them, one way or the other.

It is all well and good to have a great *Constitution* or *Charter of Human Rights* which grants people equal rights and freedoms, but Constitutions are pieces of paper. Humans are humans and live by their own rules. Those rules are generally those of their families and communities. We all want to fit in, of course. So if the rules are unjust to some people, it becomes very difficult to want to change anything, because no one wants to rock the boat. But rock the boat we must if we want to achieve equality and justice for everyone in the community.

Here's the problem as I see it, though: the hard part is changing the mind of the oppressor. If a person is in a position of perceived power, they might very well fight change. What needs to be done is to show people that it is in fact to their advantage to want change, that there is no loss, but only gain. More safety, more opportunity, more advantages for all. And, ultimately, it is to bring that change about without asking permission or trying to change narrow-minded people's opinions.

That old adage of trading *freedom* for *safety* is false. We've already done it, and certain *freedoms* (like killing) are not needed in a society where the members respect each other.

So, there have been many attempts to create so-called "better" societies, but those attempts have been based on the wrong notion of one type of person being superior to another. This is a fallacy. There is only humanity, and the imaginary divisions we create. There is only the mind, inhabiting a body, trying to cope with a family, inside a community, inside a nation, on a planet.

We've created organization throughout history to try to make better, more peaceful societies. That's the basis of religious thought. It wasn't so much the adulation of a creator that was important, but the regulation of our own actions within a community. Think of the *Ten Commandments*. If you take away the Godly aspect of them, you have the perfect recipe for getting along with your neighbors. The same goes for Jesus' golden rule. As a matter of fact, that is the common point of all religious thought: getting along with people so that you could live a more or less peaceful life.

Because, if you think about it, there are only two ways of policing a society: actual police, because everybody is out there looking out for themselves, or self-policing, which makes sure that everybody acts in accordance to their own regulations so that we don't abuse each other, and indeed, help each other. It's that simple.

Of course we want to have *all the freedom*. Of course we want to abuse each other and ourselves, but it makes for piss-poor societies, and they decline and fall. It's only when we start putting the focus on those positive driving emotions, that we have societies that drive in the same direction.

Q: What does that mean, "driving emotion"?

A: Well, think of it this way: let's imagine that you are driving, and that your passenger all of a sudden wants to grab the wheel and do it his way. What happens? You'll crash. What if you have a nation where sixteen dozen groups want to go their own way, with their own beliefs on how to get there, and all want to drive the car? You get pretty much the same result. If you offer them all the same goal, though, as well as the proper emotional tools to get there, it doesn't matter who's driving – they'll get there, or at least strive to, and help each other on the way to that goal.

A new philosophy is *not* a new religion. We have enough of those. What we need to have is a new way of thinking about the human race, and implant it, no matter what. It is putting the Human Race above petty concerns, and greed, and jealousy, and war, to have better people. Caring people. Loving people. Organizations and religious groups are umbrellas for the people under them. What we wish to achieve is making an umbrella for humans. One that puts the individual in the position to think independently and want to learn more. It is one that wishes the survival of the planet we live on, so that all who inhabit here may do so. It is also one that considers the expansion of the human race beyond our planet of origin as paramount to the survival of the planet and our species.

As we once considered our deities to come from some nebulous place in the clouds, or even beyond the stars, (without even batting an eye or thinking it remotely odd) we must consider the possibility that at some point in time there will no longer be the resources on our planet to sustain ourselves at our present rate of consumption. We may have to leave it for our ever-increasing population to expand. This isn't some weird science fiction dream. This is a reality, and like climate change and the destruction of our only home planet, it must be addressed.

All these things I spoke of are true. If you can think of a new way of doing things, it can become the new reality. People might look at you and think: you're crazy for trying! But honestly, the price for not trying to put this world right is too much to bear. I want my kids and grandkids and all my descendants, and yours as well, to have the things they need to not only survive, but to live a good life. And for that to happen, it has to start somewhere, and it has to start with someone who believes in hope for a better life, and not only hopes it, but makes it happen as well. Because that's the power of education, and community, and love brought into action.

As I said, this the introduction. If you're intrigued, I recommend you keep reading. I filled the tool box. I understand that what I'm saying isn't for everyone. I'm not here to force anyone into anything. Just to interest those who want to make a difference to have the tools to do so. I originally wrote this as a letter to my son, but really, it's for everyone.

Q: Okay. That was a long read. Is there going to be a lot more like that?

A: Definitely. Some things can't be explained in a single sentence. And yes, I do repeat myself sometimes.

Q: So how did you come up with this concept, anyhow?

Crisis of Conscience

A: As a young man, a child, really, I already knew I was an *atheist*. I was raised a Catholic, which, however horrible it sounds, is probably one part why I did not believe. I think Salma Hayek said it best in the Kevin Smith movie Dogma: "You Catholics don't celebrate your religion, you *mourn* it!"

I think that's a fairly accurate assessment. There isn't anything in existence, or in this Universe, more boring for a child than sitting in a Catholic church for one or two hours at a stretch. Litanies are boring, organ music sucks, and wearing Sunday formal is itchy and uncomfortable. The whole pomp and ceremony thing didn't do it for me. I suppose a catholic priest would cry sacrilege and tell me that boredom is a way to be closer to God. That seems a bit weird, but not entirely inaccurate, I think.

One other part of the equation was that my father was dispensed from church duties, which to me was incredibly unfair. Why should I be subjected to this nonsense while he got off scot-free? From the beginning, I think my mother thought it would be a great idea for us to do this so that I could get some sort of moral upbringing, or belong to a non-technological Borg Collective. Whatever the reason, I hated it.

Of course, there was my main objection, ever since I was young enough to think for myself: Why should I believe in one particular God, while so many had come before Him, and yet more had come after? It made absolutely *no sense!* You had to mentally cordon off millennia of History to accept that there truly was only one of those Supreme Beings roaming the Heavens, creating us, pell-mell, and then expecting us to believe in the One True One, whichever It or He or She, or a combination of all of the above, might be. Personally, I thought it was a complete waste of time adulating any of them, since, if they did exist, none of them manifested themselves in any tangible, provable way.

Even my priest, at my First Communion preparation, when I told him I didn't want to partake in this farcical exercise of eating a dead man's flesh, told me: "Do it for your mom." Shit. You got me there, Father. So I remained a Catholic in name only until we changed church and I was old enough to attract the attention of the new priest, who wanted me as an altar boy.

Finally, it was my telling my mother this old man with the creepy grin and the wandering hands had completely turned me off of any pretense at religion that made her relent.

For years afterwards, though, I analyzed and studied what made these systems work, at the same time worrying if I, myself, was Lost with a capital "L." Those of the religious persuasion will nod their heads in agreement, that yes, I am a little lost sheep and must be returned to the fold for my immortal soul to be saved. I beg to differ. I have no soul, and it is my freedom from this burdensome imaginary body part that has finally freed me.

So, for many years I did revel in my appetites – what religious people call *sins*. But I also continued to study, and to learn, and to have funny little "a-ha!" moments.

I came to many realizations, of course, the more I read about practically everything. You see, humanity fascinates me, and so I wanted to know what made us tick; this is why I came to understand religion, as a system. When I say religion, I don't take aim at any particular branch of the overall scheme, unless I mention some aspect of it that is particular to that branch. I mean solely the theoretical system comprised of tools, with the main theme and focus being a/many divinity(ies) overlooking human activity, within a sanctioned construct.

One of my main epiphanies was that it was not part and parcel of atheism to become a nihilist or an existentialist the way that most people thought it was (although existentialism has gotten a bad rap, through no fault of Mr. Sartre's).

I'd like to stop and take a moment to thank my mother for having encouraged me in my philosophical endeavours when I was twelve or thirteen, and helped me acquire the myriad philosophy books I ingested over the next few years.

This may seem common knowledge to everyone else, but before the internet was populated with all this knowledge, and not having a formal university education at the time (or now, for that matter), I believed that what belonged to religion had to stay within religion, as if every virtue that one could have, could only be attained through this means. Therefore, having given it up, I could not take part in virtues that I (erroneously) believed were the purview of the church.

To give you an example, and this was my greatest epiphany, I didn't think I could ever Forgive, with a capital "F." Of course I could take someone's apology, but it took me an Earth-shattering realization to be able to forgive something I'd carried with me a very long time, therefore erase the harm I did to myself every time I thought of this event. Silly, I know, but I was thinking in terms of the whole system of religious "thought" being alien to me, and not the whole of human experience being available to all.

What made me smack my palm to my forehead was the conclusion that all religion had done was take human experience and appropriated it for itself, within an organized system, to regulate human behavior inside a society. For this, it utilized a reward/punishment paradigm (Heaven/Hell) brilliantly, since no one could ever come back from the afterlife and tell others: "Hey, this Heaven thing is bull-pucky!"

So since the beginning of organized society, we've been manipulated to be *good*, not out of altruism, but out of fear. Remember, the afterlife is a terrible place for those who do wrong. This isn't anything new for those who, like me, have looked at the overarching themes of Godliness, holiness, religion, etc.

What has changed, in the past few hundred years, is that we've begun to base our assumptions on research and fact. We are no longer were satisfied with: "Because I said so." which was the official line of the churches and religious doctrine (and moms everywhere).

Being a system of many tools, one of religions' was the search for the original truth. Why does it rain? Because God makes it so. Why did my wife and child die in child-birth? Because God's ways are mysterious. And so on, and so forth. We've been a superstitious lot for a long time now. A lot of people still believe in the Zodiac and mysticism, like tarot reading. It's comforting, I can't deny that.

Along came this new way of thinking, however: why don't we measure things? Why don't we investigate? That was novel.

So that measuring stick we used to see how long something was, turned into a precision microscope. We have refined the tools (and continue to do so) that we first started off with. The main thing that changed, though, was turning away from: "Because I said so." to "Hey, I wonder why that is, *really*."

This new mode of thinking also created new philosophies which were not based on the worship of deities, such as atheism.

Another tool in the religious system is purpose – and that is one of the most important things human beings have. We need to find out who we are to find out what we are for. With religion, it's easy: You are God's creature and you are here to worship Him, Her, It, They, end of story.

With science, there is no such measure, since it is not a closed system.

Q: What does that mean: A closed system?

A: It means it's a system of exploration, and therefore, cannot tell you *who* you are, only what you're made of, and what makes you tick, to a limited degree. That new answers have to be sought outside of what we know within the system.

That is one of the main reasons for the title of this piece. My crisis of conscience comes from the fact that I am completely free. So what is my purpose, if it's not to worship (what is for me) an imaginary God? That is entirely up to me, and that's something that depressed me for a long time. Why? Because of the infinite possibilities – within the realm of humanity, of course. It's like looking into a deep well and becoming giddy at the idea of jumping.

There is also the *lack of realization* that to have a purpose brings an element to your life that if you do not have, might cause you a great deal of anguish.

So I come to this, the knot of the problem: why there is still so much religiosity, and a seeming lack of direction when it comes to Atheism?

No one wants to be rudderless on the open sea, especially in a storm.

Religion provides the rudder, and the boat, and the hymns to sing until the storm abates. Atheism proposes none of these things.

Religion offers means and ways to deal with society which have been successful, if based on fallacies, for eons. Atheism leaves you stranded.

Q: You're saying that Religion is better, basically.

A: No, just different. Like a bus and a car will take you there, but are different methods of transportation. One can carry more people.

Atheism is, by nature, a kind of solitary endeavour because it is not organized, and has no avowed purpose for its adherents (or non-adherents, if you prefer). They simply do not believe in the supernatural. They believe in the provable, the empirical truths that science provides. They exist within the flotsam and jetsam of what little religious doctrine has been passed through their families, existing as *right* and *wrong*, but with no all-encompassing, stronger conviction.

I propose that is the reason that, even though there is a lessening of the grip of religion on societies where its abuses have been the strongest, there is also a losing of a generalized sense of purpose in those societies. Because we don't believe in God anymore, we don't know what to believe in. So we turn to the worship of money, of sex, of objects, of power, and all those things religious scholars knew were wrong. That's a valid point, I think.

The thing is, what should we believe in, what should we work toward, and how will we get there?

Well, that's why I've written this treatise I call *Universal Wisdom*. It's proposing a roadmap to something positive and uplifting.

Q: That's where it comes from, then. So how do you go from the present world situation to what you're proposing, exactly. I mean, this won't happen overnight, right?

A: Of course. But, like I said, we perpetuate things through the ideas we propagate. It's by using a set of ideals that people derive solace in, which brings them joy, which helps them navigate a harsh natural (and human) world, gives them hope, and purpose, and helps them build something together that we might be able to get the ball rolling. It's creating a system where, even though you can't get all the answers, you can at least get an inkling of where to start searching. It all begins with the basic education we give our children, of what is good, what is bad, and what they should strive for. It's about giving them advantages we didn't have, and avoiding the mental mistakes we made.

Pretty much everything that comes after this was written for my kids, and I wrote it with them in mind. It does apply to anyone, though.

Introduction

1 Hey little ones, how are you doing? As I write this, you have no idea who I am, apart from "dad," and one day you'll read this and probably be embarrassed to hell, but I don't care. Why? Because I love you. Even though I don't know what kind of person you are, or how you will turn out, I want to put every single chance on your side, and that's the reason I wrote this: for you.

We have a tradition among human beings, those others that you've met and will continue to meet, and will have to deal with for the rest of your life. The tradition is that we try to make things a little easier for our children than they were for ourselves. To give them more choices than what we had.

We all do it in different ways, and with different results, but I believe that if I give you the right information, you might be able to avoid some of the grief that I went through.

Don't get me wrong, I won't stop life from happening to you; that would be a cruel thing to do. I only want you to be properly equipped to handle what it tosses at your face: the good, the great, the bad, the sad, and everything else.

You see, there are people who mistakenly believe that overprotecting their children will somehow save them from the vicissitudes of life (that means the poo life tosses at you). The truth is, there is no one that will take care of you better than yourself, later on. For that reason, you should be well prepared and autonomous.

Don't be afraid, though. Being a self-reliant person does not mean you are alone, far from it. It is just as important to be able to surround yourself with caring, loving people as it is to be able to do things on your own. The idea is that you have choices available in the way you deal with every situation you encounter in your life. You will be reliant on yourself and the people that are a part of it.

Yes, you read me right. You will make friends, you have family, you will work with others, and you will never be alone unless you want to be. The people you choose to associate with will help or hinder, propel you forward or hold you back. Your choices will determine whether they are good companions for you, or if you are a worthy one for them.

It all sounds very confusing, I know. That's why I'll teach you all this stuff slowly, so you have plenty of time to understand it all. I think I'm also writing this down so I don't forget anything (I have a terrible memory. Ask your mother, she'll tell you often.) and be able to remind myself the things I should know as well.

This is my love letter to you. I think it might get longish, but hey, that just means there's more of me you get to remember when I'm no longer around! Maybe some of the stuff I'll write down doesn't make sense. I am aware that that might be the case.

The thing is, at different points in your life, you will understand different things.

Have patience; that is one of the most important things you can develop. Patience.

You cannot have everything you want when you want it. Being able to wait for something is often an even better reward than getting it the moment you realize you want it, and keeping a cool head to achieve something is honestly one of the best traits you can adopt.

So please, please, please be patient with your parents, as much as we will try to be patient with you. We will try to answer all your questions, and help you achieve all your goals, I promise.

I think back on my own childhood now, and a moment of dread just crossed my entire being. That is something you will feel when your first child will be on its way, but not now.

Not yet.

You still have some growing to do, and some living, and some playing, and some learning, and loving, and discovering.

You'll also have plenty of confusion, anger, sadness, frustrations, and bewilderment, and all these things are completely normal.

I have to tell you though, it's mostly all about love. It doesn't seem so, often, but it is. There are millions upon millions of people on this earth, where you will decide where to settle down one day and make your home, and they survive through love.

That is how we survive, and thrive. If we didn't there would be none of us left.

Welcome to life, kiddos. It's everything you didn't expect and more.

Whenever I think that I'm writing my first "words of wisdom" as a dad, I get a little choked up. I have a vision of you in my mind, and I can't help but smile, thinking about you. Like every parent, I will want you to be perfect, even though you're not. I will put pressure on you to be better than you are, even though you don't want to. All these terrible tortures I will put you through, I will do because I care for you.

It's hard to know where to get started, because everything is not simple. Living your life is the most complex thing you will ever be faced with, no doubt about it. I imagine you shaking your head yes, wide-eyed, wondering where all this is heading.

Even though you will have, up to a point, lived with the truths we have imposed upon you, you will come to question those truths. Naturally, if the answers we have given you for the truths we hold dear are unsatisfactory, you'll go looking for your own somewhere else.

That's part of growing up, and becoming your own person. We couldn't expect you to become an individual if you were to only believe what your parents had to say. This is why it is so important for you to be open to as many possibilities as you can be, since restricting yourself to a single answer cannot cover all that is within the realm of human thought.

Be aware, though, that not everything that is said is the truth. Nothing is ever *perfect*, in the human world, but that doesn't mean we are not *perfectible*, we try to become 'better' all the time. Perfectible, or *better*, mean different things to different people though, depending on what their values are. The fact that we never will be *perfect* shouldn't detract you from the attempt at bettering yourself.

It is an ideal that can never be reached, and everybody dies on the road to it, but it is the journey that reveals everything about who you are.

Everybody has their own version of what that ideal goal is. Their methodology reveals their philosophy. Their philosophy is their truth. Their truth is their lives. I can't tell you what the "best way" to be is. I can only tell you what my "best way" is, and what I believe. I have no choice but to imprint in you these beliefs, because if I didn't do so, I'd be raising you with what to me amount to lies. That's why I'll have to ask you to forgive us for raising you in our image and that of the world that surrounds us. It's how I see it, how I live it, and how I would like you to do the same, of course.

Q. So you don't expect your kids to be like you?

A. I'd hope they were better than me, in a lot of ways. I'm not going to pressure them to be so, however. Like I said, their lives are their own. I'll only tell them how the world is, and how they can use that to their advantage, as well as how to make it a better place.

Q. So what is the world really like, then?

2 The world is filled with competing schools of thought. As a matter of fact, you yourself are a competing school of thought within yourself.

You rebuke the things you hold to be false, and accept what closely resembles your philosophy of *truth*. Depending on your level of understanding, you may accept or reject some thoughts more readily.

Much of the time, that personal philosophy of yours will reflect that of those around you, since doing so will help you integrate the group to which you wish to belong. This doesn't mean that those around you are *right*, only that they have the same group-think. Your opinion of those around you and the way you define them will determine how you treat them.

For the most part, you will be surrounded by friends and family who will support you and help you.

The elements that will propel you in your growth, though, will be your challenges. It may come in the shape of new knowledge, physical hurdles, or other people, but the expansion of your abilities will rely on your willingness to face these new challenges, and overcome your own limits in the best way you will know how.

Whether in the form of competition in sports, or school, work, as well as daily life, you will be pitting yourself against hurdles at some level. Opposition is what makes you test your skills and adaptability either on your own or within a group, against a limit.

If you want to create better conditions for your overcoming of particular problems, you will learn to do so, as well as join groups who have the same goals, for mutually beneficial results (such as being on a team).

The coalition/team vs. individualism paradigm is what drives much of the world (and divides it as well). There are coalitions and oppositions in every level of society. What creates cohesiveness is the *degree* to which these two paradigms are employed.

For example, if you play hockey and you don't necessarily get along with one of the other players, the level of animosity you might have towards that person will affect the way the team plays together. It all depends on how you balance the needs of the team versus the feelings you have between you.

The same can be said on a much wider scale. The way various segments of society treat each other will affect the outcome of the cohesiveness of the population itself. It all depends on if you put your interests before the teams' or not. If you decide that your interests come first, then you will do everything in your power to discredit the player you dislike, and may garner some fame for yourself. The long-term effects will be the loss of the team.

Remember that you are not alone, even though you are unique.

I might as well mention that this is not only true of those living *within* your society. Wherever you may go, you will encounter people, and the level of respect or cooperation you show them will to a certain degree determine how you in turn will be treated.

Much of your life will be spent facing challenges of varying degrees of difficulty. Your imagination will dictate how you will overcome them. The most important part is, of course, the learning process you go through in the attempt. It is not important whether you *win* or *lose*, but what lessons you take out of the experience, to aid you in facing the next challenges. I know I make it sound like life is one big competition where you have to continuously struggle for survival. It's not.

These things I describe come naturally enough, in everyday life, and are nothing to be afraid of. For the most part, you won't even notice them, like automatic reflexes.

As well, the first time you do something can change the way you do things in the future, since it is through those first reactions that you might base all thought on a subject. I just thought I'd tell you that, as special as first experiences are, they aren't indicative of future experiences. Every single situation is unique in its own right, and should be considered carefully as such.

Generalizations tend to hold you back into familiar thought patterns, which can stop you from seeing every new situation under its true light.

The challenges you face are somewhat like walls, on which you have to deploy whatever means you trust is the best to get through. Once you have gone through a wall, (whether physical or mental), you will invariably face new ones. Sometimes you will decide what your walls are, like when you play sports, join a debate team, play an instrument, or mental exercises. Mostly, they will come out of the blue, as external stimuli from life or other people.

Here is the kicker, though: The greatest opponent you have is *yourself*. Everyone is always looking for their next challenge and opponents elsewhere, except within themselves. How you see yourself will drive your actions. What you know will help you define your external methods of reaction and the way in which you implement them.

There are many different ways of dealing with your walls and potential opposition. The method you choose (e.g. to destroy, circumvent, appease, outwit, befriend, accept, or outperform) demonstrates more about your personal philosophy, than it does about anything else.

The other most important thing to know about *opposition* and knowledge, is that the more you amass of the latter, the less you have of the former. Things are difficult because our lack of knowledge prevents us from solving them creatively, or being frustrated by our lack of understanding. The more knowledge you gain, the less you see things as *opposition*, but as *opportunity*. They become less *wall*, and more *door*.

Many a method has been theorized, philosophized and sanctified. There is no "perfect" method, since we are still looking for it. There are methods that are more effective than others, within the context of various situations, and provably so. The question, then, is, for who is it better?

While there are methods of thought that favour the individual and his achievements, there are also methods that favour the group and theirs.

I personally favour the more group oriented philosophies, since in modern pluralistic societies, no one is an island. Even though the individual can and should achieve great things, it should not be to the *detriment* of his society (or that of others), or so I think. There are always levels to integration and individuality, and even though many individuals can push the boundaries that are before them, they cannot do so without the support of the structures that helped them achieve this.

This is why, to me, cooperation is one of the greatest human traits, and love, its greatest driver.

Q: That's your basic human truth?

A: In a nutshell.

Q: Where does your philosophy come in, though?

A: So, before I go on, I just want to mention terms and psychology.

Q: Okay. What for?

A: Well, when you use a term, for example, like "duck," you have a mental image of a two-legged water-fowl that quacks and has feathers. Simple enough. When you talk about terms like "forgiveness," "truth," and "love," these are much more complex issues that have psychological implications on how your brain works and reacts to things.

Q: How so?

A: Well, for example, if you haven't developed, say the trait *patience* in your life. You might be easily irritated. You might not be able to sit down very long for explanation. You might sabotage your own chances at things because you couldn't wait. So, the word and its definition have very real implications in the neurological sense when dealing with the brain and your existence as a whole.

It's important to remember the *weight* of words from hereon in, as the words, their definitions, and the impact they have on my brain, yours, and that of those around us are very important, because on the macroscopic level, they affect all of society.

How we define ourselves has *positive* and negative *aspects* on both us and our surroundings.

Q. Fair enough. And what are these traits you're so keen on?

Mental Traits I Have Chosen for Myself

3 The main mental aspects that I have discovered I needed to pursue to achieve the best balance in *my own* reality, are those of the open variety: Truth (as in, telling the truth), Patience, Love, Logic (through science and consistent mental processes), curiosity, perseverance, forgiveness, scepticism, questioning, and all others I may have forgotten.

Q. Let me stop you right there. What do you mean by "open mental aspects?"

A. Most people use the terms *positive* and *negative* emotions. They mean the same thing, and I will use the terms interchangeably. I prefer *open* and *closed*.

Q. Why is that?

A. Well, for one, consider the emotion Love. When you think of love, or when I do, anyhow, I think of someone with open arms, willing to embrace others. You are projecting outward. When I think of Hatred, I think of someone who is *closed* to others, who has built a mental wall. And so, I feel that there are *open* and *closed* emotions. The positive/negative paradigm is one I feel is in direct relation to society (positive/negative for whom?), whereas open and closed directly relates to the emotion.

Q. That makes sense. What were you saying about open mental aspects?

A. With so many things to think, and so many ways to do it, the open mental aspects – to me – are the clearest path to my desired goals, which, as I've stated before, is for a more peaceful inner life. I wanted to know serenity within myself, to acquire knowledge that is external to myself,

42

and the mental means to process it, as well as accept (or reject) it. For that I had to pick the best tools, and pursue how to use them optimally.

All in all, these aren't bad methodologies as human beings go. There are others that I could desire and they are just as important as well. I'll discuss them later. Yes, I will be raising you with these attributes in mind, since many more flow from these, and are intertwined in the hive that is your brain.

Even though I can't give you *all* the answers, no one else can do that either. You will pick *what* your opponents are, as well as your friends and allies. Because of *my* personal philosophy, you will be able to see which opponents I have chosen, and why.

As you will notice early on, others pick their *opponents* for a host of reasons, which – to me – are not always very good. They carve up their niche in the world according to how they were raised, as well as the influence of their immediate environment and the limits placed on their knowledge, just like you.

This doesn't mean you shouldn't oppose them. It just means you should know *why* you do.

Life is not solely based on friends and opponents, but at a certain level you have choices to make which affect everything around you. Opponents, opportunities, as well as allies and friends, are the end result of the personal philosophy you have chosen for yourself. If you have an opinion, one way or the other, there will always be someone who thinks differently than you do. That's okay, though. That doesn't mean you have to make an *enemy* out of anyone who disagrees with you. It just means that to a certain degree, you have a particular view about a subject, and that you are willing to defend it.

It doesn't mean that you can't change your opinion, either. That opponent you have might convince you otherwise, since their argument might be more logical and hold more *truth* stemming from facts, or empathy, than yours.

Opposition does not mean non-acceptance, it can be the precursor to acceptance. In any event, by building your personal store of information, you will be able to judge more readily whether your position is warranted or not.

Opposition does not mean to fear or hate, either. The choices I make, when based *solely* on my *opinion*, hate, and unreliable sources, are completely subjective and limited to a dependence on my closed world-view. The wider my knowledge of provable facts are, the easier it is to comprehend the mechanics of *everything*, and with that the meaning of Truth.

It is normal to be angry about a situation. That does not mean that you've stopped loving. It might in fact mean that you love something so much that its abuse has fired you up! My only recommendation is to try to avoid hatred, which is a kind of poison: easy to ingest, and hard to evacuate.

When I place myself in opposition to something, it is because I believe I have a deeper understanding of the mechanics that underlie the system to which I am confronted.

Much of the time, it is against *myself* that I am opposed. Since I want to push myself further, it is by forcing my mind to open to other possibilities that the opposition takes place. I already know *who* will *win*, of course, but in which way I do so depends on if I was able to stick to my *virtues* or not.

All virtues you choose to pursue have something in common: they concentrate your view on the long term. Vices are, for want of a better term, the feeding of instant gratification, and nothing more. When you look down the road a bit, you mentally picture the things you want for yourself and others, and it is through virtues that you have a better ratio of success with.

When you take the macro view, societies based around core *virtues* have the advantage over those who are not. It is much easier to create a complex society around Truth, or *honesty* than on *lies*. For example, since to create social contracts, truth, and its derivative – confidence – must hold sway. As well, when justice and equality are held high in the societal sphere, there is less chance of poverty, abuse of power, and violence.

It is my belief that as much as these core values are important in individuals, they are so in all human systems. The more forward-thinking virtues are instilled into individuals and systems, the better the society is for it.

It is a balance, of course, between the desires of the individual and the needs of society. To let the balance tip toward *vices* within systems and a majority of individuals creates an imbalanced society. For example, if most people begin to think only of themselves within the system, you might end up with rampant corruption, which erodes both the confidence of those outside the system, and the theft of monies and property with no recourse.

You will be tempted to allow your animal nature to take over, and think only of yourself. It is up to you to decide whether you want to be *virtuous* or not. Whether to work hard, or steal. Whether to be generous, or avaricious. You might grow into your virtues. Keep in mind that if you want to build a better environment for yourself, you need to be the example to follow.

Q. Okay, so wait. Virtues, or those *open* mental aspects you were talking about are better in the long-term? Is that what you're saying?

A. Precisely. Virtues are what religious people call *open* mental aspects. If you think about it, when they're codified into law as aspirations and rules to follow, they help a society's longevity. They keep people together, they tend the peace, and they provide a road-map to the future, by giving innate laws for people to follow.

Q. What about vices, though? Certainly there's room for that?

A. Of course there is. We're human animals. The thing is, we have to balance our virtues and vices, and know the difference. There are also certain areas where we shouldn't compromise, such as in Law, or government. If all you elect are greedy robbers, nothing gets done; your tax money is wasted on rapacious people, and the society suffers. It might be a good time to tell you this:

Humans, the Floating Point

We, as a species, are like a continuously rising and falling bobber on the ebb and flow of the evolutionary sea. We're like a half-way point between the animals and the divine we admire so much. One moment we are considering ourselves the Universe evolved, and the next, we're jerking off, watching porn while eating junk food and bitching at random strangers we'll never meet in comments sections on the internet. That's a metaphor. No need to tell me that's physically impossible.

There have been many systems of human organization that have come and gone, and we never quite seem to grasp the best one. Partially because we're all too fallible, and partially because even though a system may have started out with a good premise, it is inevitably drawn to its logical conclusion. Or perhaps more tellingly, when we do find some way to get along long enough to lead a nice, quiet life, someone comes along to ruin our shit.

Philosophers have been debating these questions for years, but we as people owe it to ourselves to look at the underpinnings of the machine we're driving, if we wish to understand where it might lead us.

For example, the two major competing schools of thought that drive the West are Democracy and Capitalism.

Q: But Capitalism is an economic theory, not a philosophy.

A: True, but it needs to force us to think a certain way to *work*. We need to be made to think that we *need* things. For that to happen, advertisements needs to tell us that there are things missing in our lives. For Capitalists to continue to thrive, things that are public need to be privatized. Democracy, on the other hand, is the theory that everyone has a vote and can make good for the entire Nation by voting for the right person. On the one hand, then, you have a socio-economic system that works well when it uses our vices as selling methods and splitting us up, and on the other you have a constitutional method that tells us we're better *together*. You have that dichotomy there, of the individual and the masses.

There is also the fact that the end-run of Capitalism is extreme inequality (being based on greed), thus making those in charge want to create for as little as possible to sell for as much as the market will take. This is all well and good if you're the captain of industry, but not so much if you're the person relying on the scraps that trickle down from that table in the sky.

Now that Capitalism has become the de facto lingua franca of most (if not all) nations on Earth, we have to contend with something that is entirely unsustainable in the long run.

Why's that? Well, for starters, there are *not* unlimited resources on the planet, and the more other nations enter the fray to compete with, say, China and the United States, the faster those resources will wither away, deplete, or end up in our environment as pollutants and carcinogens. There is also the problem of planned obsolescence and the inevitable use of things that cause more pollution (electric cars are great, but the oil companies don't profit from non-gas-based engines).

We are fast approaching an era where automation will take most of our jobs away in short order, thereby leaving us penniless, but we are expected to pay more for things, as inflation and the desire to put a price on everything ruins the lives of all save the wealthiest among us. Figure the logic of that one out.

With the election of rich demagogues, we see the natural endgame of unbridled capitalism: the businessman literally replacing the politician, rendering bribery a useless thing of the past. Who knows? As those businesspeople stack more and more of the greedy into their cabinet appointments, perhaps wealthy business owners across the country will go into politics as well, changing the laws as they see fit, to benefit themselves above all others. Pure conjecture, of course.

So on the one hand, we are mired in this sort of mediocre swamp of entertainment and sex, gluttony and violence, just like the animals we are, but some are still keeping one eye on the sky, so to speak, thinking we could do better.

We can.

We just have to break the bonds that hold us back for one second to see that there are bigger, deeper, and more worthwhile things to do with our lives.

We call ourselves *addicts* when we need to get a fix of drugs on a regular basis, but we're just as addicted to video games and Facebook, porn sites, eating copious amounts of food, and watching violent movies. And there's nothing wrong with that, in-and-of-itself! I don't care if you play *Minecraft* or *WoW* for hours on end, as long as you are aware that you could also do things that have a higher purpose (and once again, I'm not talking about worshiping a god, not that there's anything wrong with that).

By higher purpose, I mean doing things for others, whether that means family, friends, neighbors, your city, country, or planet. *Higher* to me means every other person than ourselves. And yes, we might be doing things on a small scale, but we need to think bigger.

My problem is that we are either all one way, or the other: we believe in a deity and blindly follow the religious leaders or doctrines and get things done for our in-group (which doesn't help Humanity, on a larger scale), or we don't believe in one and get nothing concrete done, either. Either way, there are a whole lot of people who are not doing very much with the time they have on this planet. And *of course* you want to enjoy it by doing something fun! And *of course* there is nothing wrong with worshiping an idealized form of the human being! My main concern is that while we're consuming mass quantities of resources and praying our lives away, we're losing our planet, and we will never repair the damage we've done, or get off of it to help our ever-expanding population!

I've said it before, and I'll say it again: I want a *Star Trek* future, and not a *Mad Max* one, and we're kind of on the cusp of either of those right now. If we keep destroying our planet so that a handful of individuals get to shit on gold toilets, nearly eight billion people are going to die. The rest will have to murder each other for whatever resources are left. I don't want that.

Q: I don't want that either. So what happens next?
A: We need counter-intuitive thinking, for one.

Counter-Intuitive Thinking

Things changed, a long time ago, when people started thinking counter-intuitively. Up until then it was: I don't like you? I'm going to kill you. Then this weirdo comes along and says: "Hey guys. Love everybody." I'm not a religious person, but you have to admit that was some fairly revolutionary stuff. We wouldn't have peace in such large swathes of the world if it wasn't for that *kind* of thinking.

If we want to survive until we as a race evolve out of being the Doctor Jekyll and Mr. Hyde of species, we have to start thinking counter-intuitively. The umbrella we cast over similar-coloured people we call our tribe has to be cast over all of humanity, and our tribe has to be the one that looks to the future with hope and hard work.

Our tribe has to be the one that actively builds that future to include the poorest to the richest, and tries to raise everyone to a fair standard. This isn't Communism or Socialism. It's Humanity. It's Universal Wisdom. To me that means the pursuit of a sustainable, wisdom-fuelled future. We really *are* on the same boat!

The goal in this case is not to create a new enemy to join together against, but to have a new goal towards which we can all work together. That goal is the survival of our species and whatever is left of our planet, and it has to start now. Or else it's *Mad Max* and *Fallout* for everyone on a global scale, and I don't think you want to live out your old age running away from roving bands of murderous cannibals.

So yes, I do think it's important that we get entertained, have and enjoy sex, eat food however we like and be body positive for everyone, and enjoy a good action movie. That's fine! That's our animal side getting its kicks. However, remember that the timer is ticking as to how long we have until the oceans rise high enough to drown us all and disease overtake the survivors, unless a nuclear war doesn't kill us first. Perhaps that might affect your decision-making process when it comes to your involvement in our mutual survival. Food for thought.

Then when we get our many appetites under control, we might start aiming higher, and working for it instead of leaving it to some hypothetical *other*. You are that person. It's up to *you*.

Q: That's a fair kick in the teeth.

A: I never said it was going to be easy, and you don't change things by telling people what they want to hear.

Q: What if I tell you I don't believe everything that you're saying.

A: I'd tell you that facts have an annoying way of being true whether you believe them or not.

Q: So where do you and I fit in all this?

A: It helps to know your place in the grand scheme of things.

I am an Atom

My thoughts stem from a primordial realization I made recently. I *am* an atom. What I mean by that is that on a global scale, I am the smallest part of a society, and as a whole, of humanity.

I was humbled as well as filled with joy by this realization.

I was humbled, because I now know that I am only a tiny part of a vast and growing mass of people who populate this planet.

I was filled with joy, because at the same time, I know that my actions and thoughts carry weight, and influence all those around me. I may not change the planet, but I will shape the opinions of those in my surroundings through all that I do, just as everybody else does, whether they are aware of it or not.

If my acts are inspiring and uplifting, others may find them so as well, and imitate them. The same goes for the terrible things I might do. I am almost entirely responsible for my thoughts, entirely so for my acts, and how I treat others. Only time will tell if I am successful, but I will never stop trying to better myself. That will be my life's goal, and will dictate to me if I lead a worthwhile life or not, in retrospect.

I have many choices when it comes to the actions that I can take, but the best ones are always the ones that harm the least and help the most. As I learn how to evolve and become a wiser person, I will pass down these experiences I have amassed to you, who will become a new atom in your community, and will either better it, worsen it, or leave it unchanged.

As an atom, I can either attract or repulse other atoms. In the human community, it is always better to attract other atoms, since our species is a social one. We are able to do incredible things with the help of others.

This requires the right attitude and components, of course, and I spent many years trying to figure out what the best ones were. Some groups have even spent thousands of years in that pursuit, and some of the things I will describe to you are partially *stolen* from their own philosophies. All of it though, is based on love. If you live your life with love, it won't seem as much of a burden as everybody thinks it is.

As an atom, you will bounce around, here and there, and you will be a part of bigger things. Your interactions within the group will affect the group, and the way you will be treated.

It is always *easier* to be a bad atom than a righteous one, but the payoff of being a good one is that you will find less opportunity to feel guilty or ashamed of your actions. That, and as an added bonus, others might aspire to be like you. Being Bad simply means you will give others the urge to follow their animalistic human nature. But once you realize that being the Good atom has far-reaching effects, you may want to stay on that path.

As an atom, you will directly change no one. You shouldn't want to. You should simply want to be the best atom that you can. That way, if someone else sees the way you are and live, they may tell themselves: "I want to be like this atom." You did not change them. They decided to change themselves.

When you are young it doesn't seem to matter very much, but when you grow up, it's the opinions of others about you which will determine your success among the rest of your community. You can either see that as a negative or a positive, but it is what it is. What is even more important is the opinion you have of yourself.

The way you act and the things you'll say to others will become the basis for their thoughts about you. The thoughts you have within yourself will influence said actions. This is your reputation. It won't matter if your in-group is small or large, but your reputation will follow you wherever you go, because people like to tell others what they think of you. It isn't the most important or determining factor in your life, but if you want other peoples' help, it'll be important to incorporate skills that make it easier for them to accept you, and trust you.

This doesn't mean you shouldn't be genuine. You really should be a good person, not just pretend. Like I've mentioned before, being truthful is very important.

Trust is one of the major foundations of friendships and any other relationship you can create between yourself and others. It is hard to build trust, because it takes time for others to get to know you and accept you. It only takes an instant to destroy that trust through a reprehensible action, and is very difficult to regain afterwards, if at all.

Don't worry, you'll do stupid things whether you want to or not, but your awareness of them is what will help you limit them in the future. A great many qualities I'll discuss here are based on human trust, and the more of these you add to your personal tool bag, the easier it will be to navigate the turbulent waters of social life.

It all begins with you, and your perceptions. Your biggest enemy is your ego, as well as your best friend. Your ego is your sense of self, and however you conceive your place in the world will define the roles you reserve for others around you, as well as your own. The conception you have of reality, whether it is there to serve you, to crush you, to uplift you, and a myriad of other interactions, affect your identity and the methods with which you will operate to further your own well-being.

When you have an over-inflated sense of self, you are said to be egotistical. When you have a deflated sense of self, you are depressive. It is by finding a happy medium, and avoiding extremes of the *closed* emotional and selfish variety that you can begin to *grow* as an individual.

Being prideful is one of these negative traits you want to watch out for. You might think you are the absolute best, if you achieve something over those who are around you. If you react in a prideful manner, acting as if you were the best that there ever was and disrespect others, you are losing touch with reality. You are letting your inflated ego run out of control. It is intoxicating to achieve great things, but it is toxic to let it go to your head.

The best course of action is to take the honours you are given and be thankful for what you have achieved.

Even though you might be filled with pride, you are not the only person who has achieved something in life, and putting other peoples' noses in your achievements is a sure-fire way of alienating yourself. Humility is the opposite of pride. It means that you are grateful for your achievements, but are mindful of the feelings of others as well as keeping your feet firmly planted on the ground.

Remember, if you want to be respected, you have to treat people with respect. This, by no means, means that you shouldn't try your best!

If you do something, always do your utmost to pour all your energies into the task you have been assigned, or that you assign yourself. You can't gain satisfaction from a task you have performed unless you did your all.

Do not do it to be better than others.

Do it to be better than *yourself.*

You are the only person you should be comparing yourself to.

Remember, there is only one person you can truly change in this world, and that is you. You have no influence over others save the example you set. So try to be a good atom, if you can.

There are many people who will be your influences growing up. You might admire sports stars, teachers, authors, thinkers, or maybe even your old mom and dad (hopefully!), but everybody is different from you, and everybody knows something more or less than you do. You are no better and no worse than anybody else, only different.

It is important that you observe others and try to emulate those you respect. It is also important that you do not adulate them. No one is above humanity. By the same token, you should ask yourself why you admire someone so much. What is it that they do that is so special? What do you have to do to become more like this person you admire? You will find that a lot of the time, those worthy of admiration arrived where they are through a lot of hard work and years of practice. Do not despair. If you truly think a person's path is worth following, you will put in the work as well, one step at a time.

Your experiences are your very own. They are what make you unique. Just think: you will have experiences that no one else in the Universe will ever have. They are your own to hold, to keep, to cherish, and sometimes, maybe, to regret. Every new experience you have will bring you knowledge that you did not have before. It is the methods with which you will deal with these experiences that will determine whether or not you will go on to the next experience more or less unscathed, indifferent, or better for them.

Following are just a few hints and tips to help you along your way. They've helped me and a lot of other people as well.

For as long as I will know you, I'll try to *explain to you* why it is important to do something and not another, instead of simply ordering you. That way, you will have the choice to continue on the path you choose, with better information at your disposal.

Be careful of greed, or rather, remember that there is no lasting satisfaction in material things. When you want to have more than everybody else, and are ready to do anything, including walking all over others to get it, you are succumbing to this very negative trait.

There is nothing wrong with wanting to achieve things in life, or even having material possessions, but not at the cost of hurting other people.

If you benefit from anything, you were probably not alone in getting to where you did. There was a whole team of people who did their utmost to get you there, and you should never forget it. We get further as a team by sharing, and by spreading the spoils of victory to those who were kind enough to get us there. The only ones who would deny this are those who are benefitting from the endless, bitter toil of others.

Be thankful. People will do things for you, throughout your life. All they want in return is your respect.

As a matter of fact, once most basic needs are fulfilled, even though many people don't know it, all they want is respect. We all follow convoluted life paths in search of the respect of others, and do some incredibly stupid things, incredibly greedy things, incredibly mean things for others to respect us.

These ways are wrong, and can only do harm. People often mistake fear for respect. Most of us wouldn't be doing these things if we were kinder to others, since others would respect us for our kindness and goodness. So, what I am trying to say, is be kind and be thankful.

Those who use negative tactics to own the respect of others only attract the greed of others who want to replace them for that position. Those who spread goodwill and kindness and are genuinely good, spread that desire in others.

Most people are good. Most people are goofy, nice, serious, silly, happy, sad, gentle, naughty, crazy, and a great variety of other harmless attributes. Some people, however, are not Good. Those who are not Good are the ones who do things only for themselves, to advance themselves over the good of others, trampling everybody else to get to the top.

You cannot avoid them, because they exist in every society. You can, however, be careful. Be careful with your money, with your feelings, with your reputation, with your life, and especially with your heart.

Do not be afraid.

Just be careful.

The best thing to do, when one has been identified, is to make sure that others are aware of their existence, so that they too do not get suckered. Yes, you will get suckered. It'll hurt. You'll swear never to trust anyone ever again.

This is wrong.

You should never generalize, you only hurt yourself this way. If one person hurts you, you can't assume that everybody else will do the same. One bad experience shouldn't stop you from enjoying the rest of your life. Most people are good, and will bring you positive feedback and experiences. Bad people will make you tougher. Forgive them and move on.

There are many different ways of showing people that you mean them no harm. Smiling is the most effective. It is positive in the sense that not only does it bring *you* joy, but it has the possibility of doing so to others as well.

Genuinely smiling activates pleasure chemicals in your own mind, so when others see your happiness, they are more inclined to reciprocate. This in turn activates their own joy. *True* smiling is the easiest way to spread love to your surroundings.

Don't be reckless with other peoples' feelings. If someone trusts you, don't trample all over their emotions. There may come a time when you have to tell them something or do something that may hurt them, but there are ways of doing so that will minimize the pain.

You can't avoid hurting other peoples' feelings sometimes, but you can at least avoid being cruel and toying with them. It all comes down to how you wish to be treated. Yes, others might do this to you, but it doesn't mean you have to lower yourself to their level.

As much as possible, try not to hate anybody. Hatred has a nasty way of becoming stuck in your head and affecting your judgement, not only about the person or people you hate, but others who may resemble them, and situations completely unrelated. If you have to hate something, hate situations. They are inanimate, and have a tendency of evaporating quickly, whereas people stick around for a very long time. Besides which, the people you might hate will feel no pain at all from your hatred of them. Only you will feel that pain, inside your mind, for the rest of your life (or until you have decided to let it go).

Learn to forgive. It is the antidote to the hatred you might feel. Forgiving makes you let go of it, and brings peace back to your mind. It is one of the most difficult things to do, because it makes you battle your worst enemy: your ego. If you win, though, you will feel better, and will harbour no more ill will towards others or yourself. Some of the unhappiest people on earth are those who can't forgive, for whatever reason they invent. It is always possible to forgive; it is only the bar of seeming impossibility that rises in the individual.

Apologize. A true apology, from your heart. You are not perfect, and you will make mistakes. You will do things you will regret, either to loved ones or even to perfect strangers. No matter how big or how small the mistake, you should apologize. It takes a lot of courage to recognize our faults, and it only takes an instant to show we can admit it. It demonstrates that you understand that other peoples' feelings are just as important as your own.

Only apologize for things that you have done.

Have empathy, for all those around you. Before you speak or act, try to imagine how others feel and think. It will help you understand where others are coming from, and their sensitivities to certain issues. As you want to be respected, this is how you will learn to respect others. As the old saying goes: "Put yourself in their shoes."

Be kind. Don't say mean things to people, unless you want people to do the same to you. Don't expect special treatment, ever. You are only as good as your actions and the words that come out of your mouth. This doesn't mean you shouldn't criticize, since you have your own opinions, it only means you should carefully pick the way that is most suitable for doing so. There are a thousand different ways of saying the same thing, depending on the effect you want to have. Many people confuse rudeness with individuality. They have somehow conflated the act of being an asshole with having independent thought. Being rude is simply a method for the stupid to feel superior. Don't fall into that trap, unless you want others to think you are a moron.

Take the time to admire the beauty that is around you. There are plenty of things you'll find ugly or sad, but if you have the opportunity to be in the presence of something truly magnificent, take it in with all your being. It will blow your mind.

Keep your promises. Your word is your bond. That means that your reputation as a person is predicated on the things that you say, and the acts you commit to uphold those words. If you make a promise, you should try your utmost to keep it, as much as you humanly can. The trust that people invest in you depends on it. If you routinely break your promises, people will no longer trust you, and will know you are undependable. You will lose their good will and be left to your own devices.

The same goes for lying. It is easier, and safer to tell the truth than to lie. Depending on the lie, you will have to add more lies to cover up the lie, and you will eventually be found out to be a liar, losing your support and friends. To avoid this, tell the truth. It is easier to remember and may get you in trouble, but it is trouble you deserve in the first place, if you did something wrong. The penalties for being found out after you lie, though, are much worse than if you come clean in the first place. As well, the human mind has a lie detector built-in. You're harming yourself as well as others by lying to them.

Don't steal. This might seem like a no-brainer, but believe me, you don't want to steal. Not only is it wrong, but it carries very strong penalties, none of which are pleasant. No matter who you steal from, everybody will despise you, period. The fact that you would commit such an anti-social act means that you might do it against anyone, therefore you are no longer a trustworthy person. You will lose everybody's trust. It might take you years to get it back. It might seem easier to take without asking, but if you didn't earn what you got, it's not, and never really will be yours.

Work hard for what you want. Earn your keep, so that you know for a fact that everything you possess was something you earned legitimately, and are proud to have done so. I'd like to put a caveat on this, though. When you take peoples' *ideas*, and make them your own, you are not stealing, you are building your mind. You are only stealing if you use them literally, word-for-word, and claim them as your own. The human community works by improvement, so obviously we need to start on some basis upon which we can build. This wouldn't be possible if we could not use others' principles and thoughts.

Think positively. There are many different ways to think, and many different manners in which you can approach a question or challenge, but the best and most productive is to think positively. If you do, then an answer won't seem impossible, just difficult. Life is constantly throwing curveballs, and your attitude towards them dictates your method of hitting them. If yours is to look at them as interesting problems to be solved, you will more readily be able to do so.

Have confidence in yourself. It is easy to doubt your motives and who you are. To truly live and not just exist, you have to go forward.

If your mind is filled with doubt over your own capabilities, you cannot take a step. Believe in you, and what you are attempting, and give it your all. That is the best thing you can do. It doesn't matter if you fail. It does matter if you don't even try. Have doubt, but do not live in constant doubt. It is perfectly normal to question anything and everything, yet it is only by resolving this questioning that you can take the next necessary steps.

Speaking of trying, do so at least once for everything. I mean that in a general sense. You *obviously* shouldn't be drinking poison, or doing heavy drugs, or jumping off buildings without a parachute of course. There is a plethora of incredible activities, things to see, experience, and live in this world, that refusing to try out of fear of dislike is a sure way to miss out on awesomeness.

Remember, as well, that because your tastes evolve, things that you used to dislike can become things you like, with time. Don't limit yourself.

Adapt. Everything changes, all the time. It cannot be helped. The best you can do is to be as prepared as possible, and then roll with the punches when the unexpected happens. You have to learn to think quickly and find solutions to whatever particular jostle you are experiencing (or crumble into a heap and abandon all hope). This latter reaction will definitely not help you win the day.

Thinking about what your options are and then picking the most viable one is what will make you a quick thinker, and someone who is ready for anything. Sinking into despair and despondency will only help you feel miserable and useless. It is unavoidable, at times, but it is dangerous to dwell for too long on these emotions. They can become habit.

Find solutions. It is very easy to avoid getting blamed for anything that happens. It is just as easy to blame others. As much as we need to accept responsibility when we are at fault, that is only half of the equation. If the situation is recurring, we need to find a way to curb it. Finding a way of solving a problem means overlooking blame, since it changes nothing, and concentrating on the fixing part. This will help you learn responsibility and avoid living with shame. No one likes being shamed.

Protect your friends. Defend those you care about. It's okay to discuss problems you might be having with anyone around you, but don't talk crap about them. If you have a problem with someone, find a way to discuss the situation with that person directly. Tell them in a nice way what it is that is bothering you.

Talking behind peoples' backs means that others will think you might do it about them. It also means that you are trying to raise yourself by lowering others.

Be honest, and if you ever need advice in any situation, never hesitate to ask me or your mother. We're here to help you. Defend ideas with words. Insults hurled at you only have effect if you let them. They are only words, until you let them become personal, so don't. An argument should never get physical. If you have no choice though, you should defend yourself if you are attacked, but only as a last resort. Please never be the instigator of a fight, but try to end it as much as possible.

Be on time. When you have to be somewhere at a specific time, do it. Other people are busy too, and have better things to do than to wait around for you to show up. Don't make them wait. You won't like having to wait for them, so don't do it to them, either.

Respect other peoples' customs. People around the world live in alternative ways than you do. What they do is neither better nor worse than what you know, it is simply different. To avoid embarrassment, or even insulting those for whom you are a simple visitor, learn what their customs are, and even a bit of their language. This will ensure you will have a much better time during your travels, because travel you will. Your mom and I love to travel, and you will be going to the same places we will, so hold on to your hats, little ones. You will see, hear, smell, go to, taste, discover, and experience a million places and things you never knew existed. You can only fully appreciate other peoples' cultures if you immerse yourself in them, so be ready for the plunge.

You are not your material possessions. You are the thoughts that run through your head. Consider your needs before you spend your money on something. Think of how long you will derive enjoyment or pleasure from this expenditure, then appreciate it is for as long as you own it. When you are done with it, either donate it to someone who needs it or sell it. Always keep in mind that you are not a consumer, you are a human being. There is a fine line between existing and owning, especially in this ownership society. Never forget that the things we own usually end up owning us.

Try to make people feel special. The best gift you can give someone is your love. Be genuine, and honest, and kind to those around you, and they will generally do the same to you. You're not alone in this world, and those who have done much to make you become the person you are today deserve your appreciation. Even complete strangers can benefit from your kindness, so if you have the opportunity to help someone out, you should. Let your generosity be its own reward. If someone wants to show their appreciation for what you do for them, let them, but don't expect it out of hand.

I know this will come back to bite us someday, and I'm not sure I should tell you this, but no one can read minds. Don't believe for a second that anyone will be able to tell what you are thinking if you do not tell them. There is nothing quite as infuriating as a person who does this. You have to express yourself if you want to be understood, and not doing so while being absolutely sure that you are, will only make others angry or uncooperative. If you ever use this tactic, you deserve to be ignored. There are times when you don't want to speak about your problems, and that's fine, too. What I am talking about is the insidious: "You should know what you did" scenario. There are a great number of people who really do believe that others will be able to intuit what they are thinking, and be even angrier still when they do not. Don't be like that if you want people to respect you. Communication is the door to understanding, and you have control over whether the door is open or closed.

Haters are always gonna hate, and that's their problem, really. Some people are completely unable to see the good in life, and spend their time trying to bring others down to their level. Don't let them succeed with you. Sympathize, but disagree. Life is not about hate, unless you let it, and then it just becomes a living hell. You can't live a great life if it becomes hell for you. You'll have to find a way for it to become better. Why let it become so in the first place?

Enjoy every age you will go through for its own merits. A lot of people spend the first part of their lives wishing they were older, and the other half that they were younger. Every age has its advantages and disadvantages, but if you spend all your time wishing you were something you are not, you will never get to appreciate what you are and what you have.

If you are strong, protect the weak. If you are not, become stronger. This does not mean mere physical strength, but mental as well.

Have a sense of humour. There is a time and place to be serious, but those times are few and far in between. Take life with a grain of salt, don't forget to laugh and make others laugh as well. Laughing is healthy and will help you stay positive.

Be happy for others' fortune. There are plenty of things that you will not have, this doesn't mean you are missing out on anything. Be glad for what you have, and work hard for the things you want, and let the rest sort itself out.

Have confidence and trust. Jealousy is a mixture of fear, desire, and anger. You should be able to trust the people around you. If you can't, you either have good reason to, therefore should not be with them. If you have no good reason to, then you should search your feelings and find a way to calm your fears. Jealousy is destructive in any relationship, and should be shed like snakeskin.

Do the work. One of your main goals in life, if you choose it, is to better yourself. There is no honour in going around the work that that involves, since you acquire nothing. Any short-term gain you might think you have is destroyed by the ignorance or lack of experience you demonstrate. The important things are hard. The worthwhile things are tough. Once you have them, though, no one can take them away from you. They're yours for the rest of your life.

There are only opponents. There are some who will disagree with you, and you should consider them opponents. An enemy is someone that is very hard to make peace with, but an opponent is a person with whom you can still get along with even though you disagree with them.

An enemy is an opponent you've decided to despise. There are human beings out there who will despise you, and you will do the same to them, even though you shouldn't. This is usually out of a basic misunderstanding or opposition of philosophy, compounded by a lack of goodwill to correct the situation, and an overbearing ego that refuses to meet the other halfway. You can avoid all this with love, understanding and empathy. Still, there will be some that you just can't bear, or who dislike you enormously in return. It can't be avoided if you have an opinion of your own.

Ignore them, and forgive them, they are not worth your time and energy. Not everybody in the world wants to have friends or share your point of view.

The same is not true when it comes to positions of power. If someone who is diametrically in opposition to your philosophy wields some amount of influence, and you see it as being detrimental to society at large, you have a *duty* to oppose them. Especially if not doing so would allow for the dissemination of untruthful information, the creation of discriminatory laws, or unethical behavior. This is where your involvement in the political process becomes very important. Still, the discourse should remain polite (as much as possible).

Be mindful of waste. The things you consume, the food you eat, the products you purchase, everything you utilize in your daily life should be appreciated. To do this, you have to not let any (or as little of it as possible) go to the garbage. This is another way of showing your respect for your environment and those who work for you. If you do your part, like everyone else, you will be contributing to the safeguarding of our home planet for generations to come.

Everything is interrelated. Everybody spends their time trying to pinpoint what particular factor is the first or main cause in any occurrence. There are usually several factors that come into play, and finding the main one is sometimes a futile exercise. It is important to know all that is involved in a problem before being able to address it, since every detail, when taken as a whole, changes the big picture. The response(s) that need to be used to fix the problem(s) will therefore also be altered.

So why all these recommendations? They seem like a lot of trouble, and might not give much in return. This isn't so. All these things I laid out before you help you in a myriad ways. They will help you keep a peaceful mind. They will improve your relationships with others. They will ease your ability to learn and to communicate. Remember, if you choose so, life can be about learning, and new, interesting experiences. For that you need to engage others. Tools that help you in this task should be something you seek out, not shun.

You are a thinking person. This is one of the gifts you have been given as a living, breathing, upright monkey. Don't waste it on *not* thinking. Too many people do that already. It's hard to figure out if what you are thinking is right or wrong, since the goalposts keep changing with time. The best thing you can do for yourself and those around you is accumulate knowledge of all kinds and make a synthesis of your experiences.

You will be a student for the rest of your life, whether you are in school or not, so make the best of it. Knowledge is your best friend, not your worst enemy. You have a better chance of doing right if you are doing it for the sake of others *as well as* yourself. Almost everything is subjective. This means that a great many things you consider depends on what you are comparing them with. The reason why people think such incredibly varying thoughts is partially based on this fact.

If you try to live by what I've written so far, and a plethora of good advice you'll encounter along the way, you have a better chance of creating a more positive environment for yourself and those around you, but it is critical that you learn more, always.

Read as much as you can, on as wide a variety of topics as you want to. One of the most important things you can do is think, then act.

Take the time to sit down in a quiet place, once in a while, and take stock of how you feel, what you know, what your desires are, and what you need to do to achieve them. During your introspections, you will realize a great many things, as well as imagine worlds, and it is these worlds populating your mind that will determine your future, since they represent who you are and what you want to be.

Everything you will attempt will be difficult, at first. As you practise, and get better at what you are trying to achieve, the parts you used to find hard will become easier and easier. As you progress, more difficult steps will be added for you to overcome. If you use your patience, and practise hard towards your goal, you will derive more and more pleasure from it. If you give up, you will never get to the fun part, and so much the pity. You may regret not having tried harder for the rest of your life. Trust me.

We have, each and every one of us, the ability to learn from the world around us. The things you learn, in turn, can benefit you in life and help you achieve new levels of understanding. Sometimes, these nuggets of information radically change your way of thinking, and you no longer perceive your reality in the same way. It's like looking into our house from a different window. Even though the house remains the same, since you've moved, everything you see is slightly different. So it is with thought, and the concepts that populate your mind. Once a concept has been introduced, you gain a more thorough, or different understanding of the world around you.

Everything I've been writing about so far are concepts. They are methods of thinking that alter your perceptions, and by doing so, make your reality a more enjoyable, or at the very least comprehensible, experience. Since reality is something experienced through your senses, you might as well make it a worthwhile endeavour. As far as we know, we only possess one life in *this* particular reality, and how we live it is directly proportional to how we perceive it.

One of the strongest elements stopping you from achieving anything you wish to, is yourself. I can't stress this enough. You are your greatest opponent. There are a million things you can do, and the only person who will stop you, will be you. Yes, I won't let you do a few things at first, but that's normal. There are things that you shouldn't do at a certain age, because you don't have the cognitive abilities to comprehend that what you are doing is either socially frowned upon or simply dangerous. We aren't going to let you hurt yourself. You will be frustrated with us for it, of course, but you'll get over it.

As you grow older, though, we will slacken that invisible leash so that you can comfortably explore your reality, without letting you go into danger. At some point, the leash will be removed, and you will be an autonomous being, like every other adult. The rules *you* will choose to live by afterwards will be your limits. Even then, you should never stop growing.

Try to live what it is to lack things. Attempt to exist without all the exterior trappings of modern life and all the advantages you usually have. Then fast for a few days. No, I'm not talking crazy talk. Millions of people around the world live without even the most basic survival tools that we take for granted all our lives. If you want to be in touch with what it is to live like most, and to be able to appreciate what *you* have, you need a basis of comparison.

Life is experiential.

For this you need to shed the excess. In the Muslim religion, they don't eat from dawn until dusk for a whole month (this celebration is called Ramadan). I'm pretty sure you can attempt something similar without going to those extremes. Besides which, it is said that fasting is good for you. As I've mentioned before, just about everything is subjective. You can't appreciate what you have unless you have had to live *without it.*

Never lose hope. It is so very easy to feel down, and think that if an event is so crushingly painful, you will never be able to feel good, ever again. This is not true. You will find love, and you will lose love. You will find love again. You will be disappointed, you will be frustrated. You might even hate the whole planet for all I know. Don't lose hope. Unhappiness, no matter how much it hurts, is only temporary, and fades with time, if you let it. Grieve what you must grieve, but don't dwell on it for the rest of your life. You will have terribly upsetting experiences, and they will become a part of your mental makeup, but they shouldn't be the core of who you are. If someone hurts you, forgive them. If someone is no longer there, remember the good times. Hurtful memories can be anchors that drag you back to your past, and won't let you go forward. They stop you from elevating yourself to a higher place. They are a burden unless dealt with properly. Don't let your pride and pain stop you from putting your bad memories to rest.

Your negative emotions can either be your best friends or your worst enemies, depending on how you treat them. If you let them wreak havoc on your life, completely out of control, you will have a hard time fitting in, feeling comfortable, or happy about your life.

You may even try to move from one physical location to another, thinking you will feel better. Will your thoughts stay behind? Or will they stay in your head, as they always have? You can tame them, though. Knowing who you are and how you react can help you in that quest.

Don't forget that you can't always control your emotions, and you need to be able to express your feelings for your own well-being, but there is a time and place for everything, as you will learn. If you do lose your temper, and hurt someone in the process, ask for forgiveness, and mean it.

I don't think it's possible to be fearless, but I do know that you can stop fear from ruling you. It has a tendency of popping up when we least expect it, taking control in tense situations, and making us do some pretty dumb things. A modicum of fear can do great things to motivate you, but as one of your primary driving emotions, it'll cripple you from doing anything you might want to try.

Learn History. Those who don't know it are bound to repeat it, and seeing as we used to be pretty dumb, why would we want to turn back the hands of time? As a species, we have made incredible progress since our humble beginnings. We do it in fits and starts, sometimes regressing a bit, but in general, we seem to be on a positive course. True, we have evolved tremendously in the past few million years (we've been around for *that long!*), which in evolutionary terms is quite astounding. As our means of communications have developed, so has our ability to disseminate human thoughts and values. But in the past several hundred years, our thought processes have been refined tremendously with the help of science and by extension, modern philosophy. What we used to use as tools of thought in the past are in stark contrast to what we employ today, much like the difference between the stone blades our ancestors used to have and the fMRI scanners we use now. With the growth of our knowledge and the precision instruments we have developed as tools, we have transformed our lives from what was once a game of survival to what is now one of relative comfort, where these tools have been implemented.

Even though you will have material comforts and physical benefits to your life, I don't want you to miss out on the mental aspect of what you are, and what you could be able to accomplish.

I was trapped in the materialistic side of life for a very long time, because sometimes there is just no escaping it. The messages surrounding you are very strong. Society tells you what you should want, and that that's how you're supposed to find contentment.

Yet the pleasures I derived from these pursuits, activities and values were always short-lived. Eventually I felt as if I was an empty shell of a human being, and powerless to do anything about it. I've felt it many times (I'm not a very quick learner, unfortunately). What I have discovered, among other things, is that I derive pleasure by achieving goals. The harder the goal is to attain, the sweeter the pleasure I experience when I have. This is why buying and owning things are such a fleeting pleasure. Since I invested so little of my emotions into the act of attaining an object to possess, I retain very little satisfaction for long.

The advertisements I see that promote products, are promises of inner peace and eternal satisfaction, or sexual reward, at times. In general, they result in short-lived joy and much disappointment.

There are fictions all around you that are sold to you, not for your good, but that of others. When you are unable to identify them as such, you buy into the lies that trap you within that system. Your awareness and ability to dissect your surroundings are your filters for parsing what is truth, and what is propaganda.

As much as this book is for you, you must realize that the processes I'm describing are in here because I've lived them to various degrees. You will go through similar processes. I'm almost sure that there are lot more like me who go through life, not really knowing what it is that they want, but certain that it isn't what is being sold to them. Since life is what you make of it, if you don't know any alternative ways of thinking, you tend to believe what you are told, even though it might feel wrong.

I'm sure there are many others, who, like me, have been struggling for something to latch onto as being worthwhile ends for which to strive. For me, the ability to develop my mind has been the first step toward that process.

The spheres of human thoughts and emotions toward which you focus, and in which you will invest your energies, dictate the way you will live your reality. The areas in which you will invest your potential are what should concern you most. One of the first problems you'll encounter after childhood is the inability to achieve true satisfaction.

Don't be so hard on yourself, it's not a myth, and it's not impossible. It just takes time and practise. When you are young, it's actually quite easy to get it. The older you grow, though, the more it seems to slip away. To a certain degree, it's like developing a tolerance to life. It's true that when you get no new experiences, the repetitions of the old ones get more and more boring.

The trouble, you see, is internal, and not external. You will start looking for ways of breaking the monotony of your life by getting new *stuff*. You'll notice, growing up, that advertisements everywhere will sell you excitement and novelty. You might even start believing that it is by surrounding yourself with more objects that you are finding new and exciting ways of living your life.

If this was the case, though, you wouldn't have to keep buying more objects. You will get used to being told what to desire by others in your surroundings. Eventually, those societal values imposed on you might become all-encompassing and you'll actually live them as if they were the end-all and be-all of your existence.

The fact is that many of them are band-aids covering the true needs you have. Some people out there really do think they need to buy objects to be happy. They just don't know otherwise, that's all. They do it to fill that empty void they have, and by buying, they cure that desire for a little while.

It comes back, over and over, of course, just like any addiction. They have been inundated with information which has convinced them that this act is the one they can perpetrate to accomplish the fulfilment of their joy. They have no other basis for comparison and that is why they are indoctrinated into believing this is so. Of course, there are times

71

when the object of desire is necessary, but in this case I am referring to the sole act of purchasing to feel actual joy.

We *are* addicts, of a kind. We find joy mostly in what is exterior to us, because many of us cannot recreate this feeling within ourselves, and this is how we live our lives. We are constantly trying to prove our self-worth by exterior means. In a sense, this is normal. We are raised to look at others for opinions of ourselves, to normalize and regulate our behavior. This has somehow become the entire basis for our self-worth, though. We can no longer look upon our own lives without having to look towards the mirror that is our peers. We want to see if what is reflected is pretty enough to be worthwhile.

In this, as in everything else, there is no one to blame, but if you want to lead a life that isn't dependent on pure cosmetics, then we should look at other options, shouldn't we?

You have a brain, and in that brain, you have almost unlimited space to put just about anything you might want to. Everything that you incorporate into that mind of yours stretches the limits of the possibilities you have, in every branch of human thought. You will never be bored if you have an active mind, and you will always have a pursuit at hand if you let your curiosity and ingenuity run wild. The choice is between what is inside you or what is outside of you. One requires you to achieve the means to surround yourself with objects, and the other the patience to fill your head with thoughts.

For a very long time, I picked the former. I can't say I regret it, since that was my choice. I have changed my mind on the subject, though, and I can honestly say that I am, in my own opinion, a better person.

I understand, though, the dilemma people are faced with. It is far easier to buy things than to have the patience to achieve anything.

That's the trade-off, unfortunately.

You either get what you want quickly and are bored with it just as fast, or take the time to get to know something worthwhile and enjoy it for the rest of your life.

It's not really a question of choosing one over the other, as much as how much you concentrate your energies to have one more than the other.

You'll always have *things*, and you'll always have *thoughts*, but both take time and energy to get. The arena in which you invest more of your time and energy will either help your material progress or mental progress. Only you can choose what is more important to you. Both are important, but the emphasis is presently placed on acquiring material possessions. Now that you know this, you have a better chance of evaluating your priorities.

Imagine for a moment that you are in a house. Outside the house, there is a dome, covering it. There are no doors in the dome, and you can't climb over it. It is opaque. The more you learn, the wider the dome gets, and begins to circle the neighborhood. You can now walk around the neighborhood and discover things that you didn't know existed before. Now that you see these new parts of the neighborhood, you can learn more, and the dome gets as big as the city you are in. Great! Now you can explore a whole city, to find what you've been missing out on. This makes the dome wider, and wider, until eventually it is as big as the entire Universe. That's a big dome! Well, whatever is within that dome is your knowledge and imagination. The dome is the limits to that knowledge. You can't have this inner expansion if you buy things (except for books, of course), only if you learn things. The even more amazing thing is that it *has no limit*. It can go beyond the limits of the Universe, because there are things we dream up every day that defy logic. Your imagination is the limit, always.

You can, of course, decide that knowledge is not for you. You can, most assuredly, stay inside your house, staring at the dome. You will wonder for the rest of your life what you *could have known*. That is entirely up to you. You might discover amazing things that you thought were impossible. You will discover horrible things that you will wish you did not know. That is a fact.

If you deny the opportunity for knowledge, you will miss out on the wonderful because you are afraid of the dreadful. Humans have changed a lot over the years. There are gruesome things we, like any other animal, have perpetrated in the past. No one is perfect, but we are getting better, over all.

Q. That's a lot of info to take in, but I think I get it. You're not saying 'stuff' is bad...

A. No, just that there are other pursuits that shouldn't be ignored, even though they're harder. In a sense, there was a shift in thinking, a long time ago. Back then, people had nothing except for monarchy and religious dogma, and then there was a revolution called the Enlightenment, which shifted thought away from religious pursuit to more earthly ones like secular rule and Reason as the basis for truth, and that was kind of the beginning of the desire for *objects*, I think, since the pursuit of a Higher Power was seen as secondary to science.

We're drawing toward the logical conclusion of society that's obsessed with acquisition. There has to be a renewed balance, because there aren't enough resources to sustain *infinite stuff creation*. By this, I don't mean that we need to start believing in deities again, of course, but that we should at least define a new Higher Purpose, one that isn't so completely obsessed with the individual and material possession. Heresy, I know.

Q. So how do you go about impressing the idea of acquiring thoughts over *stuff* and their baser instincts into people? It pretty much permeates everything we do.

A. For one, knowing it's there and how it works is a good first step. All in all, I think these are a few basic things that make you a better atom. For two:

Obsessions and Passions

In my last part of Universal Wisdom, I spoke about the choice between material possessions and gathering knowledge. There is a common theme in all humans that we share, to some degree, and that is, collecting.

A little while ago, I went to a friend's house, and we were talking about a relative of theirs who owned an apartment complex. A small, six apartment block. The thing is, I found out that he'd been kicked out by his brother, who'd bought the block. The whole conversation had started because he was giving away his books. I love books. Can't get enough. I have tons, it seems, and always find ways to get more.

In any case, that person who owned the block, who also loves books, had filled his own apartment with them. Then the basement. Then one of the free apartments above him. So much so that he'd sunk all his money into his collection. He is a hoarder.

I look at my mother's home. She has a work room where she collects books and papers and activities for kids. She makes new games constantly. She's a teacher. The place is awash in stuff. I told her that she was a hoarder. She said: No, a hoarder is a person who collects garbage, and is very messy. I reminded her of the fact that my father also collected electronic parts and gizmos in the basement of our old house, and that half of it was put away, and half was messy. He was a hoarder. It runs in the family.

I told her that most of *my* books are put on shelves, but I have growing stacks at their feet. I am a hoarder, and it might get out of control. My aunt collects craft things. Her craft corner is redolent with stuff. My wife used to get lots of clothes, before. My sister sews, and has an entire room of her house filled with fabrics and sewing equipment. I used to collect movies: the more, the better.

Of course, to a certain degree, those who collect lots of garbage or have messy homes have just lost control over their collection, but the basic premise remains the same: most people have this deep-rooted obsession. Just remove the negative connotations you automatically associate with the word. Concentrate on the mechanics.

Now, before I go any further, I want to say this: I'm not shaking my head or wagging my finger in anyone's direction. I'm only analyzing. There is nothing inherently wrong with *anything*. I mean that in the most profound sense you can take it. Yet our philosophies have taken us in one direction or another. Remember, we are at the base *only animals*, and our behavior is predicated on instinct, plus whatever extra mental baggage we've developed to behave in social ways.

I spoke a bit about Sins. If you look at the specifics, sins are just natural animal instincts: the urge to gather, to reproduce, to eat, to get angry, to relax, to show off, and to desire what others have, at the core. These things, in and of themselves, are not Bad. They are natural. The trouble, I think, comes in the form of obsession. We get obsessive about things, like when the brakes fall off your collecting, for example. If you think about your own *stuff*, or your own life, there are certain aspects that, whether positive or negative, you obsess about. In the *religious* context, they hinder people from doing what is the most important thing to *them*: worshipping God.

The church thought that people should have a *higher* purpose, that of fearing and obeying the church. I mean God.

This runs through much of organized religion. The fact that people ran from one obsession to the next probably got under their skin, and the deadly sins had to be invented to curtail these activities.

Originally, though, it was a need for social order, so that our fore-fathers coming from hunter-gatherer tribes could settle down into larger populations, into agrarian societies. I'm sure you can see the advantage of people self-policing in pre-scientific societies where clashes could endanger a settlement, or unchecked venereal diseases could do same, etc.

The fact that we have obsessions is not in and of itself bad, either. Some people are obsessed with their art, and only want to create the best of what it is they do. Remember, there are positive and negative aspects to everything. It only depends in what you are getting your mental pleasure from. It all stems from the pleasure chemicals we release when doing something we enjoy, of course.

So, obsessions mixed with a desire for objects will produce a desire to acquire more of similar objects. Obsession for sex, for food, etc., creates this sort of unhealthy imbalance that makes us seek out the objects of our desire, to the detriment of other pursuits. You could call it a dependence as well, or addiction.

I kept on collecting movies way after I stopped really watching them. So there are many elements involved in hoarding, and obsessions, not just the pleasure aspect. For my family, and those who keep their garbage, or just random stuff, there might be an irrational element of: "I might need it later."

I look at my library and think: "I have way too many books." Then that other little voice kicks in and says: "You'll need them for research." No I won't. I really won't. Well… maybe…

So I keep them all, and let them accumulate and multiply, even though people swear a streak every time I move, and bring thirty heavy boxes of books with me. I will never read three quarters of those books again, but I need them somehow. Like they are the proof that I've existed, as well. They are my mark on the world, my legacy. But so what? Like I said, there are many different aspects to obsessions, as there is to everything.

Obsessions can be good and bad, in the societal context. That person collecting so many books he'd lost his home and couldn't pay his mortgage: bad. The mathematician obsessed with an equation that will solve a major problem: good. It all depends on how you look at it.

My personal pet peeve stems from the fact that yes, we do get obsessed with our base natural instincts, but more than that, we no longer have that higher purpose I keep talking about.

I mean, the higher purpose of publicly worshipping God was always a sham and we know it. If there is a God, and he does love you, and you do love him, you don't need to prove it to others or to any authority. Do you? That's between you and your deity. So that was always about controlling the poor and uneducated through a fallacy.

What I mean is, we should be dedicating more time to things that are not purely ourselves or our families. We should find that higher purpose in our community. Who's got time, though, right? Well, people used to find time every Sunday to go to Church and put money in a basket to turn the Vatican into the biggest bank in the world. People still go to Megachurches to turn venal preachers into multimillionaires, against the tenets they themselves preach.

Here, to me, on the obsessions front, is what I see as Western values. We are obsessed about making money to buy things to add to our collections, about sex, about our phobias and anxieties, which we feed with our obsessions for food, and the only higher purpose we have, unwittingly, is giving money to, or making money for, people who are much wealthier than we are, because their obsession for money surpasses anything we can imagine. I'll leave out the politician's obsession for sheer power, because we try not to think about it. We take that as a given.

There are, as they say, alternatives. We can sit down, and look around us. We can think about our thoughts, and picture what our obsessions are. Whether or not they are truly healthy for us. Because, don't we want to do good to ourselves? Don't we deserve to treat ourselves right? For that we need to know where we focus all our energies, to gain some form of satisfaction. Easy as that.

Perhaps we need to think about the idea of *too much*, and what we need to do to curb our excesses, if they are unhealthy. To find a new focus, which will give us the satisfaction we crave, but will not harm us physically, or mentally.

The Buddhists choose the middle path, meaning not too little, or not too much. That's a road worth investigating, as a way to curtail our overindulgences.

That higher purpose I keep alluding to? Seek out an activity that does something to benefit the community. Simply put, it is investing in people who are not simply yourself or your immediate family.

If you think about it, you spend most of your time either taking care of yourself, or them. There are 168 hours in a week. 56 are spent sleeping. That leaves you 112 hours. Apart from the time you spend at work, or with your wife, husband, kids, or social media, the odds are you can find an hour of time to do something altruistic.

There is a reason I say this. The vast majority of people read this and might think: "Dammit, not another do-gooder hippy bastard." No, not at all, actually. You can keep your stereotypes. I am being serious.

The bonds that hold society together are the glue that ordinary people put in to make things smoother for everyone else. Think of charitable organizations, non-profits, and the like. Making sure that those who have trouble staying on the bottom of the ladder don't fall off. Well, they need help as well. We need to ensure that not only people do not fall off the ladder, we who are higher up on it give them and their kids a hand to climb higher than just the bare minimum.

Everybody needs a hand, sometime. Whether to get out of poverty, or have an ear to talk to, or someone who can teach them something useful. We all have something we are good at, that we can help others with. We're all teachers in a way.

Q: But why do all this? I have no time for this crap. It's bunk.

A: Well, that's the cynical view of the society you live in, is all. You don't have to think that way. You've been conditioned to. If you thought just that, though: congrats! You're well-conditioned. Why would you give your time away for free? It's simple. Because you will feel amazing.

Q: You've got to be kidding me.

A: Not even a little. Listen, there is no sales pitch, I'm not trying to sell you religion, or a product, or anything tangible. Just your own feeling of inner peace and well-being. You don't have to shave your head and join a cult.

Q: It just sounds so... I don't know...

A: Corny? Wholesome? What rebel would ever think that way, right? Isn't it weird that we've grown up to think that helping others is some sort of cliché bullshit? Like we lose coolness points for giving people a hand?

It's funny, as well, when I used to hear people say the words "inner peace and well-being," I thought of homeopathy and quack medicine, and fake spirituality, and all that bullshit. That meant I was well-conditioned. I un-conditioned myself from cynicism. Didn't need it.

What I do need, is inner peace and well-being. So how do I get it? There are many different ways, but it's just about helping, really. Giving time or, in my case, money to charities that I know are helping real people, and not just those that run the charity, gives me a sense of accomplishment I don't get otherwise.

Q: Good for you, pal.

A: I know you're thinking all sorts of snarky thoughts right now, but it really is your loss. I don't pity you, I just wish you could see how happy you could be. That would make me happy for you, in turn. Hey, that's why I wrote this in the first place: to help you. Like I said, though, you pick and choose the tools. I only provide them.

That's another thing I do now. I obsess over ways to help other people find happiness, and then I give those methods away for free. Because hey, why not?

It's been discovered that you get a greater thrill from giving than receiving. You've given Christmas presents, and waited with anticipation to see what others' reactions would be. The excitement you felt when they finally opened their gift, and the glow in their eyes when they saw it for the first time. You can feel it now, as an echo of the moment itself.

Now think of doing that, over and over. Not giving the *gift* of an object, but the *gift* of your time, or your expertise, to help people out, even just a little. It brings genuine joy to your life the way hoarding, sex, eating, or "likes" on your social media cannot.

Because the *stuff* gets old quickly, and you need more. The sex is over within an hour, and then you want more. The food gets digested and you get hungry again. The "likes" last a split second and you need more. The money you send to save a refugee's life will stick with you. You saved someone's life! How cool is that?

An hour a week is all we would need to do some real change, in your life and the lives of others. Donating an hour a week to, say, Habitat for Humanity, to help someone build a house. Or give your time to read or hang out with elderly people. Or choose a worthy charity or political party and help boost them so that we could all enact real change. Because the difference between those Sins I was talking about earlier and becoming a helping person is turning our obsessions away from ourselves and toward giving a hand to others. Getting the obsession to help seems counter-intuitive, but it's scientifically proven to work.

But the things you do for others? The thought of the joy you spread around? That stays with you. It's a buzz, and it feels good.

I have my own obsessions.

Q: Well, what you're describing sounds more like passions than obsessions. Isn't that right?

A: I think it's just a matter of semantics. Passions are the obsessions you have that appear to have some sort of positive influence on either your life or that of others. Passions are the things you obsess with that your family hasn't disowned you for. Yet.

I'll be honest, I have a ton of obsessions, but I'm trying to turn them into passions, as it were. I want to be a business owner, someone who helps others, someone who gives great advice, someone who can ameliorate who he is, someone who writes worthy prose, and someone who will have a positive influence on his community. Those are my obsessions. There are many more, of course, but to me, they are the ones that count.

And you, where do your obsessions lie? More importantly: do they bring you positive, or negative things? Mull it over, and see what you come up with.

Everything's Related

From the little dog in your neighbor's yard to the Prime Minister, to the whales beneath the sea, to the rings of Saturn, everything has correlation. It's all action and reaction, and a giant mess of relationships we can't begin to fathom or comprehend.

It's complex.

Whether it happened today, yesterday, a hundred-million years ago, or has not happened yet, relationships intrinsic or external among humans, objects, animals, the world, the environment, or even the Universe, all come together to shape and mold who we are, and everything else with it. Whether this is through evolution or influence, our interrelatedness affects us all.

For one, you can think of such ideas as the butterfly effect to understand what I'm talking about. The fluttering of a butterflies' wings can set off hurricanes on the other side of the planet, or so they say. The actions you take, positive or negative, or do not take, have consequences.

Do not be afraid into inaction. This is normal. It should just make you realize: you matter.

Two babies are born. One is white. The other black. Depending on the geographical location of their birth, their socio-economic conditions, and the education they receive, they could become best of friends when they are old enough to meet. Or they could marry after courtship. Or hate each other. Or they could kill each other. They could also become President and Vice President. There is an infinite amount of variables involved in the simple transaction of meeting for the first time, between two human beings, whose skin colour differs.

Depending on emotional baggage, education, similarity of world-view (or the opposite). This plays out a hundred thousand million times a day, all over the planet, with every single one of its inhabitants.

These relationships and animosities are not only dependent on pigmentation, as you know. Any difference among groups can be used to any effect. It all depends on who is directing the narrative, and for what purpose.

Most people are simply strangers, and we harbour our curiosity or animosity in secret, going about our daily lives. When the opportunity for interaction does arise, though, which path should we choose? Usually, it is the one most travelled within our psyches that wins out.

So we bring out a smile and a handshake if we are of an open mind, or a frown and repulsion if we are not.

It is our education and experience which will define the outcome of the encounter. Generally speaking, the more segregated the upbringing, the less likely there is to be friendship from the encounter, and this from all parties. This is why a broad education is paramount to better encounters. To better relationships. To a better world. And we can only count on ourselves as the ambassadors of this better education. To live it. To make others realize that it is possible, and laudable.

It would not be so bad if there were but *one* bigot, in this world, and everyone saw him for what he was: a small-minded fool who has never been further than the end of his driveway. This is, however, not the case. There are scores of people who, for one reason or another, can't stand humans who have skin a different colour than theirs, a language they cannot comprehend, or a culture they see as alien because they've never encountered difference in their lives save to ridicule it. This creates friction, and tension, to entire regions. For what reasons? Pigmentation. Vowels and consonants unfamiliar and frightening. Fear of the unknown.

It would be okay if there were only one religious extremist, and he'd been found before doing any damage to anyone. Just locked up and looked at as if he were slightly loopy. Cared for, even though his only purpose was to kill all those who didn't think like him. But there are many, and what possible reason could justify this kind of behavior? Interpretation. Denial of the beauty in difference. Intolerance.

I wouldn't mind so much if there were a logging company that cut down trees, just the one, and few trees ended up chopped. But this isn't so, and we end up getting junk-mail flyers we throw into the trash the moment we get them, allowing for entire forests to be completely obliterated. And not only logging companies, but all companies involved in the extraction of natural resources and creation of products. Why do we need this? Because we're consumers, and our values lie in our purchasing power. And so we must destroy to make things worth selling. To give us value as people because if we don't have money, we are worthless.

What's the relationship among these three? What interconnectedness is to be found? On a small scale, not much, admittedly. On a larger scale you have the movements of societies and the survival of the planet, and our place on it as well. The bigots who make life hell for people who are different than themselves create an underclass of citizens by denying them access to paying jobs. They torment them and taunt them, and so anyone who is not within the circle of the *elect* ethnicity is free game to be tortured, marginalized and killed (Think of people of colour in the United States, or indigenous people in Canada). They are disrespected and vilified. This causes strife within their own communities, socio-economic and otherwise, which in turn affects the rest of the population.

Intolerance wrecks economies and lives, and is driven by hate. It destroys nations by awakening the worst emotions in those who live there.

The religious extremist has a tendency to call for the elimination of others, and when he joins up with other (albeit twisted, like-minded) individuals, will easily find those they hate, to persecute, and execute. Their actions, and that of those responsible for their rise, might even cause the evacuation of entire regions to flee from their acts of savagery, causing pressure in other countries where refugees will either be accepted or sent to their death by the narrow-minded aforementioned bigots who will reject them and send them back to be killed by the extremists.

Meanwhile, one of the main reasons why the religious extremists came to power was the rise of a political class dominated by corporate special interests which pushed the country to go to war for access to their natural resources in the first place. Everything is related. From A to Z.

Everything I've been writing so far is also inter-connected on a deeper level as well. I spoke of obsessions, and what we perceive as Sins, which are our natural appetites allowed to run rampant. I spoke of philosophies, and what makes us tick, and many other things. It is hard to stay on subject for me, because, as I am saying, all that stuff doesn't happen in a vacuum. It's all inter-related.

Everything about us, within us, is connected as well – whether (logically) it be our body parts, our emotions, our thoughts, and the actions resulting wherefrom. On a larger scale, we affect our environment through our common upbringing and the values we share as a society, or share even through the rejection of society, or parts thereof. We are all in this together, whether we want to be or not. When society is small enough, everyone must pull their weight or everyone suffers. When it is large enough, we can share the burdens that arise, and spread the risk around.

Q. The people you mentioned, in the bigots and extremist's case, sound like they have very closed emotions.

A. They do, and that's one of the reasons why we have problems among populations. We all put up umbrellas over our heads, above that of our groups, to make sure the groups survives and thrives.

Q. What do you mean by umbrellas?

Umbrellas

A : We all have personal philosophies. Personal beliefs stemming either from Faith or surrounding cultural norms. We are influenced by the currents of thought that permeate our environment. Some of it is very old thought, coming from the Greeks, or Buddhism, perhaps. Some of it very young, like: You only live once, or YOLO.

Whatever thoughts we were transmitted were done so to survive in the localized geographical area in which we reside. There are various types of thoughts: geographical, nationalistic, religious, political, family-related, etc., and all of them give us an edge, or should, in our personal survival and our betterment. All of these thoughts are somehow blended together in our minds, and from them we choose our courses of action.

Now comes the tricky part: some favour the individual, and some favour the group, and we always walk a tightrope between the two.

We live in society, which means that we must interact or *get along* with many others of our species. Certain philosophical strategies have prepared us for this cohabitation, like: "live and let live," or, "do unto others as you would have them do unto you." But these are not *natural* tendencies. These are doctrines that have been perpetuated through conditioning by certain religious groups. It's not brainwashing. It's a perfectly logical strategy for having large numbers of people inhabit the same region without harming each other. But for that to work, there is a necessity for philosophies that take "the long view."

When we take it upon ourselves to lie, cheat, steal, rape, kill, take more than our fair share, etc., we are taking the short view, and are thinking only about ourselves. We are answering the call of our primal, animalistic instincts, and not trying to live up to our higher potential, to transcend our origins, to become a better being.

We leave behind societal concerns and survival to tell everyone that *our* concerns are the prime concerns. This is natural person at work. But unfortunately, we are no longer entirely natural persons. We are also societal persons, and we must work at trying to balance individuality and society.

We started off with tribes. Some genius figured out that if tribes got together and hunted side-by-side, they could make off with better loot, or hunts, and so the first societies began. But they had to make rules within that group, or else they would end up destroying each other. To avoid blowing up this wonderful thing they'd created and worked well when they all put in their lot together, they made a pact, to follow certain codes of conduct so that the group would stay cohesive.

Fast forward several thousand years. We have nations with Declarations of Human Rights. Our new pacts, which we must respect, to continue moving along the timeline in a non-destructive way (toward the people within the territory, anyhow).

What are the problems we have now? This one is a two-parter:

1) Those within the territory are not taught the same pact uniformly, and therefore do not act with the good of the whole at heart. They must live at a survival level, and to do this have to resort to those negative traits so dangerous to the lifeblood of society. This is because not all those within the territories are treated equally, and those who are below the level of opportunity have no choice but to act in manners that do not allow them to live up to the expectations that those who are. Socio-economic and racial prejudice play a huge part in the dynamics of a multi-ethnic country, but the same pressures are applied economically, by class structure or through sexual politics in other, more homogenous nations.

2) Those outside *our* territory have different rules, laws, rights, prejudices, and philosophies which, when used properly, provide opportunity for enmity and strife, even war. War is started by leaders desiring to acquire some result out of the conquering of others' territory, which in turn causes misery and death. War is also declared to polarize a disparate

and unfocused population in *our* territory to point them all in the same direction through the fear and hatred of a manufactured enemy.

So how do we overcome these two major problems?

This is both simple, and very hard (of course). As a footnote, I've been told many a times before that what I expound upon is "very easy for you to say!" Yes, it is. But for something to be done, it has to begin as an idea, then acted upon. Nevertheless, it must be said!

Let me give you the umbrella analogy. Yes, I'm finally getting around to it. If you have a tiny umbrella, it will help you in the rain. Only you can carry it, and everyone else will get wet. Simple. If you have a bit bigger umbrella, you could have five or ten people out of the rain, and you could all hold it up, making sure those under it stayed dry. What if you had an enormous umbrella? That could cover an entire country? Imagine one-hundred million people kept out of the rain, all holding it up. But what of the rest of the planet?

This is the point we are at. We had these individual umbrellas millions of years ago when we foraged alone. We made better ones to protect the tribe. Then, eventually, we created umbrellas to help large swaths of the human population. Now we must create an umbrella that covers the entire planet, and we must do it without fail.

Q. Right. Common philosophy as 'World Umbrella.' But the world is a very vast thing, and everyone believes in different things. How can you create a World Umbrella?

A. You just have to pick the right *values*, and throw them out there, and see who decides to follow them, teach them, share them, no matter what.

Q. But there are so many entrenched powers that it makes it sound an impossible task. There will always be those who want war, or who don't care to fix poverty. What do you say about that?

What the Globe Looks Like

Yes, we have been becoming, on the whole, a much less destructive species, which is laudable in many ways. We have done so through our finding common ground with other people.

We have imposed peace upon our nations and taken away the means for others to destroy each other. We have found ways of interacting with each other that avoided mutual self-destruction.

Of course, the weapons we have at our disposal could definitely put an end to this little experiment we call humanity, and may actually still do so if we are not careful.

Fortunately, in many societies, the new power-center is no longer the business of war, but the business of Business, predominantly. As the world becomes more cross-integrated beyond the borders of every nation, destruction of the other becomes a less viable option.

In my opinion, this might be why we encourage poor nations to war among themselves. Since they have no real 'value' as business partners, wealthy countries see them as the last places they can sell their weapons. A touch cynical, but not an altogether implausible theory.

It is time for a new step in the experiment, however. The time has come to see the intrinsic worth of the human being for who he or she is, independent of their value as a commodity or consumer.

The way the system works, poor countries are enslaved by richer ones to produce for them, and their citizens are kept in poverty by their economic systems which have been coerced by corporations. The goal being to pay as little as possible to reap as much profit as possible.

We will never be able to achieve any kind of peace or equality while all we are interested in is the abuse of our neighbor for our own pleasure or enrichment.

Yes, we do get four hundred dollar Smart Phones because Chinese workers are paid fifty cents an hour and are packed ten people to a room in god-awful factories.

Yes, we do get five dollar t-shirts because we pay ten cents an hour to Pakistani laborers. We are slavers. This is the new slavery.

We don't have to look much further than the private prison system which wants disenfranchised black/brown people incarcerated because they are free labor.

But someone is paying for all that cheap/free stuff. There's a balance in the scales that is completely out of whack. Those Chinese slaves are living in Hell, and we should care. The same goes for the Pakistani, or Vietnamese, or countless African countries whose labor practices we will circumvent as soon as they get the balls to bring them up to code.

Because we want slaves. We *need* slaves, apparently. We *love* cheap stuff. Maybe we need to change the way we look at human beings, then.

Would you like your brother or sister packed like a sardine in a sweat shop making clothing ten hours a day? How about your mother? Or your father?

Why is it okay for someone else's?

Q. It's not, but there's not much I can do about it, is there?

A. There is always something to do. No matter how small the effort, it is better than acquiescence.

No matter how much better things have gotten with the model of humanity we have today, there are still billions of people living in poverty and being crushed by systems that we help enforce. And that needs to be addressed.

And yes, for a lot of people, things have gotten a lot better. We worry much less about fiery death raining down from the skies than we used to during the tense times of the Cold War. Many of our neighbours have no such luck, as can be testified by the many conflicts still destroying societies across the globe.

Much of our aggression has been redirected for positive results, in our business, sports, and entertainment, which has altered the dynamics of our societies for the better. I only use this example to illustrate society as a macroscope of our personal lives.

To wit, the more *open* (inter-social) traits we incorporate in the general societal makeup, the better it works as a whole. The more we involve our destructive, aggressive traits into competitive fields that do not include violence, or at least not mortal violence, the better inter-societal development we can expect.

Society, though, is made of individuals, each with his or her own opinions, upbringing, difficulties, hurdles, joys, and all those elements that influence him or her. To have a truly great society requires many elements.

By *great*, I mean one where everybody has the opportunity as well as the drive for self-fulfilment in a way that is beneficial to all. The behavior and core beliefs of each individual dictates how well society will function, as a whole.

I strongly believe that it is important for people to have within them the traits that are desirable for that result to come to fruition.

Great societies are comprised of people whose open social traits far outweigh the negative, and who, if they are given a common project for which to work for, can accomplish incredible things.

The attitudes required for any social interaction to succeed in a mutually beneficial manner are *trustworthiness*, *honesty*, and *goodwill*. As an aside, some cynics will say that it is money that is the all-important bond that keeps societies chugging along. I agree in the sense that it greases the wheels, but it is only an exterior tool. Wherever there is a lack of it, social cohesion disintegrates if there are no other *mental bonding agents*.

Poverty is not synonymous with dishonesty.

As much as laws can be a powerful deterrent on any person, they are also only an *exterior* constraint. If the internal flaws and contradictions of the society in question are not addressed, laws are only created to repress, rather than uplift.

The fracturing of a State or Nation through its lack of cohesion eventually has to be addressed or face the dissolution of the State itself.

Cohesion can only be brought on by making its members equal partners in its constant construction and betterment. Since society begins with the individuals that comprise them, the influence they exert is inestimable.

It is a matter of common good to instill those three previously mentioned positive traits of trustworthiness, honesty, and goodwill in all members of society, since they are the ones that reduce much of the friction that is generated among many people living together. I will be teaching you about all this stuff so that you can live it yourself.

You see, even though you can behave in a thousand different ways, it's by being a kind, honest, peaceful person that you will avoid trouble, make friends, and keep them. You will go far in life with a positive drive, but you'll go even further with a terrific reputation as someone others can count on and won't harm them.

Some people still think that *their* interests are the only thing that matter, and that these traits are useless. Little do they realize how much their lives would be enhanced if they chose otherwise.

Self-Analysis

I t is not enough to say: "I'm awesome!" as many seem to do, with no particular reason. There is no basis in warranting for a high opinion of myself simply for existing, wherever or however that may be.

I can, of course, ride on the coat-tails of those who came before me and claim their victories for my own. That would be dishonest and stupid, so I discourage you from doing that. You are your own person. Don't look for an easy ride.

The same goes for thinking: "I suck." How can you know how or who you are if you don't analyze yourself and have no basis for comparison, I wonder? By comparison, I don't mean to other people, but to the ideals I've set for myself.

That's why I take the time, once in a while to take stock of where I am in my life, to see what I've accomplished, to think of what I'd love to do, what I want to learn next, how I'll do it, and what it will bring me in the grand scheme of things. Generally, I'm satisfied. I neither think I'm the best, or the worst. If I did something right, I'll pat myself on the back. If I could do something better, I figure out what I need to do to accomplish it.

If I've encountered a problem, I will set myself to solving it.

I do, however, feel a constant need to improve myself. It is my evolution. There are many requirements for this. True evolution takes many thousands of years, but I use *evolution* instead of *change*, since the decisions I make to become a better person don't just change me from one thing to another. They force me to take a step upward, and I do feel ameliorated for having done so.

The basis for these thoughts is that I, as an individual, have a duty to be the best person I can for my surroundings, as well as for myself. I couldn't be a good person if I didn't raise you to be that as well. You couldn't be a good person if I raised you as a hypocrite.

That is why, to me, being kind, honest, and peaceful are the best policies to pursue if I want to be a positive force in mine, yours, and societal life in general.

As well, putting the emphasis on logic and truth make it so that there are always means for you and I to discover something new, and to not be ashamed of being wrong. These simple facts are often overlooked as being too difficult, since it is easier to do the opposite of all of these.

Ego takes a lot of room in the equation, and it is most often *that* which people feed to pursue their own happiness. The trouble with that line of thought is that, like buying things to achieve joy, the result of the pursuits are just as empty. Feeding the ego is like trying to fill a bottomless pit.

It cannot be done.

Only personal achievement in the field you have chosen, as well as the road you have decided to take to reach that goal will instill in you true satisfaction. You won't know *constant* satisfaction. It is something you achieve. For that, you have to be unsatisfied with an element of your life to pursue it. It does, however, carry the added bonus of lasting a lifetime, in whatever area you have nailed it.

Yeah, I'm going right back into my talk about society. It's hard to avoid, since the individual is a product of society, and vice-versa. I think I may have mentioned earlier that everything is interrelated? This is partially what I was talking about. You can't have one without the other, and you can't understand things about yourself if you don't get what society is about. Paradoxes are an integral part of what humanity is, as well. I'm sure I'll be naming a few examples later. Everything has changed for human society over the years, which means everything has changed for the individuals living in these societies.

For one thing, poverty levels have shot down tremendously in the past two-hundred years. The main reasons are because of education, a fairer distribution of wealth, and incredible advances in medical technology. It took a lot of soul-searching on the part of our philosophers, however, to decide what was truly important.

The power structures, however, have remained more or less the same. The wealthy class (at the moment) pockets the political class in return for favours. They, in turn, are in charge of a mostly malleable and unknowing workforce underneath them, which sustains them all.

This, to my knowledge, is one of the main problems facing the world today. A distracted populace led by a power-hungry political elite controlled by those fed by greed, whether bankers or moneyed men. The perpetual recreation of this system is also something that concerns me, and should concern you, since it is my personal belief that by *altering* these, some of our oldest shackles, we could perhaps head into more prosperous times as a whole *species*. That, however, would take self-analysis on the part of those who controls the reins of power.

The more we know, as a whole, the better our choices are when we choose a leader. It is by making good choices that we head in more positive directions. If we consider the betterment of all peoples as a positive development, and the restriction of destruction and division as negative, we can better make decisions towards the improvement of personal, local, provincial, national, and worldwide situation. All of this starts, of course, with the individual. You, me, everybody. You have to know who you are to decide what you truly want, and for what reason.

Even though the end-goal is large, it always begins with one person, and that person is you. Fortunately, you are not alone. There are many others just like you who are looking to better themselves, and will join forces with you to achieve these goals.

You should not be afraid of the road ahead, it is well travelled, and you will be amongst friends.

Here's your alternative: you do nothing, live your life, and let things slide into the oblivion we could head into. It's not much of a choice, but it's the choice we've all got.

I hate to drop all that on you in one fell swoop, but that is the basis of economic systems we have in the majority of the world. That doesn't mean it will always be like that, only that that is what has prevailed so far.

There was a time when a regime called Communism was dominant, elsewhere, but that was the extreme opposite of the system we have now. They wanted absolute control over production, and the distribution of wealth evenly to all. That failed miserably. On the other hand, you have the Capitalist System, which says that everything should cost something, only the best and brightest deserve money, and they have it because of that reason.

It also commands that no restrictions be placed on the Free Market economy, and that is quickly becoming obsolete as well.

On paper, both look very appealing indeed. The difficulty lies in the extremes, and the intercession of *reality*. A system that is completely altruistic and controlled cannot work because it eliminates competition and stifles innovation (there's also the fact that human greed and will to power come into play).

Conversely, a system that demands no restraints and profit only for those that can control it ends in chaos for any and all who do not manipulate it.

No system can work well without some kind of balance between the needs of the many and the greed of the few. You will see the dichotomies of all World Systems, in and of themselves, and amongst each other when you are older. For now, just keep in mind that extremes in one shape or form create general misery for the majority.

My end-goal is not a diatribe of one strata of society against another. Or even to pit people against one another. Quite the opposite, in fact. I may express disappointment, as most people do, but that is not my point either. I demonstrate as frankly as I can the way that I see we are living, to encourage the positive, find solutions to the negative, and sort out everything in between.

I want to speak about the way we, as a species, might be able to surmount hurdles which were placed in our way, and are an intrinsic part of who we are.

We, of course, cannot do it without you. A species is as much a single person as it is 7.5 billion humans and increasing daily. We each have problems to solve through our lives, in order to lead better ones.

We learn how to surmount our challenges, with the limited equipment we are given, and hope for the best. Our societies must face bitter challenges to grow and prosper as well, and not only continue along the boom but bust cycles they have been following since the human race was still young.

I posit that we face challenges as a species that if we fail to overcome, we will not survive, *any of us*. Since it is the goal of every organism to pass on its genes to the next generation, it would be a great tragedy for the human race not to do so, for we would be remiss in our genetic programming.

No big loss for the Universe, of course, but sad for all of us who think we are heading somewhere.

My idea, therefore, to set Humanity as the highest ideal, would be to supersede all other ideals we live for now, whether it be money, in most cases, or deities, food, revenge, sex, or any of the other smaller pursuits that we go about chasing in our daily lives.

Even though they are *natural*, not placing anything above ourselves takes the focus off of our survival and places us in front of a mirror. We can preen and take selfies, and be all about ourselves, but if a sizable portion of the population remains unconcerned about the welfare of the whole planet, we are doomed to failure. I do not say this to invoke fear, but it is a very real possibility. I'm also not saying that that should be our sole purpose. I'm just invoking the fact that it should play some role in our daily lives.

Efficiency as Prosperity

One of the great quandaries I am posed with is efficiency. Not in the sense of *faster*, but in the sense of *better*. Every single person has their own version of 'efficiency.' I am only presenting my version, for your consideration.

In every aspect of Nature, the most efficient one will dominate and survive, in the niche which is its home. The same can be said about humanity. For example, when a new technology comes onto the market, it supplants the ones that came before it. Spoken word was replaced by print media, which was surpassed by the radio, which was killed by television (and killed the radio star), which is being destroyed by the internet.

We live within systems that supplanted others throughout time. We started off as small tribes, incorporated bigger ones, founded Nations of like people, and now live in Countries populated by people of all ethnic backgrounds. Through every process, we have adapted new methods to make interpersonal relationships as egalitarian as possible, so as to make societies as efficient (towards their own survival) as possible.

Populations have to be stable within the borders of the country for them to thrive, and help it to prosper. The more internal division is created, and segments of the population left out, the less a country can work efficiently towards prosperity. To create a prosperous nation, its people must care about the direction the Country is headed, and work hard for it to get there, *as a whole*.

They cannot do so if they feel they are being abused or discriminated against. They cannot do so if they are unemployed or very poor. They cannot do so if the dominating emotions of its people are greed, fear, and hatred.

These are the dominant emotions of a paranoid, bigoted, and ignorant Nation. Whenever you introduce one of these emotions into the National discourse, they become the dominant emotions, because negative emotions tend to be louder.

Anger screams, yet love whispers.

Love is more powerful, but anger is more violent.

Only those whose agendas are selfish use them as tactics to divide their own countries to help themselves. A nation cannot stay great if there are those who would take all from their citizens. They are then, through their actions, the instigators of the destruction of their own States. An 'efficient' Nation is one which is ruled by its educated people, and by this I mean *all* its people, not only its rulers.

The more people are educated, the clearer their choices are. The less they are educated, the more they are led and easily used. This is as true on a societal as a personal level.

You and I, and society at large, cannot function efficiently for the good of all when we do not have the information necessary to make important decisions.

We cannot make efficient decisions if we are blinded by hatred, lack knowledge, or are gripped with fear on any level. Think very hard about the way you wish to live, and what your dominant emotions are.

As well, when you make any decision, remember that you are influencing the discourse for all around you. Your choice should reflect the good of the many, no matter how much you want it to be about you.

There are strong reasons why unselfish emotions were promulgated so much within religious groups. If this had not been done, there is no chance we could have lived so close to so many people without great injury or injustice to each other.

It is the spread of these ideals that pacified many warring clans. Ironically, they also created new tensions based on the origin of the decrees, but that is a matter of politics, not morals.

The basis of our ethical behavior is, in great part, derived from the theistic decrees that came before them. Granted, these laws have restrained our freedoms to a certain point, but it has been done so for the benefit of the majority.

Who can honestly complain about the freedom of walking down the street without the constant threat of being killed for no reason whatsoever? Where prejudice prevails, and dehumanization is king, people are still murdered for no other reason than being themselves. This is the state of affairs we should be educating others about, and working to stop. Where people suffer stigma, and are shunned or hurt for simply having different skin colour, all people suffer. Where people are refused jobs, services, or even the right to live for any reason, everyone within that Nation suffers. It impedes the progress and efficiency of the Nation to better itself.

The next step in our global evolution is not how much immense wealth we can hoard, or how many people we have sex with. We should judge Nations by how much poverty or unhappiness we find there.

Then we find a way to fix it. There is no other way. We can't wait for government to fix our problems. We need to seek efficiency. In helping others. Out of poverty, into education, into well-paying jobs, into meaningful lives.

As world population grows, we will be faced with new challenges. One of the biggest involves the relatively unrestrained movement of people around the planet.

How you and I live our ethical behaviour, in the face of so many contrary views, will dictate how we will decrease the friction we create by merely existing. This requires looking beyond the physical aspects to deal with the mental aspect of human relations. The balancing act then created is one of accepting the inherent differences you have with others, while still retaining your knowledge of the mechanics of the Universe, and your opinions of them.

As no two people think exactly alike, it is presumptuous to believe that others will think the same way you do. This should not stop you from developing good relationships with others who think differently.

In this case, the opponent is yourself, and you are going beyond pettiness and judgment to get to know a fellow human being. As I mentioned before, most people are good, and should be taken for that value first, and any others afterwards.

Strangely, this is how most people act towards each other, naturally, in the first place. The divisions are generally created by the leaders of States, to promote themselves and their power first.

I think you remember my telling you that some people like to bash others to make themselves seem better? This is an often used propaganda tool to rile up entire populations. It does nothing, however, to decrease world tension. You will see for yourself, of course, what treating others fairly and honestly will do. These aren't 'tactics', but methods for living healthier lives.

The more you spread love, the more love will be spread by others. The opposite is also true. The more hatred you disseminate, the more it gets spread around.

In the Beginning...

The human being is an interesting creature. One that denotes itself from others on this planet because of a few qualities it acquired that differentiate it from its fellow animals.

Since the beginning, we have tried to make sense of our surroundings. Born naked and afraid in the African Savannah, many millennia ago, with no sense but that of our own survival to guide us, we created stories about the things that most scared us, to tame them, and quiet our minds, as well as to ensure our survival.

If we yelled loud enough, did not those dark clouds seem to be frightened of us, instead of the opposite, and glide slowly away? Did that not mean, then, that they were possessed with agency? What else, then, was animate in the arid, unfriendly plains?

And so, as time passed, we developed and grew, as much in our physical form as our mental. We tamed the beasts that hunted us, and began to eat them.

We tamed the lands that surrounded us, and eventually began to grow our foods on them.

We tamed the lupine and feline quadrupeds, and made them our pets and companions, what we know as dogs and cats today.

We tamed the Spirits of the rain, of the hunt, of the dark. Who knew what dangers lurked just out of sight of our watch fires, in the night?

Sometimes, caves kept us safe and warm, and there we could rest with less fear.

As we became more numerous, we began to define our Spirits, gave them qualities and names. Our societies grew. Always, we kept looking for answers. As well, we kept looking for the best methods of perpetuating our tribes, our arts, our beliefs, in the hopes that our human DNA would survive as a child, a clay pot, a song, a story, jewellery, or Deity. We have been perpetuating this methodology, in part, since the beginning of our self-awareness.

All that we do in our lives is based upon trial and error, and sometimes we happen upon a system of thoughts and actions which boost ourselves beyond what we are, because it changes what we consider ourselves to be (and by extension, our reality).

Errors are inevitable, of course, but there are ways of minimizing them. If I keep burning myself on the same stove-top, wouldn't I be silly to not try to find a way of stopping it?

These methods make me more efficient in my treatment of others and myself. They help my survival, and that of others. This gives me time to consider how to better my life even more. Instead of staying in the same rut, for untold years, recycling the same negative thoughts, I ascend to a *higher plane*.

The same methods have been utilized for thousands of years, and have been given various names, but their purposes never varied.

What I have simply done was to collect all the most positive aspects of our human traits, and explained why you should reproduce them, in your everyday life.

Since we are the basic building blocks of society, you and I, it goes to reason that adoption of these traits are not only beneficial for ourselves, but for all those around us. There is nothing magical or mystical involved. It all begins, therefore, with a look at the basics.

The World Lenses

remember, a few years ago, having a conversation with a friend of mine. She is a very salt-of-the-earth type, and doesn't believe in any kind of fancy sort of deferential talk. She felt sorry for the way I had to 'bow down' to the kind of snobby people she despised so much, in my work.

I am a server, and as such, I get to see absolutely every type of person that walks the earth. She couldn't stand the kind of person I just described above, feeling that they looked down upon others or saw themselves as better than everybody else. She said that if everybody was the same, we wouldn't have such idiosyncrasies and differing points of view.

She also knew that what she was saying was a fallacy as she said it, to her credit. She had studied psychology, but her surroundings and upbringing made her think a certain way. She saw the world through a certain kind of lens.

She could not help but be a product of those surroundings and ingrained systems of thought, even as she fought them. I thought about this problem a lot, I guess, perhaps unconsciously.

The problem to me was not snobby people, as much as the barriers we create between ourselves, when we see differences as a negative.

I know, in my experience, that absolutely everybody is different. There is no way that everybody will ever be identical. Besides of which, this would be disastrous. Imagine meeting an infinite amount of copies of yourself! Even the most narcissistic among us would get bored eventually.

It is our differences, among peoples, among educations, among backgrounds, that bring out the best and most interesting qualities that human beings have. It would be a crying shame if someone came along and tried to force everyone into the same mold.

That does not mean that it hasn't been tried, of course. It's just that with historical perspective on our side, I see that a lot of blood, sweat, and tears have been spilt in the pursuit of making all the round pegs fit into the square holes.

By now it's become obvious that everything that has gone into writing this book has been about my point of view.

My lens.

It can't be helped, of course. All I am doing is trying to explain which lenses I view the Universe with, and why. That's both extremely simple, and incredibly difficult. Simple in the sense that I can tell you how I interpret the Universe, and the way I *think* the world should be, yet complex because I realize that it's not that easy, and that there are variables that I don't know, or haven't taken into consideration.

For example, if we were to view life through the lens of it being a game, we as the players, and the planet as our playing field, we would see many different competing opponents.

We would see that all peoples are busy playing various different games, depending upon where they are situated on the socio-economic, ethnic, and geographic scale.

The poorest are playing the survival game, where their lives are at stake.

The richest are playing the acquisition game, and the power games. Somewhere in the middle, between extreme wealth and extreme poverty, people are trying to live the day-to-day work and family raising game. To me, that should be the baseline for all humanity: neither awash in wealth, nor dying to eat.

Now, if we are to be mostly objective, there is nothing *inherently* unnatural with any of these situations. What makes it wrong is our ethics, morals, and views. They are part of the greater game called *Life*, where the only rules are the ones we set for ourselves, or don't, as is often the case.

When we realize that not many people are playing with the same rulebook, that's where problems arise. Here, I am not speaking simply about justice or equality, but something even more basic than this.

The basic rule-book I speak of is based on possessing the same, common information available, based on *fact*, independent of the purpose or meaning we ascribe to it or them, and our Universe, such as we *think* it is.

The amelioration of the lenses through which we view our lives, ourselves, our World, and everything in it, depends on everyone being given the same facts. This might give the players everywhere the same broader view of the board upon which they play.

It is by seeing things clearly that we can understand situations more precisely.

It is thus, through these better lenses of understanding that we create our own rulebook, based on our influences and decision-making process, and afterward ascribe our own meaning.

Whatever influences we've had in the past has shaped our worldview. Because we are human, our lenses are skewed, or unclear, and there is fault in the very basis of our understanding of how things work, simply because of our natural biases. It is therefore important to seek out information that is fact-based, for our lenses to be sharp, and unbiased, to be able to see a truth as objectively as we are humanly capable.

The lenses we wear tell us things. Whether the world around us is a hostile place, whether it has inherent meaning, whether it "loves us" or not. All the things that go through our minds, telling us things about the Universe, skew the way we look at it. Some of our most basic thoughts are the bedrock of the foundation of our worldview, and some are tweaks to those thoughts. In any case, we are one-hundred percent confident in the way that we think, even though most of it is opinion.

A lot of it comes down to how much of what I do is about *me* and how much is about *us*, in the greater sense, and how I *feel* about it.

So my quandary is not to "level the playing field" as it were, because doing so is, in any event, undesirable and/or impossible, but giving you, the player, the opportunity to use the best *rule-book* possible. Handing you an accurate topographical map, as it were. I want you to have the best lenses, so you can have the sharpest focus. This in turn will give you the opportunity to make better decisions.

I'll give you an example: what if you wanted to build a furniture set. You're given a box, with pieces and tools, and instructions that take you step-by-step through the process. What if your glasses didn't allow you to differentiate between the tools? You might be able to build this furniture, but it a) might not look very good b) it might take a very long time to build. It might also fall over and hurt you the first time you sat in it. Not very efficient, on the whole. If, however, your lenses allowed you to properly identify your tools, you would build that furniture in no time, with little difficulty, and it would look stellar.

Life is not a piece of furniture, but the way you live it, among other humans does depend on how you view them and choose your interactions and actions. It affects them and the way they interact with people like you.

As well, if you can't see the difference between *truth* and *lie*, your lenses might be a bit smudged, and could hinder you in your day-to-day.

If your lenses do not permit you to see further than a foot away from you, you might have difficulty planning for the future.

Offering your kids better lenses is something parents try to do to make their job of interpreting the world easier.

Of course, this book doesn't contain *all* the information you need to improve your worldview. It's a starting point. It's to show you that lenses exist, and that it's up to you to pursue knowledge that will be beneficial. Or not.

You will view things in a way that some other people may find familiar, but is very much your own. As for the rest of the tools I would like to offer, others may already live a part of them, but certainly not all. Realizing the existence of the tools is a first step in your acquiring them.

I try to explain these tools in as precise a way as I can, in as simple a way as I know, so as to make it as comprehensible as humanly possible.

The process is simple at first, (as you saw the rules I laid down at the beginning of the book) because it is basic mental exercises. It gets more complex and arduous as time goes by.

Like any good game should be. I'm hoping the rules won't seem too overly difficult, or incomprehensible. They might, but not because of how they are formulated, but because of what they ask of you, the player.

Everybody is *built* differently, but we all have optimal ways in which we could operate that would make our lives that much simpler: this is understood.

The thing is, though, once all the rules are internalized (because sometimes a rule can be known, and understood, but not really felt or lived), the next step is to apply them in the real world, and that is where things get interesting.

These rules applied to the game of your life will be added attributes in your mental arsenal. I know you probably don't think of your life as a game, but I'm just using that as an analogy.

What I want most of all is for you to enjoy the time you will have on this plane of existence. At least, that is my most ardent hope. Being aware that you have your own biases, your own way of looking at things, and that everyone else does as well is the first step in making your journey an easier one.

Now, I freely admit that I use analogy and real-life experiences to make clear what may seem obscure and abstract. That is of course, how we learn: by example. So, when I say that life is a game, I mean no disrespect to you, or even to anyone who may be struggling for their lives. *Game* is a word that describes a system. I could simply have used the word Life, but not have had the same effect.

Whatever connotation you may associate with it, good or bad, is not my purpose. I merely am attempting to write what I feel in a way that I believe is comprehensible. So when I say that life is a game or that we see it through lenses, I am only simplifying a very complex subject to make it palatable and graspable. I want you to understand me, not for it to seem like I am making light of anything.

As mentioned above, we – each and every one of us, including you – have to overcome hardships in our lives. From the day you are born, and even before then, you are given both physical and mental, as well as genetic barriers that you must successfully overcome and adapt to before you will have the capabilities to confront the next.

Naturally, if you have not learned to overcome certain hardships, you will keep having difficulties for the rest of your life with that particular hurdle, and it will only get more difficult with time. Of course, there are age-specific physical and mental challenges you will have to face.

We also have a tendency of repeating history, because we fall back on the same old human reactions, over and over. You are taught and raised, from day one, by fallible meat-pockets with minds (yes, your mom and I are just that). Knowing that history is another way of making your lenses clearer. It is easier to understand present situations if you have the knowledge of what came before.

We have needs and desires, loves and hatreds, and a slew of other positive and negative features, all donated to us by our own genitors who received it from theirs, so on and so forth from the dawn of time. They skew out lenses one way or the other.

All those things we have are natural, inborn traits.

They are inherited features that form the human baggage, helping us in every way, shape and form to conquer, survive, tame, outwit, destroy, and navigate the natural world.

They are traits our ancestors developed over millennia that were passed on to us.

The greatest things they handed down to us were symbolic thought and language, two traits that sprang up in their minds and were handed down to their kids because those who had them, spread them around and were the more successful survivors. This may explain why our particular branch of Hominid is the surviving one, even though we know that others coexisted in the past.

Evolution is a race of efficiency. The fact that we were able to imbue symbols with meaning gave us writing, which is the reason you are able to understand what I am writing now. All the knowledge of the human race is contained in the pages of books, and your worldview becomes less and less murky the more you read.

It is not necessarily the strong who survive, but the most efficient beings in their particular niche. Whenever a creature has overcome the barriers that kept it within a particular ecosystem, and thrived to new levels, new barriers are thrown up, as other creatures vie to use it as food, or disease may come into play, or natural disaster, or this creatures' food supply has run so low as to have disappeared, thus killing the species.

Humans are part of that game, but have been so successful at it that now its greatest enemy is *itself*. The further we go along, the less of a factor disease is, and soon it will be solely other humans and a complete collapse of the ecosystem which will be responsible for its demise. We need to change the lens with which we view our world to be able to survive, going forward.

We are therefore faced with maybe three great challenges, which are in fact only related to one cause: The human being as our opponent, starvation as our possible demise (or running out of resources), and the destruction of our ecosystem (which would bring about the destruction of our resources).

In these three cases, humans are the root cause, so I may as well concentrate on it for our problems as well as possible answers. The first thing I ought to do, though, is ask questions. It is only through questioning that you and I may come to answers. These will not appear out of thin air, or through osmosis, so we might as well start with the beginning.

Asking Questions: The Whys and the Hows

As you will go from a phase of existing, to a phase of experimenting, to a phase of questioning, within a few short years of your birth, so has every human child before you. At first you will be all but primal need. The need to be nurtured, to be fed, to have comfort, to be kept from harm, to be kept warm, to eliminate what your body does not need, and to basically be.

Your communication method will be the scream, the cry, the coo, and the smile. This is what you will be, what you will know.

After you develop further, you will realize more about your environment. You will explore it, with all your senses. You will experiment with every single parts of it, because of its novelty. You will put it all in your mouth (can't wait for that, too).

All the while, your mom and I will be there to stop you from harming yourself in your explorations, and guide you in the best way we know to bring you to the next step of your development, then the next, with as little damage as possible.

At some point in time, in your youth, you'll begin to speak. This will be your new trick, your new magic tool. Communication will open doors to you, and to some degree, lessen your frustrations, because if you could communicate your needs, you could have them fulfilled.

Seeing as you will be a tiny little bundle of ego, you will want everything, and sometimes you will be rebuked, which will cause, then, your frustrations. But will we, your parents always be willing to buy you toys at the store, or candy from the shop? No. Will we endure your constant whining to have what you want, and that, immediately? No. Should we? No.

It will be important for us to teach you that there are limits, since this is how we learned to cope with not having what we wanted, you will have to also deal with this unbearable fact of life. As well, our putting our foot (feet?) down will help you in developing a handy tool called patience.

Nevertheless, at a certain stage, usually around the time you will be three or four, which is a crucial time in your development, you will begin to ask why. This, after the stage where all you will say is: "No." Your parents' favourite word.

So there will be a question for everything. Why is the sky blue? Why is that dog barking? Where are we going? Are we there yet? On and on and on, to our great delight. Now, some parents, to their credit, try to answer all these questions as patiently as possible.

Not everybody is gifted with this almost supernatural power, how-ever, and just say: "Be quiet." Others, who are not as polite, say "Shut up!" So their kids are. They become very quiet. They never ask another question again.

That's not true, and I know it, but it is my belief that that particular reaction may cause in many people, (adults now), the urge not to question. To fully accept what the situation may be, no matter how harsh, and to just take the brunt of whatever comes their way. Their curiosity is shut off for the rest of their lives because they were told not to question anything at the crucial time when their questions were all-important.

They might complain, of course, about a situation at hand, but they do not think about questioning why it is so, or why they feel this way about it. Most of all, they will not attempt to do anything to remediate the situation.

You might find this a ridiculous way to be, or you might wonder why a person might act that way. I say it is normal not to question. We were not taught to question, in a general sense. We were taught to accept.

Our school system plays a major part in our lives when we are young. It has not, unfortunately, changed very much in the past hundred years. We are still made to memorize dry facts and numbers at a time when our nature is one of play orientation and openness to discovery. It is no wonder then, that only the most dedicated among us would continue even trying to learn after having had to endure thirteen (now twelve – aren't you lucky?) extremely boring years of our young lives in this pursuit.

As children, we are more or less under the decree of: "Because I said so." How are you supposed to react to: "Because I said so."? Some kids with rebellion, frustration and anger, perhaps, because no logical reason was given for the decree.

Or conversely, with morose acceptance and a reluctance to ask any more questions.

If I, as an authority figure, cannot give valid reasoning for ordering something, does this not demonstrate a lack of respect for you, out of my own intellectual laziness? Does this not sow in you the urge to rebellion?

By the way, I am not advocating that you should rebel against your parents or teachers at *every* occasion, but listen to and understand the *reasons* we will give you for the actions we will take. If you do something we disagree with, you will be told why we aren't impressed, but you will still be punished, if the situation calls for it.

Every action causes an equal and opposite reaction, in Physics, as well as parenting. It all comes down to fairness, though, and the opinion authority figures have of it.

Even though I have the final say over the outcome of any confrontation, you won't be left in the dark as to why the conclusion was reached. This is unfortunately not so in many places (such as the school system), where questioning is seen as some sort of act of rebellion. Keep in mind that teaching methods in public schools are slow to change, and do not be discouraged by your teachers' answers. You will have time enough to find your own. In the meantime, be respectful of your peers, if you value being respected yourself.

Actions are always taken for a reason, even though those reasons may not be apparent, are unknown, are hidden from us, or are just plain stupid. However, we need understanding of a situation to be able to accept it. So you, my child, may grow up with "Because I said so." and you will have to accept it for a *short* time. As you become older and more receptive to logic, explanation will be given. I realize that it will not do to keep using that same refrain for very long.

That attitude can only be a downer on the mind of someone who is on his or her way to becoming an autonomous person. When it becomes gospel, "Because I said so." kills the natural human urge of curiosity, and creates complacent, Play-Doh humans, good for obeying without question, but unable to create anything original.

The problem with this line of logic is that adult human beings cannot operate satisfactorily, healthily, and sanely without proper reasons to do so. If I came to live my life unquestioningly, it is because that is what I have grown accustomed to. To do otherwise requires an effort that I feel is superhuman, but is not.

There are many differences between the minds of an adult and a young child, but mainly that a child has no experience and very limited logic. It is therefore imperative for me to stop you, as a child, from doing things that may be harmful to you. The toddler is not at the level of development where he knows *why* he shouldn't do something, and his or her frustration stems from the denial of access to the object of his or her desire.

As a thinking adult, on the other hand, I will automatically know that if I am refused something, there must be a reason why, even if the reason given is valid, invalid, logical, mythical, spiritual, etc.

My frustration will hinge on being given little or no valid reasoning for an action, depending on my knowledge of cause and effect, the points involved in a particular instance, and my ability to correlate it with the event. If my natural tendency has become that of not questioning, I can accept anything I am told, because any reason I am given is valid. I do not even give it a second thought, no matter if it is logical or not. I can only grow frustrated if I realize that what I am being told has no bearing on that particular case of cause and effect, because I can bring my prior knowledge of the situation into the equation. The problem is compounded if I do not know what the root of the problem is, or that a problem even exists.

If I do not question my surroundings, then perhaps I do not question myself, therefore remaining ignorant of the troubles I may be having.

What I mean in this case is not that ignorance is bliss, but rather, my ignorance is letting my problems run roughshod over my mind, and I don't even realize it.

This idea is not so farfetched, since I spend most of my days acting and reacting to situations that appear before me, without truly analyzing the ways in which I behave to respond to these various stimuli. How much time do I actually spend questioning myself, my life and my own motives? Am I truly satisfied with what I am living, or is it simply that I have not taken the time to question it? Would I be satisfied with the answers? If not, what would I have to do to make it any different?

Plato said that the unobserved life was not worth living. I tend to agree. You can go a very long time without wondering anything about how you are living and being perfectly oblivious about the whole thing.

When you do start questioning, though, you might realize that you aren't all that happy, and that you aren't sure how you got this far, this unhappy. You might then decide to return to your previous state, but it'll be too late.

What has been learned cannot be unlearned. The only thing left for you to do is to make things better for yourself. You might have to undo the conditioning you went through as a child, when you were not supposed to question anything.

Don't worry, I won't make you go through that. Your questions will be answered, as much as humanly possible. The reasoning for decisions will be just as readily available, when you will be old enough to comprehend it. Never give up, though, on trying to find answers and questioning *everything*, even yourself. I know I'm going to regret that recommendation. Just kidding.

The problem is compounded later on in life, though, and is lived by too many people. You will be surrounded by those who do not question. They've been conditioned to accept.

One of the things you may want to do, to help them, is to make them question. This is one of the most painful things people must go through, later on in life, because it means going back on years of their experiences as potentially being false.

It is one of those thresholds that are painful to cross, but to become a better person you have to know yourself, and for that to happen, you must question everything. The thing is, a new era of questioning does not negate a lifetime of knowledge. It is only a new step, which leads to another new step, and so on. If it is seen that way, there is no loss, or pain. It is a new time in your life, where new knowledge has come to enhance the old.

Take, for example, a friend of yours who might be crying, and you ask your friend: "Why are you crying?" and your friend to answer: "I don't know." That answer might be entirely true, but nevertheless, if your friend is crying, it is because your friend has a problem, whether or not he or she can identify it. This is the root, the basic stuff of understanding. This kind of situation happens a lot, but we don't think we can do anything about it, or it is too difficult, so we keep going, not in ignorant bliss, but ignorant sadness.

I had to relearn to question everything. Not just everything around me, like my job, my school, my parents, my religion, or my society. I also have to question myself, often. The question is the first seed that needs to be planted in your mind, for there to be any beautiful answers to grow.

When I say the word Mother or Father, you have an image in your head of who your mother and father is to you, and if you think a little further, you will circle the track of what you know about them, in your head. Your mother is a wonderful woman with many amazing attributes, and your father is a towering God-like figure who possesses the power to lend you the keys to the car.

I have a different picture, a different interpretation, of course, from yours. The question is, why do you think this way, and what ideas are associated to those particular images?

Whether you like it or not, for good or ill, the images you have of your first teachers, us (and others), skew your view of the rest of the world. We are your first lenses. All will depend on what our actions will be, but also what your reactions will be, since no one reacts in the same way.

Example: You might enjoy bedtime as a child. Why? Because I will read bedtime stories to you.

Conversely, going to bed as a child might be a terrifying experience.

Why? Because you are afraid of the dark and won't have a night light (I am a cruel father, I know).

Or even going to bed as a child will be annoying because you won't get to play anymore AND your father will read one of his stupid books.

All situations depend on your genes, your upbringing, and the way you react to all of the above.

When I was young, I didn't have much control over who I was, or how I was. I did as I could, and that's all that mattered to me. The point I am slowly meandering towards is that there came a time when I was no longer this little creature that reacted. I became a big creature that acted, save that that is not *entirely* true.

I still reproduce the same or near-same gut reactions I had as a child growing up. Except that as an adult I am able to *question them*. I would have to delve into my own psyche to understand what made me react in unconscious ways to everything that happened around me. If I am unhappy in certain situations, it is because of the way I naturally and automatically interpret the information I receive.

My reactions are only the external expression of what is hard-wired into my brain. You and I and everybody else have fears, loves, and a veritable cornucopia of emotions, all connected to previous experiences, reinforced by our everyday lives. It is not enough for me to suffer through my reality, though. I must also shape it to my will, to the extent that I am able to. This, you will understand when you gain the ability to manipulate your own mind to do your bidding. This will be the moment when you realize fully and completely that you are the master of your own body, destiny, and decisions.

Basis of Fear

Much of what makes my life a harsh environment is my fears. I suppose it will be the same for you as well, since you are inheriting half my genes. Whatever fears may possess you are creepy, nasty, and disgusting.

They stop you dead in your tracks and force you to flee the scene, or make you shake all over. They make your skin crawl, sweat profusely, and make your heart race. They will make you have nightmares. They completely take over your body. Even though fears may stop you from doing things that put you in danger, they also make you think twice about doing things that might be good for you, because of unfamiliarity. Strangely, the more you will know about the things that you fear, the less you will fear or hate them.

Could it be that it is not any particular thing you are afraid of, but the lack of information about it that worries you? Is it at all possible that your mind fills in the blanks about that lack of knowledge with the most horrible eventualities, just so that the object of your demonization can pose no danger to you, just in case?

Better to err on the side of caution, our minds seem to tell us, as they freak the hell out of us. If that is the case, then it is quite natural that the more we know about everything, the less fear has an easy grip on our minds.

Unless you enjoy living in fear (I'm fairly certain you don't), then you'll agree that if my assessment is correct, it is in your best interests to delve deeper outside as well inside yourself (no matter how scary that might be), to face those demons that make your life difficult.

It is hard.

It might even be painful.

It is also incredibly liberating, once you have seen your fears for the kittens they are, and not the monsters you thought you'd find. For that you have to go looking for the answers, no matter the fear. You have to ask question upon question, trying to find the root of the thought.

I might ask myself the superficial question, the question with an easy answer. One that comes to mind automatically, such as: "Why do I fear (insert fear here)?" and the answer might be that "I find them (slimy, creepy, dreadful, scary, etc.)." This answers nothing, unfortunately, in any deep sense. It is a surface question with a superficial answer.

Trouble is, things in and of themselves are not creepy, or scary, or disgusting. They are simply objects, animals, concepts, or people to whom I give attributes. They have no purpose other than to exist, and it is my interpretation of their purpose or existence that makes me fear and hate them, because of something they represent for me. Something deep inside of me that I have trouble facing, that comes out when I see the object of that fear.

Obviously, not everybody is afraid of the same things. But everybody is afraid of *something*. It's that something that I need to face, and it is only by asking the why of the why that I can face it.

For example, I am afraid of talking in front of large groups or being interviewed (true story). Why? Because it makes me nervous. That is the superficial reason, the one that comes easiest to mind, but if I want to know the root of that fear, I have to delve deeper: Why does it make me nervous? They might dislike me, or judge me. Why might they dislike or judge me? Because I believe I have no intrinsic worth as a human being, and that scares me to my core.

I use a personal example that I used to believe, but you get the point. I might still dislike public speaking, but it's not as palm-sweat inducing as it used to be when I did classroom presentations.

You have to really dig up the bones of the past to get to the marrow of knowing why you are the way you are. You are trying to get to your basic operating system. The visceral you, the one that orders you around when you are not consciously giving orders. Only by knowing that part of yourself can you become cognizant of the impulses that force you to recreate yourself around you. Why do I hate such and such thing, really? Why do I like such and such thing, really? Why does this leave me indifferent? What causes my anger?

Everyone reacts in their own way to any given stimulus. Whether that reaction is dictated by millennia of evolution or simply learnt from your youth is sometimes hard to disassociate or discern, but the attempt should at least be made.

There are, of course, more than four emotions in the human spectrum, but the same general principles still apply. Once you realize more about yourself and the way you are thus (and you might never know everything, some parts are buried so deep), you can begin to look around you and see that other people, even though they are not exactly like you, operate very much in the same way, from the bottom up.

They all have childhood experiences that made them the people they are today. They all have genetic predispositions toward acting a certain way, as well. This does not mean that they are perfect little angels and that you should love them one and all, even though that would be great.

Or that they are the devil and you should despise them, either.

This just means that you now know where they are coming from. They went to the same school as you did. Yes, the school of life is a real school. All that you realize is that everyone around you is human, at the core. You don't exist in a vacuum, after all. You are part of a larger world. This may bring you to a feeling of acceptance of everyone for what they are: Human.

So take some time to reflect upon yourself: who you are, where you are (in your life), what you need (not what you want, there is a slight difference), and maybe write down the basics of you, somewhere. What you like and dislike, and how you feel about everything and why. Even if you don't come up with the deep 'Why' right away, it is enough that you ask yourself the questions. Sometimes writing things down makes interesting points show up that you had no idea existed. I know this is a learning experience for me, it should be for you as well.

It is always the hardest, but, "The journey of a thousand miles begins with the first step." The thing is, we should ask ourselves: "Why shouldn't I question myself, and take that first step?"

Q. Wow. That's a lot of hard work. What's in it for me?

A. Mostly pain and heartache, and then a sense of liberation and elation.

Q. Why the hell would I want to go through that?

A. Only you can answer that question. I did it because I was tired of not knowing why I kept making the same mistakes over and over, without fail.

Confronting yourself is the only way to get the answers out of you, and grow to become something different. Yes, it's hard. Yes, it might hurt to find some truths you don't like. In my case, it sure beat keeping doing the same thing ad nauseum.

You're faced with choices, all the time: keep going as is, or question and change. If you're a generally happy person, there's no need to question. If you're not, you might be better off to. It comes down to your will, your desire to grow.

Your will to happiness, or at least contentment. Your resilience. Self-questioning is that first, vital step toward healing what might be broken. If you don't know it's broke...

Q. You can't fix it. It just seems so hard! And painful!

A. Yep. Like everything worth doing, it is. We live in a world where everything is pretty easy to acquire, when it comes to information or material possessions. The real difficult part now is looking in the mirror and transforming the person we see in it.

I don't blame anyone who doesn't feel ready, honestly! It took me years of covering up and avoidance before I faced myself, and it hurt. When you consider the alternative, though, pain is not the worst thing you can face.

The scariest part is that once you've cut the chains to those things that were holding you back, those things you didn't even know existed before you questioned yourself about them, you feel liberated.

And looking back, you think: it wasn't that hard (even though at the time, it really did feel that hard)! To me, it's like going skydiving. It's not the falling from thirteen-thousand feet that's tough: it's taking that step out of the plane. Most people don't ever get to fly, because of their fear of stepping out of the plane.

Q. So how do you recommend looking at the world when you've faced yourself?

The Basics:
Everything as Tool

All the thoughts you'll gather in your life are the tools that will allow you to navigate through it. The more tools you appropriate, comprehend, and manipulate, the simpler your life becomes. Since frustration often comes from lack of comprehension, gathering as many mental tools as possible will reduce your aggravation as well.

Tools – whether mental, physical, abstract, or otherwise – are information. You are surrounded by information of all types, and your interpretation and reaction to it determines how well you are able to assimilate this input, as well as render it into a tool for our own good. A tool is not a human invention. It is a concept; a *construct* which is disassociated from an *agent*, but used for its benefit. For example, a bird (the agent) might use a stick (tool) to build a nest (tool). Or a person (agent) might use his arm (tool) and hand (tool) to throw a ball. Almost anything can be considered a tool. You only need to consider it so.

The hammer that you use to hit a nail is a tool. But the nail you use to hang the picture frame is also a tool. The frame that contains a beautiful portrait of your family is a tool, and the paper and ink on which the picture is printed is a tool. That picture is a tool to remind you of their faces, once upon a time, and the feelings you have towards them, so you hang them up on the wall.

These are a series of concrete tools, physical tools (apart from the love you have for us, that's abstract). You can touch every single one of them.

What other kinds of tools are there, you ask? Art is a tool we use to describe our feelings of beauty, or anger, or any number of emotions in a physical way.

122

Music as well, and they are both used as tools to communicate these feelings. Abstract tools are tools of communication, like emotions. Such as when we use love to communicate our attraction to someone else. We sometimes signify our love by giving a gift to someone we are attracted to, as a physical sign of that attraction.

If you look around you, wherever you are, all you will see are tools, in one way, shape or form. A tool, by definition is something that functions in tandem with an agent toward a goal, whether intended or not. Every single tool can have one or more purpose, or use.

Sure, I can use a hammer to whack a nail, but I can also remove one with the other end. I could get creative and use it to hit a drum (to destructive effect), or maybe incorporate it in a Rube Goldberg type machine! Every tool has an intended purpose, yes, but you should not limit your imagination by only seeing things the way they are meant to be.

A great many things can be used in a wide variety of ways, and they only require for you to see them in manners other than their intended purposes to become different tools. Your imagination is the limit of your tool-making and using abilities. Your driving emotion also repurposes the tools at your disposal.

Tools are, as I've mentioned previously, composed of information. In essence, the application I make of the tools, or information, is reliant on the purpose of the individual who has command of said tools. This is why secrets are so powerful. They are tools that can be used by a person possessing them to potentially perpetrate great harm. Power over a tool is power itself. Information in and of itself, though, is harmless. So, what we do with the tools is what we think about the tools, in a sense. What we think about the tools is what we consider them to be. We forget that they are nothing until they are directed, and give them intrinsic power, in conjunction with their innate purpose.

The education we have been given about any potential tool determines what benefit or harm we are capable of, the type of actions we take with said tools being the most important act we can perpetrate.

The secondary necessity, then, after my conscious realization of all the tools that surround me is my learning all of their potential uses, and then to apply my creativity and positive acts to make them an extension of my mind and body.

You have choices, of course. You can take these words of mine and use them against people, to manipulate and control, to be greedy and enslave others' minds.

You can decide you do not care, throw these thoughts out the window and do everything the way you want to.

You can also be the kind and gentle, alert, and intelligent person I hope you will become.

The truth is, you'll be a bit of everything, because you are not perfect, and perfection is impossible. You and I are *perfectible*, though. We can decide to use the tools of knowledge at our disposal to become *better* human beings, to like ourselves more, and to expand the love we have to our surroundings. It all comes down to the lessons you will take from what I have said, and what you yourself will live.

You have the ultimate control over your reality and the tools you acquire and use.

Keep in mind that people are not tools, and should never be treated that way. Respect others, always, and treat them as you would be treated. It is possible to join forces with many for a common goal, but not at the price of viewing those who join the endeavour as merely tools.

If you look deeply enough, and ask enough questions, you come to some fairly simple realizations. We all have basic needs that we have to have met, somewhat like when we were children.

The only difference is that now, a lot of people have forgotten how to ask why, or dare not, for fear of the answers, and therefore cannot begin to ask how.

I would rather believe that situations are very complicated, because I do not possess the tools to solve said problematic situations. Indeed, sometimes the complexities of a situation can be daunting, but if I am looking to solve a question that is causing me problems, I am probably better off *finding* the tools to accomplish this task than to avoid the question altogether.

What I found was that I required more than just basic survival and day-to-day life to be content. You and I know how to survive. We do it on a daily basis, no problem there. How can I achieve contentment, though? What tools might I want to acquire to become better adjusted to my environment? When I come to achieve the tools that make my basic survival and comfort possible, I need to begin to look for and create new tools to improve and make more efficient my life and that of others.

As an individual in the company of many other individuals, I am faced with stresses every day, which, depending on the tools I keep on me, and within me, make it so that I can relieve or minimize those stresses.

The tools I could create for myself, however, are some that could make me not only survive, but thrive as an individual. When I am merely surviving, I have no goals but that of survival. When I create new tools, I create new realities within myself, which unlock even more potential I have hidden within me.

Every tool you learn to operate is a new door you open to the world you live in. You create tools, propagate them. You do so to offer your help, to find purpose for your own life, and in the end to support yourself by doing something you enjoy, through your work or your art (which can be both).

Not everything is possible, but you'll never know unless you try. Everything worth doing requires effort. You make the effort to get out of bed every day and do what you have to do to survive. Why wouldn't you make the effort to make your life a better and more interesting place to live?

Sometimes the choices you have to make are very difficult, but you have to *choose* to move forward. It is not enough to *find* the methods that will be beneficial for solving your problems and facing life. They must also be implemented, for good or ill. The achievement of your goals is just as important as their creation.

A word on technology: As in everything else, technology in all its myriad forms, is there to help us: to make our lives easier. It cuts down the time it would have taken for us to do a thing to a fraction, allowing us more time in the day to do other, perhaps more meaningful tasks. Instead of taking half a day to go to the river to wash our clothes, we put them all in the washing machine and let it go to work for us, for example.

What technology does not do, however, is tell us how to live our lives. It does not give us purpose, meaning, or a more empathetic worldview. Just because we have washing machines, does not mean we've developed the empathy to separate tasks evenly among family members so that everyone does their share.

It's important to remember that technology, in all its glory, is nothing but a tool, and we, the users, must make choices to use it well, and more wisely, if we want to create a better world around us.

Organization: Systems and Structures

When you have many individual parts working together as a cohesive whole, it is a system. Sometimes the system is somewhat clunky and awkward, but works nonetheless. That is the perfect definition of a human system.

Since we are not machines, we cannot work in perfect unison. So much the better, or else we would not progress or evolve one way or the other!

We have systems within our bodies, working to help us live, and understand our surroundings.

Computers, societies, watches, governments, our Universe; there are quite a few things that when considered, function through systems. I mentioned watches, since your mother, for our wedding day, offered me a beautiful skeleton watch. This is a watch in which you can see all the different cogs and wheels, springs and bezels that work together with the intended purpose of keeping accurate time.

This watch, to me, exemplifies a simple and elegant working system (as well as being a symbol of your mothers' love). A computer, when you look inside it, is composed of: a power source, a graphics card, some memory, a CPU, a hard drive, an internet relay, a whole lot of wires, and a cooling system. As well as all the component parts connected to it, such as a monitor, a keyboard, and a mouse, sometimes a printer and a scanner. Together, they form a very powerful machine, with which we can accomplish just about anything we want.

Every single part of the computer is in turn made of smaller parts, which make up the system for that particular unit: silicon chips and circuit boards, current converters, and so forth. Some people joke that they have the most expensive porn-watching machines, and to some degree they may be right, but it all depends on what they choose to do *with* their system.

The system is there to generate results. How you and I realize that potential remains solidly in our court.

A car works in much the same way. It is a multitude of internal parts, all working together to produce the result of motion at a higher speed than, say, walking. Some use it to go from point A to point B. Others to go faster than others, but for no particular destination save the finish line.

Society works in major part because of the systems that are in place to regulate it. The Justice System, so aptly named, is there to mete out what we consider reward or punishment in a non-arbitrary fashion. It begins with enforcers and investigators (the police and inspectors), goes to the judges where cases are heard and defended by lawyers, and may end up in Punishment (Prison).

Arguably, not all Justice Systems everywhere are equitable, fair, or just, but that is not the point (Every society does what they can with what they have, in the only manner they know). It is up to *all of us* to make the system as impartial as possible so that some do not escape justice, and others yet get harsher sentences.

What is, is that that is what they are there to *do*. If the people in-volved at one stage or other of the whole process are not doing their job correctly, then the whole system suffers, but that is not the fault of the *system*. That is the fault of the parts that comprise it. If the system has any flaws, it is generally the result of the motivations of the people that are involved in it, the way in which laws are written and interpreted, and not the *purpose* of the system itself which is at fault, unless that system has been perverted to suit the needs of those who run it.

In any event, they are part of a system, one that was created to help run a Nation, which has many different parts, and work in a multitude of different ways, all more or less in unison. The purpose of Human systems, therefore, (it can be argued) is there for whoever has the power or the will to use it, through the agency of those who will let them.

As a computer is only as effective as its least competent part, so is a human system only as effective or fair as any of its members will let it become.

One of the problems lies in the fact that we can change the parts in a computer, for faster CPUs, or hard drives, or memory, but we can't *create* a better human. The person who joins the system has to want to be a better part in improving the system at hand. This can be a daunting task when faced with other, less motivated, or perhaps even, more selfish parts.

The problem is compounded when the parts don't particularly care about their influence, positive or negative, on the system. If you want to have a better working system, be that better part, without letting yourself be discouraged by the other, less helpful parts.

Structures, on the other hand, describe how the system is organized. Think of the way a building is built so that it withstands whatever wind, rain, snow, or earthquakes may come its way. If a system describes all the parts working together, the structure is representative of the frame within which the system operates.

Our body structure makes it so that we may carry around our internal organs without fear of them falling out.

Think of how a corporation subdivides its different departments for greater efficiency. Most societal structures are top-down intensive: The boss is at the top, with managers below, and employees at the bottom, taking orders. A few are cooperatives, where the members are in charge of making decisions, or elect a few representatives to make decisions for them. Democracy is a kind of Co-op, with more people near the top to duke out the best course of action. The 'majority' elect people to do their bidding (in theory, anyway).

A classical monarchy is one where the King or Queen is on the top of the pyramid and makes all the rules, a bit like in a corporation. Except that in older times, there were fewer laws to restrict his or her actions. The most reproduced human structure is that of a company, where the boss is at the top, dictating orders to those under him or her. For now it is just important to know that these structures exist.

The physical labour-force structure of a world-wide corporation might work thus: The management system might be, say, in Toronto, Canada.

129

The manufacturing aspect could be situated in Shenzhen, China, and the technical support might be located somewhere in Bangalore, India.

All of these systems, management, manufacturing and tech support, exist towards the same goal, the dissemination of one or several products. They can exist in various physical spaces around the world because of the communications network that now criss-crosses the entire planet, whether on it or in space.

There are more and better phone lines and fiber-optic cables being laid down as well as satellites being launched every year. They make for a more efficient means of communication, which in turn renders a globalized system easier to manage.

This is the process by which the structure of the World Wide Web is distributed throughout the planet. It has become the ultimate means of communication with the global community, at very little cost to the consumer.

Open societal structures use it to spread information instantaneously everywhere at once. Closed societies fear its message of openness, and the corrupting effect it will have on the peoples the ruling parties wish to keep under their control. The internet is therefore the great equalizer. It is no wonder so many want to put restrictions on its uses.

As an aside, when someone says they hate "The System," they are, of course, riling against the society in which they find themselves alienated. They do not realize that since any kind of working societal or natural model is in fact "The System," and their true message is: "I don't fit in here, and I hate my life." This can stem from many different reasons, but is mostly indicative of a lack of purpose in themselves and understanding of systems in general. Everything that we can think of that can drive a society is a system, whether it is communist, socialist, democratic, autocratic, oligarchic, tyrannical, capitalistic, as well as all the other myriad possibilities and admixtures of the above.

That's why when people say they'd like to "take down The System," to me, it's like they're saying they want to burn the house down because they don't like the colour of the walls.

The most important thing we should remember is that any system is malleable. It can be changed for the better, or for the worse, and it all depends on how much energy we intend on spending toward that particular pursuit. It is always harder to make a system better, because making it worse only requires we do nothing and let it slide into our natural tendencies of sloth and greed.

Anarchy is also a system, which, depending on your interpretation, can mean either total lawlessness, or simply the absence of government. In the first case, it is a system that can only last for a very short time until order is returned. This kind of Anarchy is the law of the jungle (still a system!), brought upon society by those who can only see changing whatever system is in place by attempting its complete destruction. The second kind is simply means to abolish government for an individualist, and therefore egotistical, manner of living.

Whatever societal system is in place, it is the product of thought-forms and hypotheses brought forth by thinkers and put in place by those who had the willpower to do so that made it the way it is. Whether that system is majority-ruled or has a minority-dictatorship matters not one bit: they are shaped using the same formulas, and possess much the same underlying structure.

It is the result of many competing ideas versus few that will direct and push societies in one direction or the other, and the outside influence of money that will shape the way policy is made.

In human society, the reins of power are put in the hands of those who have proven themselves the most capable at seizing power, no matter the method. The amount of power that remains in the hands of the ruled is entirely dependent on how much they fight to keep it there. Conversely, the power attained by rulers depends on how much of it they can grab.

Even if the original thoughts of the founders of a country were of noble intent, and imbued their citizenry with rights, a citizenry which pays no attention to its leadership will eventually lose those rights, since power flows upwards, not down.

It is therefore in the best interest of all peoples to pay close attention to the way they are ruled, if they wish to alter or retain control over the dynamics of the system. They must also make sure that they have a plan to implement, if ever they succeed in regaining control of the system which may have slipped from their grip.

The structures may remain similar, but it is the will of those who are the agents of power within that system that will determine if the system will work for the general population, or for those who control it from the top.

Revolution is the unfortunate result of too much power having been taken by the ruling elite at the expense of the ruled. This terrible political act of making violent revolt is the only option of the oppressed against those who would crush dissent through violence.

As a few tyrants could tell you if they hadn't been eliminated by their citizenry, "It's not worth it to have everything, since I now have nothing to show for it." The balance of power swings both ways, and the human will to basic fairness brings the pendulum back in a big way when it has been pushed to its limits for too long.

Every system has an optimal method of operation, and that goes for human systems as well. We are all looking for that perfect method, since we believe we have found the optimal structure (democracy) within which to place it. The basic structure does not matter, though, if those who operate within its bounds do not realize the needs of both rulers and ruled and aim to fulfil them for the benefit of all.

Q. I'm fairly aware of the various forms of government. Why do you feel you should mention them?

A. Well, I did write this originally for a younger person, and wanted to give them a basis of understanding of what was going on in the world. There are a slew of systems out there, from totalitarian to democratic. To me, the most fair is the democratic system. It works because one side is always looking over the other's shoulder, however many sides there are. There is a competition of thought processes, which can actually help us move forward. This, of course, only works if the political system isn't tainted with corporate money. Then it breaks down and the people are forgotten. If you have a system in place, and it's somewhat tainted and sick, it's important to think in advance what you'd like to replace it with. Is it better to replace a monarchy with a one-party state? Or a corrupt regime with anarchy?

There are people out there who only want to overthrow governments. They want to stick it to "the man" or take down "the system." What are they offering as a better alternative, though? Sometimes it's not the *system* that's at fault. Often it's the people with their hands on the levers who have corrupted it. To me, wanting to take the whole thing down is like saying: we've caught some employees stealing from the till, let's burn down the city. If you look at the Communist revolutions in China and Russia, which replaced monarchies with single-party authoritarian rule, it wasn't a whole lot better for the vast majority of people. A one party system can only agree with itself, and there's no way to change thought-direction without revolution and the destruction of that system.

Even then, when you've gotten used to systems of strongmen, the resulting democracies might be complete shams, as in Russia.

It makes no sense. What you should be doing is replacing the people with others, who will return the system to its rightful working condition, and by that, I mean a system that is for *all* the people, not only the wealthy and powerful. For that we need the right knowledge.

Q. How do you go about gathering that knowledge?

Sediments, Trees, and Foundations: (Analogies for Knowledge)

I f you've ever had the chance to look at ancient sedimentary rock, formed by mud settling at the bottom of what was then oceans, you may have seen that there were horizontal lines going through it.

They were deposited there a very long time ago, over millions of years, which hardened until they were solids. Year after year, more sand and mud was deposited over the previous layers and hardened as well, creating this pattern of layers we see in the rock. In a sense, thought does the same thing (metaphorically), whether in a personal, a societal or a historical sense. What I mean is, we build on the past.

We take the most ancient sources as the most solid, and therefore the most reliable. You could not go forward if you did not have a base of thought upon which you could construct your own personal philosophy.

You can call it culture, or religion, or Philosophy with a capital P the fact remains that much of what we do today relies on thought processes that were laid down by our forbearers a millennia ago, and passed down through the generations.

Even without formal training, we all have a personal philosophy, which can be anywhere within the boundaries of rudimentary as survival tools in the woods, or as complex as Stephen Hawkings' or Plato's mind.

It is there, and it serves us in all that we do.

You lay down the major sediments in your youth, and then, gradually, with all your experiences and reactions to stimuli, you add more layers. You *build* your personal belief system.

Like the sands at the bottom of that primordial ocean, the more ancient thoughts congeal and become occluded from your consciousness.

134

Your belief system is not entirely your own. It is based on that of your parents which is flavoured by theirs, all the while sprinkled heavily by societal demands, education, views, and prejudices.

Add to these, as well, the history behind the very basic beliefs that we, as a whole nation, or segment of humanity hold dear. Everything influences everything, whether directly or indirectly, gets passed to you, and is laid down as another layer of your convictions and thought processes.

When you have enough *sediment* in your mind, you plant the *seeds* of your own knowledge, and it grows out of the fertile soil that was laid down.

When I am certain of my beliefs, the tree I planted grows well, and with all newly added information, new branches sprout. A tree that is planted in poor soil may not hold up to the winds of scrutiny, and a poorly grown branch of knowledge may fall before information that makes it obsolete. It will be replaced by one with the *correct* information.

There are no sediments or trees in your mind, naturally. There is development of your ideas through every stimulus you receive, though.

To a lesser or greater degree, you get to choose how much stimulus you get, and how much you let it affect you. You can help that tree of knowledge grow, if you so desire. The more love and patience you have, the better your tree will grow. The more you are able to forgive, the easier it is to clip off the dead or diseased branches that harm it.

The more you feed it a variety of information, the more powerful and strong it will become.

Just as your thoughts – and that of those that came before you – can be compared to sediments, they can also be seen as foundations.

You are constantly building a comfortable place in your mind that you call home. Before you started building the house, however, you lay the foundations to this edifice. The stronger the foundations, the more unshakeable it will have become with time, as the cement of your ideas become solid.

A good contractor may want to build his house so as to leave room to expand his foundations, though. His house can then be enlarged without threatening the old structure, only ameliorate it.

There should always be room for new and beneficial information, so that I do not need to tear down the house to make room for it. I have to make the house bigger. If I take on the tack that my mind can be expanded, I need not view any information as threatening, or useless. I can add it to my ever-expanding house.

Circles and Tracks

The way your mind works is by electrical and chemical impulses. Most people know that, I think. But if you think of the brain as a three dimensional structure, what you see when someone is thinking is neurons firing in whatever direction they need to go to activate nodes that contain knowledge.

The more you think, the more you create and improve the conduction of tracks and new bits of information for these tracks to get to. If you begin to cross-reference the information (think of two things that don't necessarily go together) in your mind, you get new paths with new information to play with.

So, if for some reason you start thinking of baby rabbits playing football on the Empire State Building (or something equally as ridiculous), you might get a little brain buzz.

That's because you cross-referenced and created a new neural pathway, or just activated one that was dormant all this time.

Humour is a prime example of creating new neural pathways. The way humour works is that a person will say something, and create an expectation in your mind of meaning one thing, but then say something different than what you expected, and will leave it to the audience to create the link between thoughts, giving them that little buzz of joy when they realize what was meant. When someone says they "don't get it," it is because they were unable to bridge the gap created by the humourist.

So the mind is also like a super-efficient train line, upon which you can construct new stations (thoughts) and new rails (neural pathways), if you so choose. The more you build this railway, the more efficient (and interesting) your thoughts become. The more interesting your life becomes, then, since it is through your mind that you perceive your reality.

Your life is boring most of the time because there aren't enough things to keep your mind active and working efficiently. We often depend on outside stimulus to keep us interested, and as soon as we have nothing around us to cause this effect, our brains effectually say: "Now what?"

This can easily be remedied by learning to do things that need very little in the way of physical objects or outside stimulus to keep our minds occupied and firing away happily.

Boredom is the true hell, or so they say. If this is true, then my lack of willingness to learn new and interesting things is my acceptance of letting my mental impulses stay idle in the Grand Central Station of the Underworld.

There is obviously also the dark side of thought, which I like to think of as negative circular thinking. When I am feeling down (it happens), I tend to go from one bad thought, to all my bad thoughts, and then over the first bad thought again, getting gloomier and gloomier. The train won't stop. When it does this often enough, it seems that the train will never leave this circle of negative thoughts, that the ruts are too deep. If this state of affairs persists, over a long enough time period, it becomes depression. If realized early enough, it can be altered.

If not, it should be treated as quickly as possible before it becomes a health issue. Having access to decent psychological help is a must. There is nothing wrong with feeling down, but you should seek help if the problem persists for too long.

There is nothing embarrassing about needing or seeking out help to solve our mental distresses, if in fact you ever should desire to. When something is wrong with your body, you go and seek the help of a physician. The same thing applies for your mind.

Everything you think about is on self-reinforcing tracks, or spirals, negative or positive. Since the mind is great at creating better and easier tracks to follow, it would make sense to concentrate on the positive, even if this seems counter-intuitive or simply very difficult.

No, this is not a cure-all, and should not replace clinical help, ever. I'll say it again: if you feel that the problems you are facing are too great to handle, seek help. Tell someone. You have a family, friends, and there are professionals out there who specialize in helping those with mental issues. Seek them out whenever necessary.

Your health greatly depends on the way you think and how you approach problems, and the more you consider problems to be riddles to be solved, the better chances you have of solving them, thus continuing to be healthy. There are things that are physically impossible to solve, granted.

But, as problems are thought-based and soluble, if we ourselves are flexible enough to adapt to new situations, most things aren't impossible to solve save those we think are.

Positive thinking is not the end-all and be-all of your life, but it is a crucial tool in adapting to new and unexpected situations. It stops you from breaking down in critical situations, and forces you to think of options.

Positive thinking alone does not *solve* problems. It simply stops you from despairing or giving up too easily.

The biological basis for negative thought is that when we are in dark moods, we think much more about our problems, concentrating on them as a means of survival.

The trouble is that if I don't have any readily available solutions, I keep thinking those negative thoughts, attaching painful memories and other dark thoughts to them, effectively making them all-encompassing and self-feeding, on an endless loop.

The trick is to concentrate on the problem at hand, not start following the other negative tracks, getting off the negative path as quickly as possible and trying to get back to a positive line of thinking before falling prey to the negative spiral.

The most important part is to reinforce the positive tracks as much as possible so that the negative tracks become weak from lack of being fed electric impulses.

As much as I can 'feed' a particular train of thought, I can also 'starve' another, making it less and less potent with time. This will make it so that if I do go back to my negative thoughts, they will carry much less weight, eventually.

It is also very important to go through with the positive solutions I may find to a problem, since it is because of inaction that I may find myself disappointed in the first place. The adoption and implementation of a positive course of action helps me begin my ascent from the well of negative thoughts I dig for myself.

Levels:
How Deep Can You Go?

What I mean by levels, and I'm sure you are aware of this, is the inner, or deeper, meanings of things. For example, everything, or almost, that an author will write in a story has a surface meaning, and a deeper meaning.

The words that are written, very often, are representations of something different, more profound. There can be more than one depth to any kind of situation. If you think about it, almost every time you speak to someone, there are deeper meanings to the things that we say to them, and that they say to us.

When your mother tells you: "I love you!" she is expressing in three words, three concepts, and an overarching theme, that she directs towards you. "I" "love" and "you" combined, make for a sentiment that is always pleasurable. The underlying message is that she cares for you.

It is the thought that engendered the action of speaking those words which are considered the deeper meaning.

Most of your thoughts and actions are far more complex, and often stem from your unconscious. Your mind has deeper levels, to which you cannot always directly access. These are the parts that should interest you, because they are your *real* drivers. They are part of the forgotten basic operating system of your mind, buried deep in your unconscious.

When I listen to (and understand) people, I know that their words express who they are, and what they want from me. I have to look deeper into the meaning of their words to understand what the true message is that they are trying to convey.

If someone says: "I hate (insert object of hatred here), it's bad!" for example, I should be wondering: "Why does he or she think it is bad?" beyond the stated reason.

There is always a truth hidden behind words, and I should be curious to know what those truths are, since they reveal to me who others are, as well as their purpose. It is important for me to realize that there is often disconnect between what people say and do, or tell you and the *truth*.

The same can be said about whole systems as well: Any organization has goals, and to obtain results towards those goals, they will use communication.

Disconnect happens when they tell you they want a certain thing, yet act in a completely different way. If you want to know the deeper meanings of things, it is good to also observe a person's acts, as well as to listen to what they are saying, since, sometimes the two don't really add up.

I often pay much more attention to what is said than what is done. Simply because I would like to believe that what is said is the truth, and I do not want to delve deeper to find out if it is.

If I am not the kind of person who enjoys being duped, it behooves me to observe events in a truly scrutinizing manner.

I should be attentive to the deeper meanings of what individuals, societies, groups, or political parties are doing, underneath of what they are *saying*.

Even though this is usually not the case, certain people may want to take advantage of others' trusting natures for purposes that are not in their interest.

History is replete with such examples of master manipulators. Many were taken in by Hitler's honeyed words, just as he was systematically slaughtering millions of people. Mao Tse Tung was apparently also someone who got his wishes, one way or another. Fortunately, the world isn't populated solely by sociopaths.

There are many examples in everyday life of minor personalities who are committed to saying one thing and doing another, and if I wish to stop deluding myself about their intents and sometimes nefarious acts, I really do need to start paying attention. Or else I will merit the uncomfortable situations I will find myself in through my own inattention.

No one else but Hitler was himself, of course, but it's through your scrutinizing more carefully the people you trust (and those you might not) that you can avoid promoting those that share the same manipulative traits.

The goal is to discover the *truth*, one way or the other. I cannot do this if I do not have the ability to analyze deeply in an objective manner.

Every story you hear or read, every show or movie you watch, every game you play, every interaction you have affects you in imperceptible ways. It is the underlying messages that you internalize in some minor or major manner, depending on how deeply it resonates with the core of your beliefs.

When you think of subliminal messages, the first thing you think about is a short segment of film, barely perceptible, which has been inserted into the regular show, to make you do or think something you hadn't previously considered.

This has been known to be done in the past. The subliminal message does not need to be hidden as a blip or temporary glitch before your eyes, though. In fact, this has been proven to be mostly ineffectual.

Most often it is the message *itself* that makes you conform to the wishes and desires of those who want to see a behavior or thought pattern reproduced *en masse*.

The main theme and outcome of the story is a confirmation of your belief system, and you take it in as reinforcement to what you previously thought.

When a story has no underlying message it is not a credible story, since it does not contain elements that we can project ourselves into. It becomes a message devoid of meaning for its audience.

Unfortunately, I can have my credulity stretched very thin by any kind of true story, yet still believe it, if it is in my best interest to do so.

Until I snap out of the self-delusions I create for myself, I will continue to believe just about anything that is thrust upon me as truth.

This applies equally to any type of messages I am subjected to. As long as I remain a passive observer, I do not see past the surface of anything.

I am prone to gobble up any type of information as if it were healthy and sane, whereas if I took the time to be a bit more discerning, I might realize that what I am ingesting is in fact junk.

This is why it is important to be able to look deeper under the surface of your surroundings to see what the iceberg really looks like. Once again, being able to ask why, and on many different levels, is the key to being able to go deeper than the surface of the world.

You have to recognize, of course, that not all things are imbued with a nefarious agenda. Very often, in the western world, the levels we find under the sub-strata of thought are there simply to make you buy something.

The advertising world is very good at passing messages on a level that we are barely aware of. At the same time, they reinforce the image of society that we have, by recycling symbols in ways that we might not have been conscious of. Being aware of the underlying messages make us aware of our surroundings. Like waking up to the fact that the forest we are traversing is composed of individual trees, each with a life of their own, we realize the various purposes directed toward us.

Benoit Chartier

Countering Extremism Percentages, and Spectrums: How Average Are We?

Absolutes frighten me. The idea that objects, ideas, people, or anything at all, really, can only be in one of two opposite states at any
given time causes me no end of anguish.

People who think this way are limiting their perception of the world
to the simplest form they can possibly imagine. Think of the duality of
Good versus Evil, black and white, or man and woman.

There is so much more than that, but we're taught to oversimplify. In
doing so, we are missing a great many details.

Obviously, there are yes or no answers to many questions. Yet, when
I take the yes or no approach to more complex equations, such as human emotions, I am being thoroughly disingenuous.

For example, if an anti-social type were to say they hated *everybody*, I
could ask them if they hated their mothers, and to no one's surprise they
would say "Of course not!" So, that's not *everybody*.

Things have a hard time being one hundred percent. Sometimes they
are only ninety-nine percent, but that is a far cry from everything. When
I stereotype and say: "They're all like that." for any stated reason at all,
I am in fact *lying*. Not all people of any group follow the stereotype that
is perpetrated. That is impossible. You might think I am splitting hairs,
here, when I say that ninety-nine percent of people can be the same but
not all. That it is all a matter of semantics, but I would beg to differ.

It does make a difference in how I perceive a situation, or a group of
people, or a set of objects, when I know the parts and percentages that
comprise them. There is never really a homogenous whole, that there is
room for dissent, that you can't put everybody in the same boat.

145

Being absolute just makes it easy to *judge* everything, especially in a negative light. I put all similar things in one basket to save myself the trouble of having to ask questions about the true nature of people, places, and things I *judge*.

Seeing things through a different facet puts reality square in my face and makes me re-evaluate my position, hopefully for something less extreme.

That is something I do not like to do, because it causes uncertainty. Those who deal in absolutes are absolutely wrong, all the time. Knowing the statistics for any given incident, or population, or event, anything you can think of, makes you aware of what is involved in that process. If being less sure about yourself makes you a bit uncomfortable, it also makes you a bit smarter and more aware.

If, say, over fifty percent of Americans believe that the human being was created a little over ten thousand years ago, that's still not everybody. I personally know a lot of people (but not all) who judge the American population solely on that aspect.

They generalize the fact that many Americans believe in Creation, thinking that it is the whole population, making them risible. Yet they do not realize that an almost identical slice of the *Canadian* population does too. Of course, there is an element of "Us versus Them" involved, but it by no means minimizes the use of overgeneralization, and is actually an intrinsic part of the argument.

When I am being guided by my sense of superiority, as undeserved as it is, that is very much when I tend to go for absolutes. Be careful in your generalizations, and your opinions about people derived from those generalizations. They reveal a lot more about you than they do about whoever *they* are.

Knowledge of the figures involved may determine that the people you were told were against you, are in fact nowhere near the threshold of most of them hate us, or whatever fallacy is being bandied about.

Absolutes are wielded to good effect by those who have little or no grasp of what is truly going on, and only care about instilling fear in those they wish to have as followers, by manufacturing an enemy.

In telling us that something is entirely one way, they are trying to make us believe what is quite definitely not true. Whether it is in the interest of directing our anger, or anguish, or even our passions, you should be careful in trusting those who speak in absolute terms. They have an agenda of their own.

It is always better to be well-informed on the issues you want to support than to step blindly into the beliefs of others, if only for the fact that it might be a trap that could very well come back to bite you, and hard. This method is how wars are sold to the public, usually coupled with a healthy dose of fear.

Spectrums

I f you are a human being (and I am hoping you will be), the odds are, you will have seen a rainbow. If science interests you, you know that it is a splitting of sunlight through a lens created by the atmosphere onto water droplets, which shows every single vibrating wavelength that comprises it, translated to our eyesight as a variegation of colours.

What does this tell us? Well, for starters, there are more than two wavelengths in the universe, as well as more than two colours in the visible spectrum. This is something we already knew, of course, but in the grand scheme of things, it just means that there are more than two of every-thing.

Just like percentages, spectrums take into account the wide difference between things. Yet it does so by going through every detail contained within a category. There is actually a huge spectrum of all possible known things, ranging from thoughts, emotions, actions, reactions, objects, in-sects, animals, planet types, bacteria, and everything else under the sun (as well as over and beyond it).

The other things I spoke of contain more or less of the ingredients that comprise them, in each of their respective categories.

If we were to use emotions as an example, we would see that all our emotions are derived from anger, disgust, fear, happiness, sadness, and surprise. Since our mind is controlled by various chemicals being released within it, each subtle admixture becomes a different emotion. Each of our more complex emotions contains certain doses of these chemicals, and our body reacts correspondingly to the chemical reaction produced. There is a whole range within the gamut of human experiences that easily fall into the qualities of spectrum, we only have to recognize them as such.

We always tend to fall back on opposite views, for simplicity's sake. The problem with oversimplification is that it clouds the issues, as if there were only two ways of looking at anything.

We don't live in a Yin-Yang world, no matter how much we wish it so.

If you were to answer a store survey about your shopping experience, it would not be so convenient if the two categories for your experiences were: A: Good, B: Bad.

There would have to be more than these two views inserted between them to aptly reflect what type of experience you had. Why should I then fall back on oversimplification when nothing ever is?

There can be simple *answers* to many problems, but it is not by using simplistic tools of analysis and a reductionist view of complex problems that I can get to the root cause of *any* dilemma. Even the colour grey has over 65,536 levels, at 16-bit resolution.

That should tell something about the intricacy of life as a whole. Even though it is more difficult to view things in shades than in absolutes, I should at least have the mental honesty to realize that there are more than two answers to everything, and that I colour my world with the way in which I act or react towards any given stimulus.

The possibilities that I open within my mind are the limits with which I can view my reality. Perhaps I should then begin thinking in ways that are optimal, and not only expedient. Two-toned world-views make reaction time much faster, sure, but we as a species mostly no longer live in life-or-death situations as common occurrences.

Yes, there are times when I must restrict my thinking to very simple options, for the sake of survival, or just quick reaction time. Even then, I have choices that will determine the outcome of my life, and that of others, so why limit myself to the notions of Good or Evil? You and I are somewhere in the middle of those two extremes.

If I consider Good to be a perfectly altruistic, honest, empathetic, hard-working, loving person, etc., and Evil to be a purely selfish, angry, lazy, spiteful, conniving, jealous, etc., entity, then you can probably imagine that we are a bit of both, without ever reaching the ultimate peaks of either poles.

What has been known for a while, now, though, is that striving for the

Good side, as it were, created an environment of inner peace that can't be achieved by letting yourself succumb to the Evil.

I did say *succumb*, as in, let yourself slide into it. It is fairly easy to do, since all you have to do is follow your natural instincts.

Why, then, would you even attempt to go for Good, if the natural way of things is Evil?

For starters, even though the pleasure you derive from the *letting go* is intense, it is only temporary.

As well, it is self-destructive when indulged in too often. You hurt yourself, yes, but also all those around you by dipping into the behaviors described as Evil. The Christian and Catholic faith labelled those negative acts as *sins*. Today, we'd just say they are *anti-social*, because they are harmful to the rest of the group.

The Good or 'positive' path is therefore harder, but much more rewarding in the long run, to you, as well as the those around you.

Just as sitting around on the couch all day feels good, going for a jog will make you stronger. One is easy and feels good, the other demands effort but pays dividends.

Even though I don't think I need to constantly improve myself, non-stop, twenty-four-seven, I know that I will derive more pleasure for a much longer time if I head towards the positive rather than the negative. You don't have to worry about it too much, because you will do both, whether you want to or not.

You should keep an eye on how much you allow for the negative, though. It may be indicative of a deeper problem you have, that you need help to solve. You are somewhere in the middle of that human behavioral spectrum, and your thoughts and acts make you go from one side to the other. I try to take another step on the positive side whenever I get the chance.

Q. Listen, I realized quite some time back that you're very much on the left side of the political spectrum. Are you trying to convince the rest of the world to be as well?

A. If you mean by that that I think it's a good idea to care for people in a wider capacity, I do. We tend to have better survival rates *as a whole* when we pool our resources.

Q. What about individuality? Don't you believe in the rights of the individual?

A. I do. I'm still an individual, aren't I? It's important to able to think for oneself, and act on your own, but when you live in society, it's not enough to think only of yourself. For the sake of the individual, and that of the group.

Q. What if *the left* wants to take away our freedoms?

A. What we consider freedom derived from our *free will*, the ability to do what we wish to do, and *responsibility*, what we *should* do, are the paradigms I'd like to introduce. Many, in this our modern world, have taken *freedom* to mean that they should do whatever it is that they want to, no matter how hurtful it is to others.

The religious aspect of the equation have invented 'predeterminism' as the opposite of free will, meaning that what we do, in the theistic context, has been pre-ordained and is therefore unchangeable (or at least punishable). Once that mental constraint was lifted, it was only a matter of time until those who did not live within the spectrum of religious thought would come to the conclusion that since their actions were not pre-ordained, they had the liberty to commit any act without fear of reprisal.

Sadly, it has come to pass that those actions still have an influence on the course of human events. It is proper to think, then, that the true opposite of *free will* is not *predeterminism* or *repression*, to a degree, but *responsibility*, and in that optic, the freedom to take action should be weighed in the balance of the influence it has against the potential negative impact it may cause to others.

Repression is an outside force coming into play, trying to stop a *perceived* negative trait *en masse*. Think of laws that are passed stopping people from murdering others.

Responsibility is an innate, personal trait used to gauge our influence on our surroundings, not because I am fearful of retribution, but because I am responsible for my actions in everything I do, as a human being.

Q. Are you saying that I should think about those around me before I commit an act?

A. ...Just as those around you should think about you before they do. Being empathic and mindful of others only gets easier when everyone does it, but it doesn't mean you shouldn't do it because no one else is. This philosopher once said: "Do unto others as you should have them do unto you." That's still valid today.

Q. You're talking about Jesus, but you're not a religious person.

A. I'm not, but I can spot a good thought when I see it. There's a lot we can learn from the classics. You have to pick and choose, though, like a lot of modern religions do.

Q. What do you mean by that?

A. Well, no Christian follows the Bible implicitly. If they did, they wouldn't wear clothes made of mixed fabrics, or eat shellfish, or a slew of other things, *including* owning slaves. We pick and choose the things we wish to follow. The trick is to find the best possible ideas and stick to those. To me, the best possible ideas are those that help the most people.

Q. What if I want to be selfish and do things for myself? Can't I?

A. You can do anything you want, realistically. What will the repercussions be of those actions? What if your idea of fun is going on a hill and shooting empty cans? What if you miss and hit someone?

Q. That's stupid, though. I would go on a shooting range to do that.

A. Right, because you're thinking of the consequences of your actions. You're responsible. You're thinking about how your actions affect others. The important thing is to do this in other situations as well, in our daily lives.

Experience Plus Empathy

You'll go through life having experiences. Naturally, those experiences will inform your decisions about future experiences. All in all, you can say your existence is experiential. You seek out experience in one way to give yourself pleasure, whether through entertainment like music or games, bodily through sex, or through something that might alter your mind like alcohol or drugs.

You also have experiences thrust upon you, and those can be good or bad: death of a loved one, getting a disease, receiving gifts, birth of a child, etc.

Everything that happens to you, or that you seek out, affects you.

We sometimes forget that what happens to us, or that we do to others, affect others as well. When we are able to allow ourselves to feel the emotions that another might be feeling, we are said to be empathetic.

This empathy is simply the ability to put ourselves in the mind-space of another, and to imagine what they might be thinking.

A good friend loses their parent. How do you feel about that? Can you imagine what it would be for someone to have this burden? Empathy is a hard thing to possess, since it demands of us that we should take in other people's pain. It is easier to shut ourselves off than to let in a stranger's negative emotions.

However, when we do allow ourselves that empathy, we direct our attention toward the wider world. We decide that it is not only our pain that counts, in the end. Of course, empathy can mean sharing positive emotions as well, but for our purpose, let's say that a lot of it is to appreciate what negativity people might be living.

Empathy makes us less selfish. As a matter of policy, in a wider sense, it makes the individual realize implications for the entire population, and thus decisions stemming from an empathetic point-of-view have more chances of helping society at large.

Just to illustrate a point: in the United States, healthcare at this juncture is not free. To receive medical care of any quality, a person must have insurance, or else they pay full price. A certain segment of the population does not want to pay for healthcare through a socialized system (paying taxes for everyone to have access).

Their thought process is: why should we pay for everyone else? Fair enough, but here's the problem: when family members of theirs fall ill, and no longer have insurance, there is a great gnashing of teeth as to why there was no Universal Healthcare.

In other words: "It's fine if it happens to someone else, and I don't want to pay for strangers, but boy would it be useful right about now for myself or my family."

Empathy is one of those *open* emotions so important in society to bring all its members closer together, so that they protect each other on a wider scale.

This is the advantage of empathy, and for many other reasons, too. Yes, it is counter-intuitive as a global system, but as I've stressed before, the more counter-intuitive tools we use on a global scale, the more of a difference we can make. We don't take away from ourselves by feeling what others feel: quite the contrary.

What is more, the less empathy we feel for those around us, the easier it is to Other people, or *make them less human,* a tactic used by politicians and hate groups who wish to target populations for destruction or enslavement.

And we do. We *other* people to a greater or lesser degree all the time. Because of sexual orientation, tribal affiliation, religious group, political party, ethnic background, social standing, and a slew of other artificial reasons for which one group detests another, and it's wrong in every single case. We do it because it makes us feel falsely superior, and we are wrong, every single time.

The Whole For the Part

S ometimes called "Making the good the enemy of the best," we take a whole subject and treat it as one big monolith, which is indivisible from itself.

Q: I have no idea what that means. Can you explain it?

A: Of course. Let's say, for example, you're watching a movie, and you like it. It's quite good, say, but at some point, an event happens in the movie that was poorly executed. From thereon in, you might become disgusted with the whole thing, even though it was just that one scene, or that one item on the menu that ruined it for you.

You transform that small bad experience into the whole show. The part has become the whole. I get it. We do this for a lot of things, though.

Take my experience: I wasn't really into Catholicism to begin with. The fact that the last priest I served under was a creepy guy sealed it for me. From then on, Catholicism was Evil, and I rejected everything to do with it, with no regard for what *good* it had to offer.

And no, Catholicism is not just pedophilia. It is a myriad of tools that help people live out their daily lives in peaceful harmony with their neighbors.

Another great example is the way Muslims, who are the followers of Islamic Religion are treated right now. There are 1.8 billion Muslims in the world, most of them living peacefully, or trying to, and a handful of awful people running around calling themselves Muslims, who are mostly a danger to other Muslims, and the rest of the world fear the 1.8 billion who've not done a thing wrong. Taking the part for the whole is destructive, as it does not take into consideration the myriad good things involved with a particular group.

Of course, I do say this with a caveat. When considering the whole for the part, I don't include individuals, as there are people who have done great things, but are still monsters. There's *nothing* good about a person who trained Olympic athletes and molested them whenever he could.

There is a kind of balancing act involved in taking into account large organizations, or groups of people. Are they mostly good, or mostly bad? What part are you considering? What is that group trying to do to better themselves?

Seen through a negative lens, every group has something horrible going on. Canada mistreats indigenous people. America is racist. Christians are homophobic. The Japanese are misogynistic. Buddhists are murderers. Muslims beat women and behead people. The list goes on and on. You can find something wrong with every *group*, because of the things that some individuals, or a part of the group does within it. If the negative aspects were taken as a *whole*, every single group treats others with contempt.

So not every Canadian mistreats First Nations people, and not every American is racist, etc. There are groups out there working to make things more fair, and I recommend you join them. Have empathy for those who aren't treated as equals in this world. Help change the education that makes it so.

This iniquity is avoidable. But it takes time to work things out, and self-realization to change things and make it better for everyone. In the meantime, be aware of the bad, but don't lump in everyone from a group into the terrible category, unless that group's purpose is avowedly to destroy other groups. There are no good nazis or nice fascists.

Benoit Chartier

A Happy Medium

There are multitudes of ways that I *can* be, given my thoughts on spectrums. My own, very personal belief is that I should try to meet people halfway. I should always be ready to give a helping hand, if that is what the situation calls for.

I should be serene in my thoughts, as much as possible. Serenity, to me, is to have a calm mind, with a positive outlook. I do not want to be overly excited, tremendously angry, extremely nervous, or very sad *all the time*. My desire is for a clear frame of mind where I can spend less energy on worry or anger or sadness to solve the problems I have at hand.

In a sense, I'm looking for a kind of Zen quality to my thoughts.

I don't want to constantly be over-thinking things beyond logical conclusions, either, or putting a negative spin on any possible outcome.

I want to take things as they come, and adapt to the new situations that appear before me with the tools at my disposal.

I want to work hard when I have to work hard.

I want to enjoy my life, and the world around me as much as possible, and help *you* discover it with your mother and I.

I want us to spend time together and communicate. If there are fights, there will be fights, but we will calm down and apologize and put them behind us to concentrate on our positive future, not our negative past.

If there are issues in our community, I want to be a part of the solution, and have civil discourse to achieve that end. If there are problems with our government or planet, I want to take decisive action that will remedy the problems as efficiently as possible.

All this, I want to do in the smartest ways I can figure out, without having to necessarily go to extremes, since to me, those are only tools of *last resort*.

I want to follow the middle progressive path. The path that looks to the future with a positive outlook, a toolbox full of methods to get it, and the will to fight for it tooth and nail if and when it comes down to it.

However much others may try to, no one has the power to alleviate my problems except myself, to change my own mind, and it's up to me to take care of them the best I can, when I receive the tools to do so.

The great thing about the society that you and I live in, is that *the best I can*, means with others helping as well. We are stronger together.

Choosing the middle path, for me, means to not forget myself when I am with many, yet not forget the many while I am myself.

The identification and implementation of methods of self-fulfilment are my path and my goal, as well as the implementation of methods to help others achieve that goal.

I've found that in this day and age (and I'm sure it's been like this forever), we mostly concentrate on our own self-fulfilment and pleasure. It's important for me to remember that these things are some of the many aspects of life, and not the end-all and be-all of it. I try to keep in mind that to truly enjoy my own life, there are those who need my help, and in giving them that help, they get to enjoy theirs.

Once again, having something above us as a goal might help us start moving along the road to something grander than this static plateau we've reached in the past hundred years.

Benoit Chartier

The Psychological Imperative

All controls of who you are reside within the mind. What you consider emotions are physical reactions to mental stimulus. When your logic tries to override your emotions, or vice versa, it is simply one part of your mind battling another for dominance.

Our bodies have developed over millennia into the beings we are today, and our minds are no exception. They began as very simple constructs. As our diets and evolution made our cranial cavities shift over time, our minds acquired new shapes and new additions, slowly making us more complex creatures.

This capacity for complex thought and basic emotions which we take for granted today is responsible for all the good and all the ill we cause to ourselves, to others and to our environment.

The human mind is the most powerful tool we have ever been given (I say *given* in a metaphorical sense), and this would indicate that our thoughts are the most important things we have, as a species.

How we direct them is another matter altogether. Looking back on the past several hundred years, you can observe real change in the way we have analyzed, dissected and resolved complex problems for which we previously had no tools to do so.

Evolution of the mind is therefore not only possible, but continues to happen to this very day, and will continue until our extinction. We have a psychological, genetic imperative to improve our minds in every way, shape, or form that we possibly can.

Whatever genetic mutation happened in our ancestors those many millions of years ago, it is that which caused us to question our very existence that has made us the dominant species on this island we call Earth.

159

It continues to do so, for it has been sent down our family tree to every single member. Whether you decide to listen to the insistent voice within yourself, or not, depends solely on your desire for true satisfaction or simple, mediocre facsimiles.

The most important and self-defining moments of your life happened when you were too young to remember, yet those events are ever-present with you in your subconscious mind. They are the invisible drivers mentioned earlier.

As a child, events marked you, for good or ill, and how you dealt with these blows from life defines how you recreate your environment.

As adults, these formative events have been so ingrained in us for so long that we no longer question them. We no longer even remember they happened. We just take for granted that we are who we are.

We realize that we are different from others, and it is the way in which we deal with this reality which makes us social creatures. Our lives are centred firmly on ourselves, such as what we do and what we say appear normal at all times.

We do not tend to question our thoughts and actions, for they are an intrinsic part of our being. No matter what we do, we can justify our actions, because we can rationalize *anything. Anything at all.*

Think of Hitler and Stalin and Pol Pot. In the same breath, think of Ghandi, John Lennon, Buddha, and Jesus. Whatever stimulus helped them become the people they were, is the same kind of stimulus that may affect you and I to be the people we were, are, and will be.

The vast majority of humanity never goes to those extremes (and in the latter cases, so much the pity) because they are content with the thoughts they are imposed.

The ultimate common thread among all those people though, is that they all saw *problems*, they all thought very hard about how they wanted to *fix* them, and then they went ahead, with the tools they had at their disposal.

With all the psychological and genetic baggage they personally carried that affected their judgement in doing so. We know what the results were, for all of them.

The first three, because of their distrust of the human being, or of parts of humanity, crushed and destroyed large swathes of it to create their versions of Utopia.

Their egos were firmly facing toward themselves, and they needed those egos to be fed constantly. Their hatred and fear of others drove them to destroy them.

The other four lived through love, and an ego that was firmly facing humanity, feeding it their own love, and their legacy lives through us today, as various philosophies and positive influences.

If we picked apart all the various philosophies that have existed, they were predicated upon certain common themes. All of them related to the mind, there can be no doubt about that, since everything you can possibly think of stems from that place.

Each of them thought that we, as humans, were all based on emotion or thought, and everything else that followed from their discourse was a logical dissertation which spread into the various meanders.

No, Hitler, Stalin, and Pol Pot were *not* philosophers. They were politicians and warriors, but they had to have had a personal philosophy, which they tried to implement, however terrible the methods they employed.

One of the major differences between those three and actual philosophers, is that the latter attempt to think in *universal* terms, and not solely their own egos, as the former did. There are as many philosophies as there are people on earth. Everybody is different, to be sure.

There are right or wrong answers, when it comes to human thought, and they are all subject to evolution of the *proof* that sustains them over time. They are just varying degrees of truth through provable facts, emotions, logic, ego and altruism.

Everything and everyone is on a sliding scale or spectrum. New facts, within the context of scientific discovery, when they can be proven time and again, become the *truer* facts, and the ones that came before, their antecedents. This doesn't mean that fact is subjective, per se, only that as our tools to discern it through the imperfect animal that we are become sharper, the facts themselves becomes clearer, thanks to our newer, better lenses.

The question everyone asks, or should ask themselves is: "Which is the best way to be, in this reality?" That has been the prevailing question amongst thinkers for a very long time (even though they framed it differently).

I believe it is understood that we can be anything at all, and we adapt to any type of situation with great ease. The above question keeps evolving at the same rate we do, and those who believe they have found the answer would like to think that there is nothing more to know.

What they fail to see is that our reality will never reveal all its mysteries, but the search for the answers is what had driven the philosophers that preceded them to do so.

They do not see that their search is not over, and that even though many great truths have been found, others are yet to be discovered, and that every new generation reinvents itself.

The belief that the Universe popped into existence recently, and is unchanging and static is very reassuring, but it is a fallacy in light of all the evidence we have accumulated so far.

We can base our philosophies on any number of universal emotions or thoughts, but what keeps coming back, again and again throughout history, is that the cultures who adopt a fact-based, pluralistic, positive philosophy fare better, and for a longer period of time, than those who do not, as a whole. Yet all of them fall, eventually, for forgetting these things.

As we progress, there are more and more people populating the earth. Resources are strained in many places already. We can, of course, decide to head into all-out war with everybody else, take what is theirs, and repopulate their lands with our peoples.

This is the *usual* pattern we all go through, and have been doing so since the dawn of time. The thing that is stopping us from doing so now, though, is that it is almost assured that this will endanger the entire human population through nuclear annihilation.

We are left with other options, though, thankfully. We can develop a truly human-centric philosophy which will encompass all who inhabit the earth. We already have the basic paperwork down in various forms of

Human Rights declarations, we just need to do the leg-work now and get the ball rolling.

We also have the monetary means to do so, if it were not held by a handful of people who don't seem to know what to do with it in any meaningful way.

For the most part, we as the people of this planet are just mostly guilty of neglect. We only see the things that we want to see, and that makes us blind to everything else going on around us. I mention all this, so that you have a firm grasp on what surrounds you on a wider scale than what you can literally observe. You yourself will see many great changes, and will affect those changes in some minor way, through your actions.

Speaking of philosophies, I just thought I would bring this one to your attention: nihilism. The main idea of Existential Nihilism, is that there is no intrinsic value to human life, and that there is no defined point to our existence. There are a great many people who find this idea depressing, and I'll get back to it shortly. All I ask is that you put the depressing aspect of it aside for now and concentrate on the infinite possibilities this thought conjures up.

There are as many ways to think as there are people thinking. Those who are successful in making their lives worthwhile are those who do it with positive, open feelings. The need to help others to feel good about themselves drives them to create a better world.

Psychologically, these are all survival strategies. How we treat others determines, up to a point, how we ourselves will fare in this world. The more positive, helpful actions we take, the more we surround ourselves with allies who will feel more inclined toward reciprocation than toward harmful action. There is never a one-hundred percent guarantee of this, but the odds are greater than if we carried out an agenda of harming or taking advantage of all those around us. This is how we were able to build nation-states in the first place, through mutual assistance.

We could not have done so if we had had no common ground, and no compunction to assist strangers.

We do everything with logic and emotion, to varying degrees. With our healthy open emotions, we help, such as when we demonstrate love and compassion.

Conversely, with our negative emotions we harm, as when we show our hatred. The harm I cause others stems from the pain I harbour within myself, unseen, and reacting when I lose control. My lack of knowledge of myself makes it so that I do not question why I harm, I just do.

If I begin to question my nature, I can learn to question my negativity. By doing so, I recognize that it may be self-destructive, and that since what I should desire is my own serenity, that self-destructive behavior has no place within me. When I harm others, whether verbally or physically, I harm myself. I try to expunge my hatred by directing it, but it only makes it stronger within me. When I harm others, it is because I do not question my own purpose, and let my emotions direct me.

An Existential Nihilist is depressed because there is no self-avowed purpose to life. In choosing this philosophy and being *depressed* about it, the nihilist has effectively chosen to equate purposelessness with hopelessness. Depending on how you view life, you shape your own model of possibilities available to you. It therefore would be in your best interest to see no avowed inherent purpose as meaning infinite possibilities with no restraint.

I found out a little while ago about a young man, who, having developed a bent for that particular philosophy, wrote what he considered to be his life's work, then shot himself in the head, in a very public way, on a Jewish religious holiday, on the steps of Memorial Church in Harvard Yard. The title of his work was *Suicide Note*. The 35-year old man's name was Mitchell Heisman.

What is interesting is that the philosophy he painstakingly unwound over nineteen-hundred pages was one that described the purposelessness of life. Having accomplished this, he took his own.

I can neither condone, nor condemn his act, not having lived his life, or being in a position to criticize what he wanted to do with what he had.

The thing I find ironic is that he spent years writing this immense volume touting the purposelessness of nihilism, in effect having found *his own purpose*.

Even though I can agree with him that life, other than its need to perpetuate itself, has no intrinsic value other than the one we give it, I would say to this: Great! This, in fact, would seem to indicate that we have free will, and can act, completely unfettered and unrestrained in our environment to do as we will, if we so allow ourselves.

The fact that he would describe our feelings and actions the results of chemical reactions, and therefore not really his own at all I find disconcerting. I can't remember the last time I went sky diving and forgot to enjoy myself because I was too busy introspecting on the Physics involved in my vertiginous fall and the chemical nature of the reactions I was experiencing.

It would seem, according to this gentleman's philosophical outlook, that because something can be explained, it is no longer enjoyable or of any value. This line of thought would bring us to believe that we are better off knowing nothing about ourselves or our surroundings, if we are to be truly happy.

Truth is, depending on your philosophical or emotional bent, everything can be *your* truth. The truth is a very personal thing, when it comes to *belief*, as can be observed throughout the worlds' myriad religions, political convictions, social constructs, business practises, and everything that makes human interaction possible.

The over-arching theme that remains when all else has been stripped away is that all we know is human-centric, since that is what we are.

However else we may think, or convince others to think, it is a complex and somewhat anarchic process affected by every single emotion and thought we can conjure up within ourselves.

Our philosophers and religious inspirations have created for us frames within which we operate, and their teachings have become part of the fabric of our societies. Whether or not the fabric is strong depends on the convictions of the individual strands that are contained within it.

This does not mean that Science is equal to Belief. Science is outside of Belief, and to a certain degree, a more evolved (and all-encompassing) philosophy.

Whereas religion tries to explain the unexplainable and unknowable through feeling and conjecture, science reveals the knowable through logic and experiment, and is therefore in a different field *entirely* than Belief.

It is interesting to observe the battle that seemingly rages between those two schools of thought. Does it really matter if the "Spirit" you ascribe to life is in fact human-shaped and all-powerful (and not the Universe itself)?

What if I don't need to be comforted about the uncertainties of life (or death)? What if, because my future is *not* written, I *do* have choices that are very important to everyone around me, and not just myself?

What if, there is in fact nothing checking over my shoulder to see if I do right?

What if, conversely, I *do* need direction other than cold, hard facts? What if I want my *emotions* to matter in this materialistic modern world? Who is to blame me? I understand why religious people believe in God(s). I understand why scientific people don't. The problem I have, honestly, is when they become so righteous about their branch of knowledge that they believe it is the end-all and be-all of human civilization and discount the other out of hand.

I am a balancing act of every aspect of my life, interior and exterior, walking the tight-rope that leads me to the next step, and no one knows what that is. I am a combination of body and mind, logic and fantasy, emotion and self-control, internal and external stimulus, in a world that is either real or a fantasy.

What I do with it, right now, is the most important thing I will ever do.

How I do it, is the second most important.

For this I need both Logic and Love.

Science cannot provide love, but neither can religion/spirituality give me any proof. If both would somehow find common ground, I believe *all* would be uplifted.

Since I can believe absolutely anything I want to, and can motivate myself to pursue any goal I desire, in any way I wish to do so, I am the freest of beings that I know of, on this planet.

Whether my goals are selfish or altruistic, for the common good or for me alone, I can do these things with the knowledge that I am not in any way going against any pre-set goal that was put before me, for me to strive for. This, no matter how much others try to convince me otherwise.

To me, that is an incredibly freeing, very open opportunity to be the best person I can be. Your future(s?) are completely open, with infinite possibilities, and only your influence on your own actions can affect those futures accordingly. This is what makes us band together as one, or go it alone, share with our teammates, or take all the riches for ourselves.

You are without limits, and it makes you entirely adaptable to any situation or environment. You alone put the brakes on your own behavior, depending on your beliefs.

I have chosen the common good as my life's goal, since to me the survival of my species and all others around it depends on the co-operation of all.

It is only by fighting for the things I believe in that anything will change to shape that future I envision. I can pass that vision on to you, and you will have to decide for yourself what a worthy goal for your life might be, because you are entirely free to do so.

Your ego determines who will come first in your treatment of your surroundings. How you define your place in the world, and the importance you give yourself will affect everyone around you.

I have touched on the subject of those who desire power having a tremendous need for adulation and being imbued with much self-importance. This, I should mention, is a trait of the ego-maniac.

There are several different types of personalities that desire power in the first place. There are those who want it for powers' sake, and there are those who want it to help others.

It is my belief that most power-seeking people place themselves somewhere within that spectrum. Those who find themselves more on the power-for-powers'-sake end of the spectrum typically place less emphasis on those whom they do not consider equals, to the point of dehumanizing them and ordering their destruction, if not simply their marginalisation.

They would be the kind of leaders to watch out for, of course, since their aim is not to change things for the better for the population over which they desire control. Their aims are very much the accumulation of power and wealth for themselves.

Whatever upbringing gave rise to the idea of clear differences among the different social classes and inferiority of the poor, gives the power-seeker his reason for marginalizing those deemed an *unfit* part of society. Not having lived in poverty (experience being subjective), people have to rationalize their station in life.

This mentality leads to all the selfish behaviors we have come to know, and the inequality that spreads from their existence.

The overbearing ego is one of the great barriers that prevents us from wanting to help others, or realize that we are not the only creature that has importance in our environment. Of course, used well, the ego can drive us to excel and exceed. Wherever the extremes of this attitude are present in a human system, however, it creates enormous inequality among its members, which invariably results in one or more group being ostracized as being inferior or less-than-human, and left to rot in poverty or worse. It is the attitude that permits and promotes slavery and discrimination. The only thing that can counter this type of movement is the promotion of those who are at the other end of the spectrum, those who are trying to improve the lives of all. Sadly, there are fewer of these personality types than the ones I just described.

Here you are now, the person you are today, carrying wounds as old as you are. You are unconscious of their very existence, except when your temper flares up. They are like viruses that have been in your system forever and have gone undetected until now. You harbour prejudices that you direct at those you consider to be less than what you are, with no basis in truth for these beliefs.

What you define in yourself as *normal* behavior is only so because you do not know any other way to be, and how you act is an adaptation to your environment, and an unconscious desire to be like the group that surrounds you.

Yet you can be better than yourself. These elements that make you the person you are, are real. You may not be able to define them, or put your finger on them, but you know that they exist. They are there, and they are what manipulate you into action. What makes life interesting is the knowledge that you have choices to make, not just reactions to actions.

You can evolve to become a different person, following a different path than the one you are now taking, if that is what you so desire.

As a tool, psychology is one of the most powerful personal development methods in existence. Your motivations to action are the deepest set of skills in your armory, dependent on your purpose and personal philosophy.

Realizing they are there, these ingrained viruses and wounds in the system, is only the first step. The next is to identify them, classify them and then, neutralize them and tame them.

You cannot destroy them. They are you. To destroy them would be to destroy a part of your own personality. You can, though, by the simple act of realizing them, make them less effective or even a positive force in your personal growth.

All those little niggling thoughts that sabotage your good humour in your daily life exist for a reason. They are your defence mechanisms aimed squarely at the difficulties of life. When you can qualify them, you have effectively made them ineffectual or at least comprehensible.

You can henceforth see them coming from a mile away. It takes time and practise, to be sure. You need to develop a different mindset, but it is achievable with practise. What is easier to deal with, an invisible enemy, or an old and comfortable dance partner?

The problem in this case, is that it is as if I was six years old, and was being asked to solve a difficult problem I had never faced: how do I do it? I have to look at it with the tools in my possession, and in many cases, it is even better to ask for help, since, to paraphrase C-Lo, "If I really want to understand me, I better talk to someone else".

The keys to your own personal kingdom reside inside its tallest turret, locked inside a room. The door has to be opened by any means necessary for you to find what it is you don't even know you want, but now realize you may lack. You might even have searched for everywhere else *but* inside yourself.

How we approach the opening of our mind is for each and every one of us a different journey. Everyone finds information that sparks the desire for knowledge once again, and with it, the yearning for self-evolution. That is what unlocks the door.

It is said that we only use ten percent of our minds. That is an urban myth that has been repeated for ages, since the first neuroscientist, William James said: 'We only use ten percent of our *potential*.'

So it is not the brain that is full of empty and unused parts, it is I who isn't using it as well as I could. This actually requires learning, and for some, this prospect is daunting, verging on the impossible.

This state of affairs is self-induced. I do not know if that means I am simply too lazy to learn, or am so unused to doing so that the task seems monumental or just boring. One thing is certain: my lack of desire to learn is the one leading factor in my unhappiness.

If I have decided that my mind is something that is only there to perform basic tasks, I am in effect turning down a Bugatti Veyron because I am more comfortable in a Ford Pinto. Even though that incredible internal vehicle could be achieved with very little strenuous work, and would benefit me for the rest of my life.

Mistakes

What is a mistake? A mistake is an action which was perpetrated with incomplete information and ended in a false or damaging result. I spend a lot of time making the same mistakes, when searching for a correction to my problems would take little time, and would make my life much easier in the future. Much of the time, I am oblivious to the fact of my own mistakes, even though they may be glaring omissions.

It would be in my best interests to pay attention to the mistakes that I make, since that is what makes me grow (we do so through trial and error), but also try to find a possible positive solution to said problems.

Always, communication is the key to understanding what the source of mistakes are. I should not feel embarrassed to ask what exactly I did wrong, to be able to properly act in the future if a similar situation were to present itself.

One of the traps I fall into when making mistakes is that I tend to need to find a guilty party in their creation. This 'scapegoating' may help me feel better in the short term, but it detracts me from the true issue of error correction.

If my energies are concentrated on the distribution of blame, I am not attempting to fix any problems, only making myself feel less guilty. When the emphasis is on error correction, guilt or shame attributed to error is irrelevant.

The important part to remember is that I am not looking for someone to blame for a mistake, I am looking for a solution. The goal should always be a compromise between aggrieved parties.

To go forward with a clear idea of what is acceptable for all concerned, and to act upon that decision systematically when similar situations arise.

As human beings, we *all* make mistakes. Blaming either oneself or others is damaging and solves nothing. It only makes resentment or sadness the main lesson learned during the exchange, and should be relegated to the wastebasket of useless egotistical acts we do not need. There will always be a share of responsibility to be accepted by the perpetrators of whatever negative action was taken.

Responsibility needs to be taken if it is through our actions that the outcome resulted, but the accent should not be entirely on punishment.

Please be aware that what I was talking about was *mistakes*, and not *criminal acts*. The former is unintentional and caused relatively little pain, and the latter is the opposite of that.

Ignorance

I t is normal not to know something. I say "I don't know." all the time. The thing is, if I don't want to stay ignorant about something, I can very easily find out the answer, and with the advent of the internet, the cellular phone, or even, lo and behold, books, it would be sheer laziness on my part not to look it up, if simply out of curiosity.

"Let's find out!" is usually my answer after "I don't know." There should be a little voice inside you that bugs you until you know the answer to a question.

If you don't heed that little voice, it will never let you rest until you do (now that I planted that little seed of curiosity in your brain, good luck with that).

Curiosity is part of my emotional mind, and is a healthy part of it too. I had been starving it for years, and so now it has come back with a vengeance. The desire to know things is a pervasive and hard to ignore imperative. I used to, but it is detrimental to my growth.

Like wearing shoes that are too small when you are growing older, you should expand your mind before you feel like it is way too narrow on your shoulders.

Communication, Languages, and Their Importance

anguage is the most important overt human tool you have: to demonstrate the knowledge that resides within yourself, share your needs, receive concepts from others, and develop your ability to understand more.

Language defines who you are, and the limits of your understanding of your environment. As well, it helps you to formulate your understanding of your reality.

When sets of sounds are arranged as a coherent system, they help us create and share the world we live in.

As numerical values, they help us to quantify our surroundings, as in mathematics.

Arrange them into different tones and sounds, and you have created musical language to illuminate your mind in the most pleasant ways.

Use colours and shapes, and you define beauty with it.

As symbols, you create an impression of your mind on paper or screen. It is with language that you can agree or disagree, create masterpieces, build machines, model societies, create rhetoric, and tame the Universe and your Reality.

It is the mind expressed in a way that is understandable to others, as well as creating the divisions that cut us off from our fellow human.

Without communication, we would never have come down from the trees.

Without language, we would never have become self-reflecting creatures, for we could not have been able to ask other people's complex opinions and been understood. Language is the basis of humanity, and it is our use of language that defines our minds, and helps us interpret the minds of others.

We have built towering skyscrapers of knowledge with our languages, and we add to them still. As a developing species, we have evolved much, in the thousands of years since our splitting off from other bipedal mammalian families.

We have gotten taller, and our brain cases have grown a bit, but the physical processes through which we are born make it difficult for us to grow a larger brain. Yet we know that we are smarter than the generations that came before us, several millions of years ago. We know that we are smarter than very many of the 8.7 million species of living creatures that populate our little island in the cosmos.

The multiplication of brain patterns through the eons have been a factor. The passing down of knowledge from one generation to the next, building and evolving from those primitive bases has also been an incredible boon.

If we had had to start over from square one every time, with no previous knowledge available to us, we would not be where we are today. Our innovations in all areas of knowledge have helped us push the ever-receding limits of our possibilities.

Intelligence and creativity have become a dominant trait in modern humans: the modest origins of these traits are what have brought us to where we are now.

We keep getting smarter, to a certain degree. It is all a matter of percentages, of course. I'm not trying to toot my own horn, or that of humans in general. I'm just pointing out the fact that we aren't *done* growing. There has been evolution, and there will continue to be evolution. It is through setting down our knowledge for others to build upon that this will be accomplished. Our ability to communicate and willingness to share is that driving force.

Quite a few people have what we call savant traits, intelligence so strong that they can remember whole languages within a week, or paint an entire city after looking at it once, from the sky. This is due to parts of their minds being overactive, in certain areas, and less so in others. The visual and memory centres of their minds might be overactive, which

175

gives them a terrific visual memory, meaning they could draw an entire scene they saw only once with extreme clarity.

This goes to show the incredible possibilities that exist within us. Even if I am not a savant, I know that it is at least possible to have a mind that is well developed.

Though it comes naturally to some and not to me, this doesn't mean that I shouldn't attempt to further my own mental development. This is partially achievable through the expansion of my language capabilities. As the building blocks of my thoughts, language, and communication help me in defining everything.

If foundations help me expand the reach of my mental 'home,' then words and concepts are the 'bricks' with which I construct that house. The more bricks I have, then, the bigger a house I am able to build. I should not be content with a single language, since other methods of communication are new bricks to add to my collection.

Symbols

S ymbols are representations given meaning. For example, a cross, (two lines, one perpendicular over the other), is the symbol used by the Christian and Catholic faith to signify its association with Jesus Christ (He was a Jewish philosopher with strong religious beliefs who was crucified at the hands of his enemies).

The association is made between the man and his death as a physical representation of both. It is then worn or decorates the homes of those adepts who follow his teachings.

Anything we give intrinsic value to is a symbol.

A letter is a symbol, given meaning through common acceptance, associated to a sound. The letter A, as it is written, for example, is not pronounced G. It could have been, perhaps, but the symbol that was assigned to the sound was decided to be otherwise. In this case we are talking about symbology.

The reason why there are so many different alphabets stems from the evolution of every cultures' own methods of physically representing sounds through symbols.

Usually, these began as picture representing a physical object, known as pictograms, and with time, that image changed until it became unrecognizable as the original picture. This is true for almost any language, save for alphabets that were created recently for peoples who had no written language of their own (Inuit until the 1950s, Korean until 1443).

You can head into the abstract as well, if you like. An expensive car is a symbol of wealth and status, clothing of any kind symbolize the belonging to a particular social group. A representation of a tree can be a symbol of life and nature as well as growth.

Symbolism is the abstract meaning we assign to objects, or the representation of an object through abstract means. Certain books have been imbued with more intrinsic meaning than others. For example, if I burn a blank page, no one will care.

What if I burn my old University books? That is nobodies' business but mine, although I am sure some would object on principle.

What if I tell everybody that I'm going to burn a stack of Holy Bibles, New Testaments, or Qurans? Then you have a reaction. Was it the words inside that are so valuable, or the paper? Nope, it is what the book *represents* that puts people in a tizzy.

They were given a deeper meaning (the Holy Books) many years ago, when it was believed that knowledge was *sacred*. Therefore, any knowledge that is contained within a book deemed Holy comes directly from God, or The Gods. As such, it is said that they should be regarded with utmost respect, no matter what.

In a sense, it gave an ordinary object a supernatural power that assured its own survival, come what may. In certain areas of the world, people are still made to swear on the Bible, to ensure that what they say is not a lie.

Many centuries ago, though, this *sacredness* was crucial at a time when writings were the main method of dissemination of knowledge other than oral tradition.

As religious texts for many thousands of years helped us police ourselves, they were considered inviolate. The intrinsic value of the books is therefore their *divine* provenance and the knowledge contained within their pages. Especially at a time when they were transcribed by hand, making them particularly valuable and scarce. Considering the effort going into their manufacturing, it is no wonder that they were given Holy status.

Symbols have been with us from the dawn of time, and will stick with us until we are no longer a species we can properly describe as human. We get to choose *some* of our symbols, what they represent for us, how we react to them, and what we do to them, or with them.

Your mind is full of symbolic thought, and it is my belief that when you sleep, you dream using acts and objects which have a deeper meaning. Most of the time, you do not know what these symbols mean. Your unconscious mind does, though, since it deals only in symbols. It acts as the interpreter of your experiences and encoder of memory. Your interpretation of your daily tribulations through the dream state in symbolic patterns makes you aware (during the dream) of what you think.

You are looking into the window of your unconscious to see a play you do not understand. It is acted out by characters which are all different aspects of who *you* represent. These include your fears, as well as your desires, in a rapid-fire pantomime in the night.

The symbols you knowingly choose to decorate and adorn your daily life with are as much a part of your conscious self-assessment as a physical representation of your subconscious.

I give meaning to everything I have, everything I say, as well as everything I do, whether I am conscious of the fact or not. I symbolically project my mind all around me at all times. Everything I am is information, and everything I take in as well. It is in my best interest, then, to fine-tune my best tools, so as to not miss any important information that comes my way. It will also aid me in communicating *what* I am in such a way as to not be misunderstood, as well.

What is Intelligence?

feel pretty dumb sometimes, I have to admit. I have conversations with people and think: "Wow! That person is brilliant! I wish I could be like that!" Everybody has different knowledge, as well as different life experiences.

Obviously, the opposite happens as well. I have met doctors who didn't know what a finger bowl was (a dipping bowl full of water, to rinse your fingers while eating spare ribs).

These people were not stupid. They were incredibly smart, but when faced with an unknown situation, where no previous knowledge was available, what were they to do? I know people with incredible personal philosophies of life who have never been to school after their twelfth grade year.

Everybody accumulates knowledge according to his or her needs, wants, or exposures. You are constantly faced with new information. You watch the news, listen to gossip, read a newspaper (something which may or may not still exist when you are grown up) and find out about the day's events, or hang out with friends and family.

A lot of things will happen in a lifetime which will help you shape your own personal philosophy. A lot of these are passive events that wash over you causing no fundamental alterations. You may be tempted to look at others and compare your accumulated knowledge to theirs.

It is foolish to judge others by the information they do or do not possess. Since everyone is different, they will certainly not have acquired the same knowledge as you. All you can do is fill your personal vault of knowledge and not judge others for theirs. In fact, you can take the opportunity to learn from them what you yourself don't know.

You can, however, *deepen* the knowledge you have. Information that changes your personal view of life, to acquire more efficient tools of learning, requires more effort than daily automatic intake.

There are many things to be learned by this method, of course. Most of what you will learn will be done this way. However, the best methods of thinking have already been pursued by others, a very long time ago. New information keeps being explored, as well, by modern scientists. It is by becoming acquainted with all their work that you can widen your lenses, to see existence in a much broader spectrum.

Even though you will make incredible realizations on your own, you will elevate yourself further by standing on the shoulders of Giants (that's not mine, I stole it from Isaac Newton). Usually, these are the kinds of points of view and insights that you have to pursue yourself, because as good as your formal education might be, it is only a beginning.

Intelligence, among other things, is acquisition and retention of information, therefore the more influences you incorporate, the better you understand everything.

Wisdom is the ability to apply it, in the best way you know.

In a sense, stupidity is dependant on what little information you have to make decisions, even though the situation requires much more. If you fall flat on your face, get up, try again in a *different* way and succeed, you have evolved in your abilities and intelligence. You are then ready to head for the next hurdle.

Life is not really a series of tests, or hurdles, these are only metaphors, as I've mentioned a few times before. Life is a series of hits and misses, satisfying or unsatisfying results. The hurdles are the quandaries placed in your path.

Information, imagination, your body, your attitude, and knowledge are the tools at your disposal to bypass those quandaries. How you decide to approach them and overcome them defines how well you proceed to the next question or challenge. You won't have to start the race over if you miss the hurdle, but you will keep bumping against that *same* obstacle over and over until you find a satisfactory method of overcoming it.

You might as well learn how to circumnavigate what is on your path if you don't enjoy getting mentally whacked in the face by the ground.

This is how you become wiser, from the beginning, by successfully analyzing then overcoming an obstacle in a way that is satisfying to you. Then, by applying the knowledge you have acquired as a tool in any future similar situations as a template for possible action.

If I fail to identify my problems, however, I keep making the same mistakes time and again. Generally, we identify a problem as something that is detrimental to ourselves and others.

A cheating wife, abusive husband, playground bully, lying politician, or a mean boss for example, are real-life problems. They not only affect themselves but their surroundings as well.

These are examples which you may encounter at some point in time in your life. What wounds do they carry from their past which force them to pursue destructive behavior time and again? What realizations do they need to accomplish to be able to overcome this self- (and other people) destructive behavior?

Do they even realize how profoundly detrimental their acts are towards themselves and towards others around them? What behaviors do *I* perpetuate that I am completely unconscious of, which may be negatively affecting me and my surroundings?

You are constantly faced with choices in your life, and a failure to accomplish or surmount a task in a positive and constructive fashion invariably results in you either harming yourself, those who surround you, or both.

You will also be forced to face these same problems time and again until you find a way of nullifying their effects. A single problem may seem harmless to the person living it (remember, we can justify anything we do!), but has far-reaching consequences when taken on an inter-personal, or social level. I am society, as its basic molecule, and when I present myself for the whole world to see, I also present my vices.

Even though I cannot be flawless, I can do my utmost to set aside the most vicious and destructive aspects of my ego. I can realize that the existence of my negative traits are not only detrimental to myself, but to all those who encounter me. By being conscious of them, I can determine if I should wish to attempt to alter them.

If my vices damage me, they damage others, either directly or in-directly. Only *I* can fully realize that what I do is harmful (even though everyone around me is suffering from the fallout), and there is only one person who can change it: me.

One of the greatest developments in the human brain is our logic, and I should take full advantage of it to grow beyond the boundaries I set for myself. As I mentioned, I can normalize any behavior I do.

There are many ways to interpret my actions, depending on what my opinion of myself is. For example, I may consider myself to be a *go-getter*, who *says it like it is*, and won't *take bullshit from anyone*, but everybody else just sees me as a douchebag.

I can justify myself in any action I take, because I would rather think of myself as an awesome person rather than the selfish person that I truly am. This holds true for anybody, on any opinion they may hold, whether positive or negative. Out of necessity, we make normal any behavior, justifying it with reinforcement. I am entirely normal, since not thinking so would force me to see my actions as abnormal, detrimental, and subject to altering if I wished to return to equilibrium.

However, that's exactly what I have to do to be able to help myself if I want to go beyond the familiar ruts of my thinking. New information forces me to see beyond who I am and helps me observe myself from a third person point of view. I can't see the way I act unless I detach myself from it, in some way, shape or form. I can then choose to stay the same, or become a better person.

Since my life is improved with new information, I am more attracted to the positive evolution of my being.

Emotional Versus Logical

Logical intelligence and emotional intelligence are interrelated and crucial for a synthesis of a complete person. Everything we are taught seems intuitive, but that is what keeps us from evolving.

In many societies, men are raised to repress emotion, and women are taught to embrace their feelings. Both are segregated into camps.

If I see a difference between myself and another person as major, I use it as a wall to separate myself from what my mind unconsciously terms as alien, and this counts for emotion as well as any other difference we create.

This is mainly caused by a lack of information. The more I concentrate on the differences (as well as negative emotion), the more I create classifications and distinct groups which I shut out. My understanding of my surroundings depends on my knowledge of the dynamics that drive it, and the motivations of those who participate in it.

The classifications I make, as well as the emotions I attach to them are the relevant tags I assign to each part for easy understanding. If my understanding of the motivations of the people who surround me is flawed, so are my labels. You can classify absolutely everything, and you do, for easy identification, but you should *realize* that you are doing it. These are artificial separations and all your ideas are flavoured by your emotions, and as such should not be used to generalize on any topic, or person.

The exploration of my emotions, not as some alien construction but as a natural part of my being, have greatly helped me in understanding myself as well as others. You should not be afraid to do the same for whatever part of your intelligence you may feel you know less about. Not doing so is sadly, one of the reasons we give up a useful tool – whether because we are frightened or leery of exploring ourselves entirely.

Whatever roles gender or identity is supposed to play in our interactions, it is far less important than having positive interaction itself.

Most of the problems I have spring from the conflicts generated with those two warring factions within my mind. My logical mind, which analyses and controls conscious acts, and the emotional mind, which is in charge of my emotional responses to whatever stimulus arouses it.

If you feel a bit at odds with yourself sometimes, it might be because both sides are constantly vying for control.

For example, I really know I shouldn't be angry at my little sister for breaking my toy (logical), but I'm too angry right now (emotional).

Perhaps, as well, I might be sad at the breaking of my toy (emotional), but I understand that she did not mean to do it (logical).

The portion over which I have control, or lack thereof, will dictate my actions. I can have them working in sync, as well, but depending on what the thoughts are, as well as the control I have over my them, the results can vary wildly.

Just to give you another example, let's consider a case where a friend of mine is late in picking me up. I can think logically about what is the cause of my friend's lateness: (he's too lazy to be on time, he got hit by a truck, he hates me), but since I was thinking in an entirely *negative* way, I am just getting angry or sad or depressed. I still don't know the true reason for his lateness, because of my lack of information. All these interpretations are logical, but hardly positive. I often fill in the blanks with negative emotion, because I turn my frustration away from myself, and project it onto others. In this instance, it is true that my friend and his lateness could be a cause for frustration or disappointment, but without knowing the reason for his tardiness, do I truly have the right to feel so aggrieved? It could be considered that I should not make decisions without having all the information I require to take on a particular attitude.

Or perhaps this scenario: what if I was at home, late one night, waiting for your mother to return from a party with her friends? What if I convinced myself that her tardiness was because she had met another man at said party, and that she was in the process of cheating on me? The more I would think about this scenario, the more I would get angry, incensed and enraged. Then, when finally she got home I could scream at her: "WHO IS HE?" when all that happened was that she went for a quick bite to eat afterwards.

Letting my negative emotions, jealous tendencies, powerlessness, and ignorance getting the better of me could not be considered a positive trait of my personality. I have a feeling that your mother might share the sentiment by leaving me before getting hurt by this wild behavior.

The problem is, many people live with a lack of control over their emotions, and often resort to this type of behavior because they were never trained, or trained themselves, to contain it or defuse it. So one of the problems you might encounter in society is lack of self-control brought on by poor patience.

The other is framing. The overall frame of your beliefs is just as important as the impulse you have to use your beliefs, or the lenses you put in that frame. The frame could be considered the attitude you have.

For example, if I have a positive frame of mind, I encourage myself that without the knowledge about the event at hand, I should not let this lack of information make my negative emotions take over my mind. I should wait patiently until I have more information, or even try to acquire more information before deciding what actions or reactions are the most appropriate.

I make the decision whether or not my emotions control me, or I control my emotions. I can also have both drivers working in tandem, making me feel good about my awesome decisions and achievements, and not so good about my less than lofty deeds. It is up to you to make peace with these two *seemingly* irreconcilable halves. They exist, they are within us, and we might as well use both of them to further ourselves, in the best ways we possibly can.

Logic should not exist without love.

When I act logically, I should also do it with empathy. When love is missing from my thought processes, I can do terrible things to myself and to others. Of course, I may do the right thing, even without love, but

I will not feel any enjoyment at the task. The opposite is also true. When I do something with pure passion, whether positive or negative, I may get myself in trouble, a trouble which will be completely apparent once the passion has evaporated, and logic has once again taken the driver's seat.

Evolving in a World of Change

Once I know a thing, I tend to hold onto that knowledge as if I could lose it forever. I fear change as if it could destroy me, or the thoughts that are inside me. Change is a constant all around us, and that is why we create routine, to give us a sense of normalcy in an ever-evolving, ever changing world.

We don't need to *change*. What we should do is *evolve*: our minds, our bodies, our diets, our friendships, our activities, our work. These are all things that we can make *better*. This is what I mean by evolving.

Even if you aggressively hold onto ideas or habits, your own body and mind change (for better or worse) through time.

If you have an open mind, you can accept that change is inevitable. You can adjust your mind to that fact by adopting core values that need not change, even though you do. These mental tracks will help you develop new ones even into old age, and the new information will help you retain the old, helping offset mental breakdown in many cases.

Your brain is an elastic structure, and allowing it to remain immutable is akin to letting pudding congeal until it becomes a hard nugget: hard nuggets break more easily.

Previously, you'd been evolving all your life. Think of what you know now. You didn't always know the things you do, and if you care to live a long and healthy life, you will never stop yourself from learning new things.

You, of course, have the power to make it happen, or to not. Caring for your intelligence is the same thing as caring for your life.

Choosing Positive Social Traits

Your mind is one of the most important parts of your body. It informs you about how you feel, then tries to take the most appropriate actions based on those feelings.

It makes decisions, it is attracted or repulsed, and every part of it is used in the shaping of your everyday life. You began at birth, taking in your environment, and formulating opinions about it even before you were aware that you had such things as opinions.

You react to direct stimulus, and your repeatedly stimulated brain begins forming basis of reactions to events. Mostly, you are told how to react, and eventually, these will overcome your natural reactions, which *can be* selfish. Many things we do, as a species, are selfish.

Some would argue that everything we do is. Perpetrating selfish acts make us feel good. In fact, it is not the act itself that makes us feel good, but the end result. For example, a two year old stealing his siblings' stuffed bear, does not care about the act of *stealing* (that term is irrelevant to him), but of possessing something he desires, through whatever means are at his disposal.

As a very young child, I may have a notion of the concept of *empathy*, but my ego can trump it if what I want is more desirable than the resulting hurt I induce.

My parents helped me create new neural pathways, by making me feel good about *sharing*. That is something I may not have developed, left to my own devices. We taught you the traits that will help you integrate the society to which we belong. These traits will carry on through your adulthood, after you have learnt such things as kindness, sharing, generosity, charity, honesty, nonviolence, justice, loyalty, fair play (sportsmanship), calmness, friendship, patience, diligence, obligation, acceptance, forgiveness, and humility.

As well, of course, as the negative traits we may *not* have wanted to teach you, but you picked up along the way anyway. The positive will make you a better person towards your surroundings, and a more serene person yourself. This, in turn, gives you better survival chances within ours, and other societies.

These will make you feel good about yourself since they are traits, that when employed in your daily life, empower you and the people toward which you direct them.

Many of these traits are present in all or most societies, to varying degrees. Emphasis is given to many of these traits, as well as others, to form the cohesive basis around which large conglomerations of people can form and work together in relative harmony.

The more of these traits that are present as core values within any given society, the more cohesive the society will be. One of the most important aspects discovered by philosophers, religious or otherwise, was that these "outward-facing ego" traits were what was needed for people to police *themselves* within a society.

Take the "Golden Rule" of Christianity, for example: "Do unto others as you would have them do unto you." It is simple, to the point, and tells people outright that they should think empathetically.

I say outward-facing ego, because we are directing our energies to further other peoples' happiness, and by so doing, our own. At the very least, it reduces the effects of violence and injustice that may be perpetrated against us and others by those who adhere to these socially positive traits.

Curtailing the violence brought on by means of retribution is also one of its basic benefits. The cohesiveness of a society is only as strong as the bonds between every single one of its members. Those bonds can be either coerced from above (governmentally, through laws), through external policing, but they are far more effective when the social contract is observed by its members willingly and fairly, from within.

The people observing the social contract do not feel as if they are the object of scrutiny when it is they themselves who decide to renounce on antisocial acts. They are responsible for their own actions within the social contract they have signed with themselves.

These traits are named social intelligence, because they are the features we developed to act more efficiently within our societies. When many socially positive traits do not have the opportunity to be used, a society still works to a certain degree, of course. The results vary from society to society.

The absence of positive social traits can result from societal upheaval, total breakdown, or simply a failure to evolve beyond a certain level. Unfortunately, this condition can be found where people are only at the basic level of survival, as we can observe in certain war-torn or poverty-stricken countries where the breakdown or inexistence of all-encompassing societal values is widespread or has been eradicated.

Wherever violence is present on a wide scale, it is the return to survival instincts that kicks into high gear. Any thoughts of social nicety are obliterated swiftly, since it is the saving of the individual that is the *highest priority*. The egotistical mindset has no choice but to take over if the individual is to survive.

When peace is imposed, however, a new social model has to be introduced to curtail violence and anti-social acts, if the leaders of said societies have any desire to help stabilize their environment. The new social contract introduced will reflect the kind of peace the new rulers expect to gain, through the laws they introduce.

Once again, the more positive societal traits are included as being primordial to that society, the better chance it will have at becoming a more inclusive group. This in turn will give everyone within the group the chance to pursue their own happiness, with no restraint save for that of not harming those around them.

Sadly, many rulers do not consider these traits to apply to them. This is the cause of societal breakdown in the first place, since it is by adhering to ones' own rules that others imitate the example, or trust in its validity. When some consider themselves to be above the laws of their own country, it becomes time for the citizenry to remind them otherwise, or face societal breakdown, revolution, and/or dissolution.

On a different note, I do everything (or should) to the best of my abilities, but should I ever be satisfied with a plateau? Is there a point where I consider I can learn no more?

I think that the tragedy is that there are many who have already decided that they have. There is always something more to learn, about any given domain. When I have learnt everything that a subject has to offer, I usually find interest in another branch.

Knowledge is choice, not only power. Life is also about choice. I realize that the more I know about life, the better choices I can make within it. Limiting my knowledge is therefore limiting my life.

A plateau, to me, is only temporary, until I have begun to add more information and amalgamated it to what I previously knew. Since, to me, life is also about helping others, constantly learning more is a means to an end.

The more knowledge I have, the better methods I have at my disposal to help people who may need my assistance. Whether these people are family, strangers, friends, allies, or opponents, I can only make choices based on what I know about them and everything that exists. The more I know, the more effective my involvement.

Choice of Actions and Reactions

Whenever a negative action is perpetrated against me, I am presented with many options in how I can react. They are all dependent on who I am, what I know, and how well I can conceive my best course of action. Negative action causes instant fight or flight response within me, and a rising of my adrenaline.

What if I am prepared? The more I have training in confrontational situations, the more calmly I might react, knowing that getting angry, or confrontational myself, the more I might exacerbate the situation.

I do negative and harmful things because I do not have the practise to deal with these situations, and therefore rely on my primitive mental reactions to direct my actions. Having knowledge of potentially difficult situations and training myself beforehand can be a life saver, or at least a relationship saver.

I should attempt to make my conscious mind the motor for my reactions in difficult situations. In this manner, I may use my reflexes, but they become trained reflexes, and no longer simply moments of sheer panic.

Knowledge as a Mountain

The reason why many people do not attempt to learn more, I think, is because when they ponder any particular subject, they only see the corpus of knowledge that comprises the entirety of the subject. They do not see it as steps to be taken, slowly and surely towards the goal of learning that particular subject.

It is as if I asked someone to go mountain climbing with me, and they looked up to the peak, thought they had to leap to the top, declared my insanity and declined to go any further.

Of course, if that is how you consider learning, you will get discouraged, and you will abandon all hope. The thing is, learning is done in steps. Granted, the end goal remains to acquire as much of that knowledge and make it yours, but no way in hell will you need to learn it in a single bound!

The other thing that makes things more palatable for anyone who enjoys learning is this: it gets easier the more you do it. The more you put your mind to the task, and begin to take in the basics of the information that you wish to acquire, the faster it gets, until you feel that you are no longer making a conscious effort to learn.

Let's take skiing, for example: At first, if you have no idea how to downhill ski, you need to learn how to stand up without falling over, then you need to control where you are going, and how fast, as well as how to stop. You may then learn how to jump over tiny hills, or go faster and faster with more confidence down harder and harder slopes.

The more you learn, and take in, and understand, the better you get at it. The better you get, the more pleasant the feeling of doing it, making learning new tricks that much easier. The same can be said about any activity, even learning.

The thing is, learning requires something we are often in short supply of: patience. I often hear: "I have no patience." That's too bad, but it doesn't mean that you can't achieve patience, only that you've put up a mental block in trying. If you remove that self-imposed mental block, you could learn patience, but then again, it all rests upon your decisions about what you wish to achieve.

I choose to know, or not to know. If I wish to know something, I can find out quite easily. The fact that I do not should make me pause for an instant and make me wonder: "Why?"

I can either learn all I can, and make informed decisions based on the information available, or I can go along with whatever I am influenced into doing and remain ignorant of why I act the way I do.

Personally, I prefer knowing, since every new piece feels like I am solving a puzzle. There are those who don't mind, but I would say to them that the knowledge they lack is probably the information that is missing in their lives that could make it easier.

If you had the choice between looking at the same wall, day after day, or slowly building a ladder to get over that wall, which would you pick? You might never get to The Truth, but you could take one more step towards *your* truth, which, in the end, might be even more important than any grandiose claim anyone could invent.

Like everything about you, your brain is a muscle that needs exercise. It grows stronger with even less effort than going to the gym. You feed it knowledge, and it makes you feel good, period.

The kind of knowledge you feed it will determine which muscles in your mind you flex. It isn't just there to show off, either. It is your most basic tool for survival in the world. Making it healthy and strong means that you have that many more chances of gaining incredible experiences through its use. There is literally no limit as to what you can take in.

Perception and Reality

To *a degree*, perception *is* reality, because people use it to shape their own. As I've mentioned before, what you know is how you interpret your world. Logic is defeated when people argue that *all* perceptions are the *only* reality.

There are those who argue (wrongly) that just because they believe something, that makes it the truth. That would mean that there is no such thing as objective truth outside of perception, since not everyone interprets input in the same manner.

It is the interpretation that you make of an event or knowledge that defines what you know, that much is true. Even though external events have to be analyzed by the mind to be understood, not all methods of analysis can be trusted to paint reality.

A lie remains a lie, no matter how many times you repeat it, for example. It cannot become reality, however much you might want it to be.

As well, historical revisionists cannot change the past, solely out of their viewpoint of it. Facts have a nasty way of sticking around, long after the events that shaped them. This said, though, perception as a means of shaping the world as we wish it *could* become, *can* make it a reality. To the degree that life, like a tragedy, or romance, is shaped by the actors who strut across its boards.

In the past, world history was shaped by Kings, Queens, and warrior tribes, bent on Glory, and Honour. Their power rested in the ability to command armies and conquer lands. Today, most of the worlds' power rests in the hands of Businessmen, Bankers, Lawyers, and Bureaucrats. The world they see is not one of Glory and Honour, but of Spreadsheets, Efficiency, Bottom Lines, and Import-Export Ratios. The influence they have over their Subjects is one of the Cult of the Dollar. Not necessarily a bad thing, in light of the past several thousand years of mutual hatred and destruction.

Not necessarily the best thing, either, since the concentration of all energies is the accumulation of capital, and the human being is but a cog in the process of capital creation. The prevalent views shape the World, and all who are within it. Capitalism has been the great Uniter, since greed can be turned into a force for *lesser* evil than war. Which will be the next great shift in perception?

Theories are born and produced as Universal Truths. Those who adopt them take them as their own. They have names and are given qualities. Realist, Optimist, Pessimist, Positivist, Nihilist, Platonist, the list goes on and on.

We have built intricate and beautiful thought exercises that shape our beliefs about the nature of our reality. The world as it is, or the world as it ought to be, based on emotional baggage and willingness to observe through different lenses.

Whether reality is truly observable, or only fantasy. Whether we can know things, or only the illusion of their substance, as well as a million more quandaries are posed by those who have delved deeply into what we wish to discover: the Truth.

It is not a futile exercise, since it is curiosity that drives the human being forward. He reflects upon his progress by comparison with his past.

All the while, there are those who will claim that they have found the Ultimate Truths.

With our limited sensory organs, we can never discover that Truth, only an approximation of it. That doesn't mean we shouldn't try. It just means that being satisfied with one answer holds us back, as a species. It means that we've given up on the search, and that we stagnate.

We may still be evolving, physically, but it is mentally that most of our progress has been done, in a relatively short time. On a long enough timeline, our mental progress will have physical repercussions, but only if we let our minds evolve.

For this to happen, you have to shape your own future, since it is through your beliefs that the possibility will arise.

There are many things you can and can't do. It is through your ability to assess situations that you know what actions to perform, and how to perform them for optimal result. Those actions should be performed for the benefit of *people first*, not *profit*.

It is incidental, and should exist for the purpose of helping *more* people.

Knowledge is the most powerful form of currency in the world. Dispensing it is the best measure of your character. Your *true worth* is measured by your character, not by how much money you have.

Power is achieved by helping others empower themselves. If you change the world by your influence, it will become the new reality. Destroy nothing that is good and evolve yourself. Love everyone, especially your opponents. Forgive all, even yourself. Be human, and kind. There is a purpose to life, it is up to you to invent it. Think of the future, there are those who will want to enjoy it as much as you enjoy the present. If this is your perception, it will become your reality, if you work hard with others to make it so.

The Scientific Ruler

Science is one of the most objective tools in the human toolbox. Nothing we can do can reach one-hundred percent objectivity, our fallible human minds only comprehending through the imperfect tools created to analyze our world.

Science, though, in all its forms, is the tool that most closely approaches that goal of impartiality.

Since the beginning of time, we have utilized our minds to define our environment, but it is with the advent of research and experimentation that we have been able to unravel the mysteries that have been maintained for so long.

The fact that science is a continuously evolving corpus of tools should tell us that there is always something more to learn about what, who, and why we are, in and of our Universe, its origins and perhaps someday, its function.

To accept science for what it is, a precept for precision tools, we accept that we do not know everything there is to be known, but only a tiny parcel of what is on display as our reality is known by us.

We do not know what we will discover, and that is a part of the joy of searching for these truths. By making but only a tad more of our reality appear as something comprehensible helps us develop into a wiser species.

When we have decided that everything we could possibly know has been revealed, we are only showing our true fear about the unknown, and are giving up control over our lives so that others may be our masters.

Being ignorant is not a flaw; it is an opportunity to learn more. Fear of the unknown is natural, but it should not stop us from stepping into the dark areas outside the light. Once we become satisfied that we know enough, and that there is nothing more to be learned, we close ourselves to the infinite possibilities that exist without the borders of our ever-expanding library of cognizance.

Q: Yeah, but what if I don't believe in climate change? Or that the Earth is round? Or that the Earth is four billion years old?

A: Do you believe in automobiles?

Q: Of course! They're everywhere. What does that have to do with what I just said?

A: Do you believe in air conditioning? Computers? Asphalt? Electricity? Clothing? Packaged food and drinks? Gasoline? Plastic? Rubber? Nuclear fusion?

Q: Come on! All those things are readily apparent! What kind of dumb questions are those?

A: Well, since you believe in all those readily apparent things, you should know that everything that science discovers, is discovered with the same principles. So, saying that you don't believe in a round Earth is like saying you don't believe in cell phones.

Saying that you don't believe in the very basic science of geology, which is what gave us an approximate age for our planet, means you also shouldn't believe in anything else that surrounds you in our modern world.

All of these things were found out using the same principles. Some religions will tell you that it is not so. The beauty of the scientific principle is that it remains truth whether you believe in it or not.

The burden of truth is squarely on the shoulders of the person who makes the claim, not the person who denies it. So if you want to tell people that the world was invented in a minute by a rainbow unicorn, you better advance some pretty convincing proof of this.

Science is not a religion, it does not try to find ways to control the minds of its followers. It does not order blind obeisance, and is there to offer debate and refutation of its own claims.

Science, in other words, is one of the best tools we have for self-knowledge. It is the ruler by which we try to measure everything that surrounds us, to truly help us alleviate our fears of the unknown.

It exists to help us understand and cure us of our diseases (physical and mental), to make our work a simpler task, and to elevate the human being beyond its weak physical envelope. Any knowledge we seek is to better ourselves, but the tools we use are either closer to Truths which are the arena of religious dogma, or Facts which are objective and measurable, and both are not the same.

Pursuing purer Facts demands better tools, and as we refine these, we inch slowly closer to the nature of our reality. It is only by eliminating the thick clouds of illogicality that we can attain better truths, but it is only with love that we can embrace these truths without fear.

What It's All About: The Pursuit of Reproduction

ife itself is both complex and simple. It starts with the premise that it must continue, it must reproduce itself. The next step is how it does that, and this is not only for human beings, it amounts to every single living being in our planetary neighbourhood.

All living beings have needs that are important in their quest for reproduction. We need to ingest sustenance, we need safety, and we need to evacuate waste. Those are the requirements of most living things, to be able to propagate.

Higher up on the ladder of living beings, we need care and love. Those basic needs will interrupt your daily life and be more important than anything else, until you are able to solve those problems.

Fortunately, they are the easiest things to take care of. You eat when you are hungry, you find a shelter when you need safety (your home), you go to the bathroom when you need to evacuate waste, and you turn to others for comfort and love.

When one of these basic needs is not met, you must struggle to meet them, and you cannot move to the next steps in your life to evolve a higher consciousness.

If you are hungry all the time, your main concern is to feed yourself. If you have no shelter, you can't think about the deeper meaning of life. If you have no safety, all your energy is used in saving yourself. If all you do is fear, you cannot concentrate on making life better for you and yours.

Only after all those needs have been met, it is then possible to move to the next step: Living in a manner that you find meaningful.

As the title of this chapter indicates, this is your end-goal: reproduction.

Every living creature is pre-programmed to multiply itself. The human being, on the other hand, has discovered a multitude of methods to go *beyond* mere genetic reproduction. With the creation of symbolic thought within your mind, you are able to begin using the tools of your surroundings to fulfill your needs.

You can reproduce the complexity of your mind through your creativity. Art, music, sport, science, architecture, deification, and a slew of other forms sprang forth from our minds, becoming mixed as time went by.

The extent of your knowledge and creativity are your only true limits. When we developed language, writing, and mathematics, we became more complex in our thinking, and therefore were able to hand down our knowledge to our surroundings, as well as our descendants, as the basis for their own thoughts, and the further development of those who interpreted the knowledge they were handed.

We now cover the planet, as a species, and the evolution of our thoughts has served us well, for it has made us the dominant one in our particular niche. We do not stop evolving, and to a certain degree, we choose in which direction we wish to progress.

The fact that not all peoples on this planet evolve evenly, at the same rate, or even in the same direction should show the competitive nature of our race even amongst ourselves, and not the backwardness or superiority of some over the others.

We have the opportunity of aiding those in need of help. The fact that we do not, or only on a small scale demonstrates our main preoccupation: the furthering of our own in-groups' progress over that of others.

The simple fact of the matter is that we, on this tiny island called Earth, are but *one* in-group, and that, as has been shown time and time again, the more we help others, the more we help ourselves, since it is by lifting everyone out of their misery that we can move forward as one.

The need to reproduce a thought process which is mutually beneficial for all, through whatever media available, has been attempted throughout history.

The desire to overcome the divisive thought processes in action, at the moment, could be one of our main weapons against artificial division. As it stands, its use as a separator and control method keeps some nations strong, and others weak.

If you are open to the world, and the *possibility* of its *goodness*, you are open to the thought of positive change within yourself. This in turn affects others, through example. Again, my goal is not to change you, but to awaken in you the desire to evolve in your way of thinking. This is the difference between positive influence and coercion, or recommendation and ordering.

The Reptilian Brain and its Influence

My father (your grandfather) told me recently: "You can't change the reptilian brain!" First of all, what is it? Well, as its name would imply, it is an ancient part of our brain, which evolved a very long time ago, and can still be found in lizards.

It is also known as the basal ganglia. It is believed to control aggression, dominance, territoriality, and ritual displays. It is part of a larger structure called the Triune Brain. It is that which controls our automatic reactions to stimulus and the fight-or-flight response, and generally makes us do things we have no idea why we do. It is not bad, per se, it just is.

Everybody has it, it's a part of you, and it is the part of your brain that advertisers aim squarely at when they want to make you buy something.

It is the part of your mind that politicians aim at when they want you to fear the opposition.

Most people have no idea it is there, and so no one cares why they act. To a certain degree, your grandfather is right. You can't change it. It is an integral part of our genetic makeup, and we have to live with it. My personal belief though, is that if we *know* about its presence, we diminish its power.

Let's say, for example, you have a shadow behind you, whispering in your ear, telling you to do things. If you do not know of the presence of such a being, you will live your life, day by day, not questioning its orders. What if suddenly you realized he was there? Now, from that point forth, you would at least have the opportunity of questioning his motives, even if you did not necessarily know them.

205

When you desire, or fear certain things, it is your little invisible voice, whispering these things, sub-audibly to your body. It tells it to have the impulse to buy, or the impulse to fight, or to flee.

Once you are conscious of it, you begin to have choices. You can either accept these reactions that are given to you, you can work to get rid of them, alter or even control them.

Accepting is easy, because that is what we usually do. Changing that behavior, though, is tougher, because you are going against your prime motivator. Eventually, though, if you are able to transform those reactions to do your will, those new methods of reaction will become your motivators. So no, we cannot stop the reptilian brain from being our backseat-drivers. We can, however, give him driving lessons.

Knowledge, Understanding, Living, Wisdom

You can know *of*, *understand*, and *live* knowledge.

When you know of a thing, it skims the surface of your mind, and can just as quickly be forgotten. You are *aware* of its existence. You can acknowledge its existence. For example, I tell you about the concept of gravity. Fine, it exists, it's there. It's been explained to you and you know how it works. If you decide to read even more about it, you get to understand it.

If, on top of this, you decide to drop something, to test things out, then you *live* it.

Life is very much comprised of experiences such as these. We are told certain things, and we accept them. We delve deeper and begin to understand them, until, quite unconsciously, we begin to live them.

Such reactions are quite normal, and form the basis of our beliefs. Once we form the core of what we know, or think we know, we naturally start rejecting beliefs that are antithetical to what we have internalized.

This is true especially if the doctrines of the beliefs we hold to be true preclude the exclusion of all knowledge that is external to it. This is a trap, however, since we cannot grow through complete exclusion, and cannot know the existence of Truth by refusing to seek its cause.

I strongly recommend leaving room for all knowledge, even though that knowledge may be proven false. The possession of a Fact does not mean its acceptance, only the realization of its existence.

The only threat we can perceive is that of having to alter our previous thought patterns to that of the new information. This isn't really a threat at all, if I've already decided to put that information in the category of *general knowledge*, and not of *absolute truth*. I think that all the knowledge we have acquired is worth knowing, even if it isn't necessarily true.

It gives basis for comparison for the rest of what we know to be so, through experimental study. It's the amalgamation and cross-referencing of all the things I know that can help me analyze a situation to greater effect.

I can understand the issues at hand with greater depths if I know what the people who are living them are thinking. It is through this logical process that I can then make wise decisions in the next step I want to take, in whichever direction I may choose. This process also widens the boundaries of your imagination, which is one of the greatest traits your mind possesses.

Frames and Lenses

As your beliefs are dictated by others, at first, it stands to reason that you should perhaps analyze them when you have developed the capacity to do so. This will help you to truly know yourself, even if just a little bit better.

Your personal philosophy is the global representation of the amalgamation of your beliefs in an ordered, coherent system (coherent to you, the person who posits and possesses it).

Everyone has one: you are just not usually aware of it, so unconscious and automatic it is to you.

You achieve your own philosophy through trial and error, through your surroundings, and through your triumphs and defeats. It is the manual that supersedes your survival instincts.

Philosophies, and the world around you, contain paradoxes. You can believe one thing on one hand, and the opposite on the other, virtually at the same time.

It is by deciding over and over how you will react to a given situation that will dictate what your general philosophy will be. It is by the actual reaction that you know what it is.

I say it thus, because a lot of people may say they harbour a particular belief, or that they would never do certain things, but it is by their actions that they belie their beliefs.

So the way you *act* is your *true* philosophy, not what you say you believe.

After all, certain people belong to groups that preach love, but hate others.

This brings us to an interesting point: That of the frame for what you believe in. In this case, I mean frame in the general attitude you develop to deal with your reality.

Having a multitude of emotions, you have your pick of the ones you want as your favourites to manipulate your behavior. You can be at their mercy, or you can be their master.

However you decide, a very few of them will be the dominant ones, and will dictate your behavior in every single situation where action or reflection is required. No matter what your beliefs are (going back to the original question), how you frame them will determine how you will live them.

It's quite easy to see that there are groups out there who preach love and understanding, but wish death and eternal damnation to certain other groups. They may not even realize the internal contradiction of their thought processes. As I have mentioned, there are many paradoxes that can exist at the same time, in the same mind. It's up to you to hunt them down and figure them out. It all goes back to what I was saying about knowing yourself.

I remember a friend of mine telling me that on his third day of work for a new job, one of the other employees came to him and said: "Slow down there, buddy. You're making us look bad." So he did – slow down, I mean. By doing so, he conformed to the rest of the office, raising his chances of acceptance within it, yet lowering the quality of his work.

Understandably, the office (well, its managers, of course) were tired of this state of affairs. So would I, honestly, if I was waiting for an important document to come to me.

So they started cutting back on jobs. They cut, and they cut everybody who was 'redundant'. So now there were a lot of unemployed workers, and sure, they would find jobs, but what of those who kept them? Now they would have to do the job of two or more people, so would they be doing it faster, or better?

Perhaps they would find incentive to, for a few months, until the leaders realize that they needed staff to do the work that is falling behind, and might have to rehire more employees.

So what changed, exactly, in the system? There were less people for a while.

My point is that how we view what we do or who we are, we do through a lens. When you are a part of a group, you tend to try to imitate or emulate their actions, to be accepted.

You therefore shift your views for that of theirs, therefore altering your lens. When I am at work, I see through my work lens. At home, I see through my family lens. I have vacation lenses, love lenses, hate lenses, religious lenses, business lenses, rich lenses, poor lenses, etc.

I try to fit in by adapting to the lens I use to look at my surroundings. I am not the same person with my wife as I am with my colleagues, or with my friends, or with you. I see every person differently, through the lenses I choose to wear to view them. It distorts what I see in everyone.

The problem with this changing of lenses is that I feel as if I *fracture* myself to *be* many different people. To a certain degree, these *people* are all different facets of my personality, but they are not a unified whole. I strongly believe that I can't be entirely content with who I am if I can't be the same person with everyone. Some people call these lenses *masks*.

The focus is on you being a different person, seen from someone else's point of view. Even though it is true that we act differently, it is because of our viewpoint that is changed. Therefore, it is not so much how others see us that is important, but how we view various situations.

If I want to be the same person towards everyone, and comfortable being myself, I have to evolve. For that, there has to be one, over-arching lens, and to me that is the *human* lens. Once I have installed that *primary* lens, behind all the other ones, everything comes into clear focus. You could call this lens *acceptance*, but only to a certain degree.

I see everyone being absolutely the same basic being, yet all different. I no longer need to be different facets of the same personality, or switching lenses. When I accept and love everything as it is, I can't be bothered to pretend to be someone else, or to get angry for no reason.

I accept, yes, but this doesn't mean I shouldn't react, or take everything as being immutable. It just means that my reaction is based on the realization that everything is the way it is, more than a rejection of reality.

Remember, if you accept your reality as it is, you have no need to feel anger or fear. You have only possibilities to alter it, if that is what you wish to do. So what does this have to do with workers and getting laid off?

Well, for one, when I look through the lens of acceptance, I can choose who I want to be. Just because I accept that the office situation is one of sloth and unproductivity, does not mean that I accept to become a part of it myself.

Since I do not feel the fear of peer pressure, I can be my own person, no matter how others think about me. Yes, I could be just as uncooperative as the others. Since I realize that real people are counting on my hard work to get on with their lives, I would be remiss in my duties if I were to become a lazy bastard.

This means that I have a conscious realization of my responsibilities and duties to perform. It was a waste of time to fire all those workers, even to save money, since there were no real internal changes within the system.

What they needed was the right motivation, or lenses, to do what they had to do. The same situation will occur, over and over again, since the basic system in place was not altered for employees to feel an urge to strive for something above mediocrity.

The way I live my life always depends on how I look at it. My world-view lenses tint every aspect of my life. I am a bit of every aspect of my mind put into action, to a higher or lesser degree.

Whatever I feel will give me an edge in my survival and that of others, are the tools I will employ to achieve that goal. I know that the whole spectrum of human action is *natural*, but that not all is *desirable*. I know, for example, that wanting to create the most homogenous society, based on everybody thinking the exact same thing is undesirable, unattainable, and disastrous.

There will always be dissent, and there should be. Religious systems have coerced human thought for a very long time and refused novelty. It was only by questioning that we were able to bring science to the fore.

A system that denies changing, questioning, or evolution, is a system

212

that is doomed to fail on a long enough timeline. As well it should, since thought is constantly evolving.

A Utopian System based on skin colour, creed, wealth, or sexual preference, is just another fascist control mechanism. It is predicated on the idea that there is such a thing as a *better* human, in comparison to all the other *inferior* ones.

Such an animal is a fantasy borne of a selfish and spoiled mind. The only better human I *can* create is the one I, as an individual, wish to become. There are many ways we have tried to achieve the best of all possible worlds. All of them failed, since they were based on the fallacy of the superiority of one group over another.

There can be many more attempts, but all will fail unless some basic truths are learnt and internalized: I am no better than anyone else, only different. It is better to help than to hinder. I have to care for others as much as I care for myself. I can be a better person. Love, always. Accept, forgive, ask for forgiveness, let go. Essentially, denying the extremisms of my ego, and negative emotions taking unbridled control over my being, makes me a better person.

The lenses through which I observe life are as varied as human experience. They colour my actions, reactions, and emotions in one degree or other, for good or ill. Every possible type of person on Earth will see his world tinted one way or the other through the lens of his or her society. When you travel and are confronted by other lenses, you will feel the clash of beliefs.

You may think your lenses as being the best ones, the clearest ones, and sometimes, the only ones that should exist.

You will be wrong.

You may reject others because they are different, and, through your prejudice, may think they need to be destroyed. Those might be some very narrow lenses you are wearing. The artificial boundaries that I create for myself alone, make it impossible for any kind of Utopian future to ever come to fruition.

We think in terms of the elimination of a part of society for the benefit of the whole. We raise ourselves by lowering others. "*We* are better than *they*." Why? Because our ego dictates this to us, and makes up reasons which we believe are valid. "We, Liberals, are better than They, Conservatives." "We Conservatives are better than They, New Democrats." "We, Catholics, are better than They, Christians." The whole of Society (world society) strives to create unity *by putting up new barriers*! "My thoughts are better than your thoughts." That is the basic message. "Come to my team, and we will conquer the world."

Or, "I am better than you are because of such and such reason, and you need to think like me." This is a normal trait. It is not a desirable trait, but it is a normal trait. It precludes specialness on the part of one group over the other (rich vs. poor, Christian vs. Islam, American vs. Everybody, Canadian vs. Everybody, Everybody vs. Everybody), that is as artificial as it is divisive.

As soon as you say: "I am better than you because," you fabricate a reason for the other group's defeat. They are different, therefore bad, by extension and extremism, therefore must be stopped. This is *natural*, but not *desirable*.

The trouble is in the lenses we use: they are all deforming lenses. The lenses we use are that of the citizen of a country. Or the member of a political group, or the associate in a religious organization, the people of a village, the colour of my skin, or a myriad of irrelevant divisions that were invented in the interest of preserving *our* genes, but not anyone else's. Since, of course, *their* genes are undesirable.

Once I realize that I am *human*, at the core of it all, everybody becomes the same basic creature, no matter who they are, and what they do. We all live in the same house, and we are the most dysfunctional family out there.

To any extent, we are *all related*. Once you understand that absolutely everybody is descended from the same family tree, it makes pursuing a mate a bit creepier, but nonetheless, it is the truth.

When we say that everybody's opinion is right, and everybody's *opinion* is wrong, it is absolutely true. An opinion, a pure opinion, not tainted with any facts, has no value whatsoever but to the person who proposes it or those who accept it. It is negative for the opposition, and it is positive for the parties who opined it.

Everything depends on what side of the fence you are sitting on.

Once *facts* are inserted into the equation, the party who uses them have the advantage, because they are approaching what is known as the *truth*. They, therefore, have the upper hand. This usually does not deter the opposition from using tactics called lying to make their point heard. Sadly, those who cannot tell the difference between a *lie*, a *fact*, and an *opinion* are those who suffer the most, since all three, to them, are equivalent.

The matter is even more complicated when that lack of knowledge is used by those in power to further their own agenda. The power of the lenses we use will define whether or not we are able to see situations from a different perspective, or if we are blinded to the truth.

Directional Ego

A belief is my world-view on how to meet my needs, in whatever area I may hold it.

You believe in something because it meets the needs you set before it, whatever the thought, object or abstract phenomenon present. As a baby, your methods of communication are severely limited. There is crying and there is cooing and babbling.

Nevertheless, these actions are enough to get through to the people who take care of you that you need *something*. At this point, there is not much of belief as much as natural reaction.

With time, though, and depending on the care that was imparted upon you, as well as your reaction towards that care, a rudimentary belief system is formed. These will eventually become the core of your beliefs, and will be carried through the rest of your life, until new beliefs are introduced or perhaps are destroyed through some traumatic event.

Beliefs are shared through family, and their interpretations are influenced strongly by the recombination of genetic material which our genitors have imparted upon us.

Our beliefs are a mixed bag of core values which are dictated by society, tied in part to religion, schooling, work ethics, and a host of other sources, but principally, they are a private matter; they begin with you.

Whatever has been given to you in the beginning, as your primary operating software, becomes the basis for everything else in your life. Beliefs are a reflection of other peoples' thoughts about yourself:

When I was a child, my parents thought, and told me, that I was a *good boy*, even though I pushed my little sister down the carpeted stairs on a few occasions. This is something I used to do myself (roll down the stairs), for my own pleasure. They didn't know about this, so I remained a *good boy*.

Yes, she survived, and has no profound *physical* scars to show for it, but my belief that I was a *good boy* never wavered, because my parents told me it was so.

Now that I am older and perhaps a tiny bit wiser, I realize that what I did was attempted murder, and I am glad that she survived the ordeal of growing up with me as a sibling.

Nevertheless, during those blissful years, my opinion of myself was dictated by those who oversaw my rearing, and not so much my own self-reflection, which I believe I was incapable of at that age.

It is only later on in life, when I began to think about thinking, that I could observe that what I may have thought or believed was wrong in the extreme.

I know for a fact that I did not wish to kill my sister when I was a child. I just thought that giving her a shove down the carpeted stairs would make her a less annoying person, somehow (or I was venting frustration).

As a seven-year-old, I am not sure how I may have come by that conclusion, but there it was. As a thirty-year-old, remembering my behavior makes me cringe.

Not only my beliefs, but my unconscious acts and desires inform my body to react in a particular way, which may or may not be detrimental to myself or others. In youth, you do not have much mental control over your emotions and impulses; the signals of stimuli go directly to the centers of our brains that control emotion, and you react.

Today, I would look a bit foolish for crying if I did not get ice cream. As a child, most of us did not have that self-restraint that informed us that our behavior was reprehensible. It is only through practise, brought on by our parents denying us certain things we desire, that we gain patience and understanding.

As well, thankfully, as a sense of decorum while in public places (at least). Being sat down and made to wait for things was the training we needed to impart upon us a sense of self-restraint, no matter how tenuous it was.

That being able to delay your need for satisfaction is what makes it possible to help yourself by helping others. If you have no patience, you can only think about fulfilling your own needs, at once. With patience, you can help others fulfil theirs, and perhaps (but not necessarily), they will reciprocate in the future.

At the very least, they will have a better opinion of you and you will be better known for your *positive* acts than your *negative* ones. This is the cause for much personal satisfaction.

Perpetrating a selfish act directs your ego firmly towards yourself. You are taking from someone else, to gain something. When you are being altruistic, you are helping or giving to someone else, therefore opening your ego towards them.

You achieve the same feeling of reward for both actions, but in the altruistic situation, you gain the net plus of having helped another being. That other being may get the urge to make an altruistic gesture towards someone else.

In the selfish situation, the person who has been swindled might want to adopt the same kind of attitude, seeing as how it is more *effective*. The acts that I perpetrate are self-replicating. Even though the rate is not one-hundred percent, it is higher than zero.

The main difference is that in the selfish case, the odds are higher that the person affected by the selfish act will perpetrate one himself, than the recipient of an altruistic act committing one in return.

Taken as two isolated events, the influence is minimal, but taken as society-wide phenomena, there might be cause for worry. If everything I do affects others in the way they act towards others, then letting selfishness, as a societal trait, run rampant, would be very detrimental to the fabric of society.

You could say the same about any other egotistical/selfish act. The question is, do I care more about myself, or about others?

We can do many things to make ourselves feel good. As well, we can do many things to make others feel good. The more we learn to help others, the more we instill in others the desire to do the same.

The more we take for ourselves, the more we make it seem permissible to do so for others. In the end, we have to decide for ourselves whether we want to be kind or to be selfish, but we should remember that by being selfish, we are closing our options towards others.

For example, I used to work with a woman who would listen intently to everything everyone had to say, and would duly report all those things to our manager. At first, we had no idea where the hellfire coming down on our heads was stemming from. After having identified the obvious cause, we no longer trusted this person as someone in whom we could confide. Her egotistical manoeuvring to raise herself in the organization had effectually ostracized her completely.

Now, I am not saying that if she had had true reasons to rat everybody out for malfeasance that she should not have done so. All I am saying is that if that had been the case, she would have done so to correct wrongs, and not raise herself by lowering others. In any event, her scheming was neutralized by the fact that afterwards, no one would trust her any further than they could throw her. The management, eventually, tended to disregard every single little crumb of a complaint she would bring to their attention like the cries of the Shepherd who cried "Wolf!" when none were there.

If, in fact, her goal had been to enlighten, she could have considered a different tack, such as being a good example to follow, and refused to act as the other staff who did those things she found deplorable, or explain to others her method of thinking and the reason for her actions.

It is important to remember that you can direct your ego at will, either toward yourself, or toward others. You can either be open and help, neutral and do nothing, or closed and be selfish. Just remember that out of those three options there is only one which is beneficial to all.

A lot of emotions are based on variants of the open-helpful or closed-selfish model. How you decide to react to any given situation reflects the lessons you have learned through your either acting selfishly or generously.

Generally speaking, acting generously and openly is a very good survival strategy. There are, of course, situations where this is not the case. I can think of several cases where the appeasement of certain tyrants and egomaniacs where acting generously and openly only helped serve their own selfish ends.

That has to come into account when you do decide to act, or react. The positive effects of open-helpful actions and reactions should not be underestimated, though. They are the underlying structure of many of our institutions of law and society, of family and all religions.

They are the positive effects that make our lives functional. When a few, or many of these positive actions are missing (such as trust, kindness, generosity, altruism, care, empathy, honesty, etc.), we are said to be living in dysfunction. In this example, dysfunction relates to family, and the allowance of parents for abuse within the family circle, but it can be writ large, societally, if those in charge permit abuse or encourage it, in my view.

Is there room for negative emotion and reaction, such as selfishness and distrust? The question, of course, would have to be "What is the situation in which such an attitude might be desirable?"

Generally speaking, we are amongst trustworthy people. When we enter a situation in which we may feel threatened, it would be prudent to be careful of our deeds and actions. You do not necessarily need to be distrusting, selfish or any of those other negative, closed emotions, but you should be on your guard.

If you are indeed in a situation where you are threatened, you should take a defensive position which shows that you will not be pushed around. Yet, you should not take any actions to exacerbate the situation, unless the other party heightens the threat level.

So no, you do not need those emotions on a regular basis, but they are still useful in extreme cases. They are part of the fight or flight response that fills you with adrenaline and forces you to react without your conscious control. Apart from a life-threatening situation where running away is the last option, you should not have to run.

It is by creating a self-replicating and self-diffusing altruistic ego-boosting mechanism that we raise others and make their lives worthwhile. Whether it is by respecting your elders, or being a good role-model, sharing your time, or any other positive interaction, having proper values tightens the bonds of friends, neighbours, families, and communities.

Negative Affect, its Outcome, and Possible Solutions

There are some pretty nasty people out there. They are angry, driven by hate and fear, (and full of themselves). Some of them hate people of different faiths, some of different sexual orientations, or even skin colour. It doesn't really matter what they hate.

All of these traits stem from the emotional offspring born of the unhappy union between negative affects. Whether it is racism, sexism, homophobia, or a wide swath of ridiculous stereotypes, at some point in time, a person may decide to marry their Ignorance with their Hatred, and the resulting bouncing baby is called Intolerance, aka prejudice.

Intolerance grows up thinking that it is better than the object of its hatred. It makes Intolerance feel good about itself to put something beneath it, since it is not really sure about itself. A lot of time, Intolerance grows up in the same house as other Intolerances, and so is nurtured by this 'healthy' environment.

Intolerance is allowed to continue because no one knows how to get rid of it. It's easy, though. Intolerance is allergic to ridicule. When it is pointed out and exposed, (often and loudly) for being the ridiculous thought that it is, it shrinks.

It is only allowed to grow in an environment that will allow it to spread. If it is shown for being a stupid idea, it's not so proud of itself, and slinks away into the shadows where it feels safer.

Knowledge, real knowledge, destroys it. Knowing how people live around the world, and being among them, seeing how they live, accepting them for who they are, those are the cures for Intolerance.

When people are allowed to know very little of what goes on in the wider world, they have no basis for comparison. They can only make up stories in their heads, which have very little bearing on the truth or facts. Lack of empathy and understanding are the breeding grounds for hate, ignorance, and fear.

So, you shouldn't have to worry about yourself, so much. We won't let you go without knowledge or empathy. When you do meet someone who is like what I have just described, though, you might understand a bit more what makes them tick.

You don't need to hate them, or pity them, even though it might feel good to. It is unfortunate that they have chosen that path for themselves, but you can't force them to be different. Forgive them and move on, all the while disagreeing with what they represent.

Most of them have an inaccurate and perverted view of what *purity* or *naturalness* is. This somehow conveys on them the title of all-knowing judges of humanity. Of course, there is no such thing as a pure Aryan or anything else for that matter, when you go back far enough, in any direction.

We are all derived from the same ancestors, and there is nothing they can do about it to change that fact. They may feel confident in their specialness, but that *specialness* is misguided and false. There is only one pure thing, and that is pure Human, that keeps developing and evolving, but only if we encourage it.

There are those who hate homosexuals. They base themselves on things people wrote thousands of years ago, who obviously knew nothing about nature. Yes, it does exist in nature. The thing is, honey, the only people who should be condemned are those who actually hurt others, not those who love each other.

The direction some despots went towards in an attempt to coerce the *proper* genes to come out on top as *the best in the world*, through some well-directed racism and political Nationalist control, the use of eugenics and ethnic cleansing, all show that some believe there is, albeit in a twisted and sadistic way, a *better human*.

That better human *cannot* be achieved by the destruction of others. It can only be done through the evolution of the self. By killing anyone, we are potentially destroying the future of the human race. We have no idea who will evolve as the future of our planet. My hope is that it will be all of us who will have that chance, even though I know the reality of how we really are. As long as we keep putting up those artificial barriers between us, of race, colour, creed, wealth, sexual orientation, and even between men and women, we can't progress.

As long as we keep trying to hold others down to further ourselves, we are all in the same pool trying to drown each other.

Don't be sad, at least you have the choice to be a positive influence! You can't expect the best from anyone but yourself, so do just that. Don't despair about the evil people do to each other, but don't do it yourself. Accept the world as it is, but work on making things around you better. That's all you can do, ever. If you do that, then maybe others will too. It is never a guarantee, but the odds are in your favour, unless you don't even try.

Poverty and Wealth, Money and its Uses

There are many factors affecting the world in a negative way, at the moment. Poverty is one of the worst things that can happen to a human being. If he or she has no money, he or she cannot eat properly, and has no way to go beyond survival mode.

There are then learning disabilities that can occur (if education is available to this person) through the lack of proper nutrition. A deficit in education means that that person will have difficulty getting out of poverty.

It also means that without proper sexual education, she (obviously, women and girls) may become pregnant at an early age, and not be able to continue her education. Lack of education *may* engender sexually transmitted diseases.

Lack of access to medical attention can cause premature death in the family, especially among the very young. As a result, a woman in an environment of poverty has to have many children in the hope that some of them survive.

This is one of the reasons for overpopulation of poverty-stricken areas. This, in turn, puts a stress on the food supply, which causes malnutrition. Lack of education can sometimes mean relying on illegal methods to acquire necessities, which fills the jails of that nation with the poor.

It augments the feeling of helplessness one feels when we are stuck in an untenable situation, leading to heightened drug and alcohol abuse. Poverty is one of the prime causes of conflict within a family, augmenting dysfunction.

It is a snake eating its own tail. It is a self-perpetuating machine made of human misery. As well, when someone who falls on hard times has been added to the ranks of the poor (for whatever reason), it is very difficult for that person to extricate him or herself from that predicament, and he or she can expect only hardship from thereon in.

The difficult pill to swallow is when we are told that *nothing can be done about this situation*. That it is inevitable, or even worse, that it (may be?) *self-induced*. I wonder what the poor think about the idea that they brought it all upon themselves. The only possible reason I can fathom for our not having solved the problem of poverty yet is because we don't want to get our hands dirty with a *real* problem.

Strangely, countries have become *stronger*, historically, by sharing the wealth more evenly among their citizens. It would make sense to think that the more people who are employed, and healthy, the more consumers there would be to purchase the products we are made to think we need.

The less poverty there is, the less dependence there is on governmental assistance. The less poverty there could be, the less crime there would be. Less delinquence, more education, less despair, more happiness, less drug abuse, a stronger economy, more confidence, and a renewed sense of purpose in the nation, cannot honestly be seen as unworthy goals by any right-thinking person, can they?

But that requires education, and taking care of so-called *dirty* people. What a drag. As long as governments and people in general have a low opinion of their less fortunate countrymen and women, no positive change can take place. No change, no end to misery.

Monetary assistance is not enough. A new education is required to change the patterns that control the lives of those who have been recreating the same thing they have lived for so many generations.

You will have to deal more and more with the widening gap of rich and poor wherever you decide to live, since wealthy companies have decided it would be cheaper to send jobs overseas than to keep investing in their home countries.

The main reason being that at least over there (wherever the jobs were sent), there are very little restrictions as to the treatment of employees. They can do the same job for peanuts, augmenting the profits of those companies that took their business there.

The main point of business *is* profit, and the human in charge of making the product is basically a machine of production, whereas the buyer is a machine of consumption. If the company can give as little money as possible to the machine that makes the products, while charging as much as they possibly can to the consumption machine, the resulting cash is called Profit.

Profit is the most important goal in life, at the moment, so equality of people is made difficult by this process. Of course, it's better than the previous human goal of *exterminating everyone who isn't exactly like me*, but it is our new hurdle to equality.

Tell that to the board of directors and investors of any large corporation and watch them recoil in horror. The mere thought that someone might want to hold them accountable would probably make them very uncomfortable, if it were at all possible.

Luckily for them, they've bought every politician they need to beat any kind of change someone could want to bring to their business practises.

Money being a medium of exchange, it makes me smile that so many people want to hoard so much of it. I can understand that having a modicum of wealth can be an exhilarating experience, and can ease life a tremendous deal. I do know people who are wealthy, and I do not begrudge them their having worked hard for it. The people I know, though, share their wealth, and help those in need. They pay all the taxes they owe, and don't try to hide their money in tax shelters and shell corporations. The more I have money, the more I am *responsible* for what I do with it.

Those whom I know are business owners, and as such, pay their workers fairly, and care for them like family. At least they understand that to be a part of a larger community, they have to be implicated in it. Such is not the case in many a corporation, it would seem.

Money is a currency. It is a medium of exchange. It is a promise, written on paper, that the government will honour the debt that one person has to another. It is a unit of account, and a store of values. This means that you can use it to buy goods. It defines the price that something should cost. You can also put it aside in a safe place and use it later. Currencies have varied wildly, in our past. Some of the earliest monies were beads and seashells. They went on to become gold or other precious metals, eventually became paper, and is now a great deal of numbers, floating on the internet. Currencies are not only money, though.

They are what we put our *confidence* in, to pursue as a worthy goal. The *currency* pursued by religious institutions is souls. The power elite within the religions, orders us *conversion* and *baptism* as their medium of exchange. The people who do accept their word as law then become *saved*, and become a store of value.

The politician pursues *favours* as his medium of exchange, and votes as his unit of account. His resulting *power* is his store of values.

In all systems we choose to observe, it is the trust in the methods employed to assign value to different acts or objects that define the worth of its goal.

If I believe that I will truly be saved by Jesus Christ by joining the Church and following His teachings, I am investing my *trust* in that *goal*. When I do, I invest all my energies to accomplish the ends of the hierarchy of the Church. It is a similar process for any religious organisation I might choose. I simply used the Christian church as an example.

The same can be said if I put my confidence in the acts of my government. I trust it implicitly to work to further my well-being. Fortunately, there is room for dissent in the governmental system. If I disagree with what it is doing, I can vote for someone else.

Historically, disagreements within religious organizations have resulted in a fractioning of those institutions. The similarities don't stop there though. For almost all systems that require our participation, there is a common thread. The power they wield require us, as people, to support their ends, yes. They also require our money to further said ends. Any successful system requires both people and money to keep it in charge.

There is nothing strange or nefarious about this, it's just how systems work. A business couldn't work if it had no employees, and they get their money from the customers who buy from them. There could be no government if there was nobody who trusted the people in charge and paid them to lead them.

There would be no church, mosques, synagogues, monasteries, shrines, etc. if people didn't go, and donated their time and money for its upkeep.

As well, there would be no wealth if people didn't spend their money on the objects that companies produced. Those with power want money to influence others so that they can acquire more money, in the hopes of gaining more power. So that they can get more money. With that money they will be able to buy more power.

My question, after this very long and boring introduction is: Why? This will sound like the most naive question that a person can ask, but it is actually right to the point. What is so incredibly important about having the most money and power if the only goal is a pissing contest with the rest of those who only want money or power to get more money and power?

It seems to me to be a bit empty and trite to have this vision of life, but then again, I'm not living at that level. I can't imagine the vapid emptiness that would inhabit me if all I cared about was adding more numbers and acquisitions to my person. Sure, I want things, and so should you! The difference is, I don't think it's right to prey on the poor to get there.

Maybe I'm crazy, but those whose primary goals are the upward spiral that I just described seem to have lost touch with reality.

I'll just give you a quick example. The government, theoretically, should be in charge of helping people who elect them. What if they are busy helping their constituents who donated incredibly large sums of money to curry favour with them? Those who have donated the large sums obviously want something in return, which they couldn't get unless they donated that money. They are, therefore, buying the vote of the official they've paid off to do their bidding, whereas his primary job was to work for the people. This no longer being the case, it is those who donate the most money who benefit the most from *democracy*.

I am not shocked or surprised by this, only thoroughly disgruntled. If this is the case, then the people within the system have given in to greed, and those who support it the way it is, need to take a nice long vacation away from power.

There are two major schools of thought when it comes to ruling: "Everybody gets their fair share," and "Do everything you can to get as much as you can." Unsurprisingly, the former is usually poor, and the latter, wealthy. The wealthy prey on the weak because they can, and since they have the politicians bought and paid for, they can get away with it.

This method of rule will be the destruction of the planet.

For as long as the wealthy will carry a handy little politician or two on them at all times, like a get-out-of-jail-free card, don't expect anything to change.

Profits before people is what is polluting the Earth, which is one of the causes of Global Climate Change. Those who want to maintain the status quo are driving the car towards the cliff. If they don't(?) realize it at some point in time, it'll be too late.

If you have the chance to do something about it, don't stick your head in the sand like the majority of elected officials. If you want to become rich, be fair. If you want to be a politician, be incorruptible. If you just want to live well, be aware.

It doesn't matter to me what you want to become, as long as you are the best person you can be. Money is the best tool in the world, as well as the worst, depending on how you perceive and use it.

It is a tool.

The more you have of it, the more powerful you are, this is a given. What most people tragically forget is that with great power comes great responsibility, not only for their wealth, but for all those around them. Money acquired solely for the purpose of furthering yourself is the greatest squandering of human resources that exists.

Government, Religions: Various Systems of Thought Control

D
epending on your first relationship with authority (your mother and father), you'll either adapt well to the systems in place, or reject authority out of hand. You have to realize, though, that authority in itself is not *bad*. It is only a tool, like all the others. It's the way it is used that can either be for your benefit or detriment.

There will always be limits placed on your actions, and this for the well-being of everybody else around you as well as yourself.

Remember, you'll live in a community, and the rules and education that will be imposed on you and those around you will be to reduce the friction that naturally occurs between people.

I used to think that all forms of imposed restrictions were terrible and should be abolished (guess what kind of relationship I had with grandma and grandpa).

With time, I started realizing that we, as humans, are a fairly selfish and violent species, and that left to our own devices we'd probably kill each other off at the first chance we got.

We could not have developed the agglomerations we have where millions of people live in relative peace with each other if limits to our aggression *hadn't* been imposed. Limits on behavior have to be put in place so that every individual (and that includes you) can enjoy relative freedom, as much as *everyone else*.

It is somewhat of a tight-rope act, but it comes down to mutual respect and self-control. Of course, there are battles within every system to say what is right or what is wrong, and depending on the point of view of the groups involved, these subjective *rights* and *wrongs* vary wildly, according to the laws they have set for themselves.

Here is a good rule of thumb, though: Be aware of what various groups believe in, and what they want as an end result to their policies. If these ends are altruistic and involve the destruction of barriers between people, there is a better chance that they have a good cause. This is not always the case, though, so do your research before backing up any movement you find worthwhile.

Religions (in any way, shape, or form) are the oldest structures of systematic and self-replicating methods of control and assembly. They were our first attempt at explaining the unexplainable, as well as a focal point, through deification, of our common energies. With time they became the single most powerful forces for human unification.

They are a catch-all for the reason for existence, method of creation, and ultimate fate of the human being. Even though not all of them have quite the grasp on evolution and science that they should, they are still a very good working model of what human assembly should be like.

Humans should hang out together with like-minded people, and not just on the Internet. Science not being a religion or belief structure, there is no human institution dedicated to the assembly of like-minded modern thinkers who want direction and a sense of community in the physical realm (apart from schooling, of course), although TED does come close.

This is a pity, since all that creative energy is wasted. If someone were to pursue such structures, there might be a strengthening of the social fabric, instead of the dissolution we are witnessing today.

As human behavior is more or less predicated on the selfishness of his/her acts, all systems governing our actions are based on the carrot-and-stick method: Good behavior gets rewarded, bad behavior gets punished.

Within religions, it is an Almighty and Impartial Arbiter (or many) who dictates exactly what happens to the core of our *immortal being* (the method we've found to cheat oblivion and our morbid fear of non-existence).

Through the writings of all the sages who imagined our reality, we have come to the modern age of man. Whereas our knowledge of the Universe, its birth, its materials, its methods of assembly and destruction, its mechanics, and its ultimate demise are slowly being revealed to us and are ever evolving. Human emotions have evolved much more slowly.

We are still, at our core, animals with desires and fears who have grown big strong brains. How we manage these basic elements of our genetic makeup is just as important as the logic that drives us, and the barriers we erect among our disparate groups is perhaps a sign that we are not as emotionally ready to play nice with the rest of our brethren as we would like to believe.

Unless our education is radically altered to include other points of view, and our egotism continues to stand firm against the onslaught of logic and universalism, we will remain petulant children who will pout and fight when we should be trying to find common solutions and goals. We can either be Of Nature, or be Human.

It is a comforting thought that all knowledge is contained within one book, but as any library will show, human cognizance is not limited to a few hundred pages.

If you ever do need a thought system to guide you in your life, I recommend you choose one that preaches love, has no elements of violence save in extreme cases, and is based upon the idea that your thoughts and actions are the arbiter of your fate, where you are not judged for who you worship as much as what your interpersonal skills and benefits to society are.

I'm sad to say that a lot of thought systems can't take any critiquing, are intolerant of variations in their adherent's behavior, and some even preach violence and retribution (even while they say they don't).

As well, when you imagine there is an atemporal, omnipotent, and omnipresent being floating above you, judging your every move, it might make you leery of taking actions that might anger It and put a check mark on the negative side of your eternal scoreboard.

Some people even have the audacity of blaming an Evil Entity for their misdeeds, as if they had no control over their own actions. You are, and always will be the controller of your own future, to varying degrees.

What you do, and how you do it, will define your life and the lives of those around you. Don't worry about what comes after life. Be a good and just person, and let the afterlife be whatever it is, if anything at all.

If you only worry about what comes after, you can't enjoy the now. If you act only for future rewards, or to avoid punishment, then you are truly selfish and don't deserve *any* rewards.

Let your actions be their own rewards, and your happiness derive from that of others.

If altruism is a kind of selfish act, it is the best one you can have, because it does not only reward you, but spreads joy to all those around you.

God(s), as *physical* manifestations, are highly illogical since they have no provable physical influence on the Universe. If they exist at all, and they do, it is as thought processes, made true by our desire to be able to think of and achieve the ultimate Good.

These Goods have varied widely, depending on the aspirations of the people, and shaped by the places that commanded them. It stands to reason that if there is an *Ultimate* Good, it is outside of the human limitations of religions that it can be found, since all religions reject thought forms that are not identical to their own.

This makes them closed to evolution, therefore *greater* Good. It is not through adoration or worship that it can be attained, since it is not, in fact, an actual being. It is therefore outside of our control.

Goodness can only be attained through acts and thoughts that are Universally Good, not only those constrained within the tenets of any closed system. Acts of violence perpetrated in the name of Good are necessarily political, since no Good is present in their enactment.

The fight for the survival of one Good over another is only another facet of human fear, greed, anger, and jealousy. *If* there is such a thing as an Infinite Being, our worshipping it affects it not in the least, and in turn gives us nothing, since it was present before our existence.

Joining a religion to adhere to one facet of Good alone is just another *rally around the flag* exercise that limits our scope of action to those who believe in the same limited Good.

Those who would claim they know the intentions of an Infinite Being are in effect saying that they comprehend it, have harnessed it, and therefore possess it. However soothing that thought might be, no one can harness an Infinite Being, or direct it towards ones' enemies, especially if it is said to be innately Good.

You do not need to believe in God(s) to be good, only to be aware that you can strive for an ideal that is beyond what the average of Humanity is willing to attempt.

The fact that these arguments were couched within the limits of religious belief only demonstrates that we have had a very limited understanding of ourselves for a very long time. Most religious believers are quite respectable people, and should be, for their intention of being Good.

It is the extremists (whether religious or not) that you should be wary of, since it is their actions, through their interpretations of reality, that carry weight. Their thoughts, and therefore acts, are programmed by those who have high-jacked the meaning of Good for their own political ends.

It is ironic, then, that extremists of *all* stripes claim to have Good on their sides while they commit the most heinous of acts towards those who claim the same, or to the innocents around them. To limit yourself to the entirety of one belief or another means that you may be tempted to incorporate those aspects which are in effect not Good. This is so, since all groups inherently discriminate against anyone that does not share the exact same beliefs.

Keep in mind that to be Good, therefore aspiring to the *idea* of Godliness, as people wish to do, means that you are open to *everyone*. Labelling yourself in any way narrows your lenses and those of others. I realize the impossibility of avoiding labels. We define ourselves through them. Every sticker comes with a price, after all.

I did say that all human systems are forms of thought control, and I do mean that in the nicest possible way. A few hundred years ago, there were laws in place that made it legal for us to duel to the death if someone felt wronged. In the end, it was not the aggrieved party that won, but the stronger of the two that prevailed. Or the better shot.

A few thousand years ago, ancient Egyptian kings married their sisters and half sisters, to keep royal blood in the lineage. This became disastrous, since it weakened the gene pool of the entire family.

Several decades ago, segregation policies were common practise around the world. These racist policies have since been changed, and only those who know their history have any clue this went on. Of course, similar policies are still there in practise, under different names.

All that this shows is that there are laws that are unfair, and methods of actions that are stupid and self-destructive, that we have changed, and keep trying to change as time goes by.

You aren't aware of them because you aren't born with an innate knowledge of the past, and only the present and its various rules and regulations, methods of learning, and general guidelines are what concern you most.

You accept them because they are there.

They are mutable, though, and constantly change as time goes by, through the power of those who hold power. Even so, they are methods of controlling behavior that has been deemed destructive or detrimental to society, therefore were curbed through law, which eventually became common practise, and within a generation, how things *always were*.

As a child, you will have been full of energy, and it will be our duty, (your mother and I), to direct your energies into directions that will be conducive to your personal growth, your respect of others' rights, and your sense of belonging in this world that will be yours and everyone else's.

These are also forms of thought direction. I'll call it that instead of thought *control*, since I won't force you to think a specific thing, only direct you to a more positive way of doing things.

They are not Good or Bad, they are what they are. Depending on what kind of child we would like to see become a mature adult, we will want to impress upon you the rules that our society plays by, some it should (according to me, of course), and those it is beginning to forget. Every parent does it, to a greater or lesser degree, their own upbringing as a template, the help they receive from various sources as guidelines, and the genes the child carries which will inform how he or she will react to these various influences. There are always constraints and directions, outlets and allowances that are made when you are raising a child, as I learning for myself.

With the information I have gathered, all these methods I have described so far will inform the way we plan on bringing you up to be a well-adjusted, adaptable, responsible human being. Only time will tell if we will have been successful, but if previous experiences regarding what I know are any indication, we shouldn't be too far off the mark.

When I grew up, my mother made me clean my room. I hated doing it! Eventually, I appreciated knowing where to find my clothes and toys, and I kept my room as clean as possible. It was my responsibility to clean my room every day, and I will teach you that responsibility as well.

As I grew up, I was given more responsibilities and duties to do around the house. I had to set the table, help clean dishes, take out the trash, mow the lawn, sweep the floor, put my stuff away and clean my room! I found this to be terribly unfair, of course, as you will too.

What I did not appreciate, which I do now, is that my mother had many duties to perform, which, when I helped out, reduced her workload, while teaching me responsibility, hard work, and diligence (if I didn't do it right the first time, I had to do it over). These things prepared me for adulthood, since there are a great many duties and responsibilities involved in working well, raising a wholesome 'family unit' (whatever that means), saving for the future, preparing for the unexpected, and being a productive member of society.

I now realize that I'm not only in charge of me, myself, and I. I can't just care for my wife, you, our house, and our car. I have a responsibility towards my neighbours, my community, my province, my country, and my planet, as well. When I avoid these duties, all suffer from my negligence.

It is the belief in the unimportance of the political process and those who participate in it that allows for the powers that be to slowly fritter away the rights people have garnered over the years. Just like any human system, if the higher echelons are not held accountable, they tend to lose track of what their purpose is.

I'm here, and you're here, to make sure that they have their eye on the ball, since we have our eyes on them. It is my duty, and soon it will be yours, too. I have a hand in the shaping of the frame within which we all live, through my involvement.

If I am selfish and serve only my own needs, I neglect my family. My planet and society is my extended family. By doing my duties as a citizen, I am exerting my power (therefore control) over the system that oversees everybody's well-being.

Serenity Through Self-Control

You have an incredible tool bag of options available to you in the quest for self-fulfilment. You have the ability to hone them to fine sharpened points for your own well-being and survival. They are all natural, since they exist within the realm of possibilities. The contentious point is, which ones are desirable, and to what degree?

When laws or edicts are devised in society, they stem from a desire to either enhance or repress behavior.

Depending on for whom the laws in question are implemented, they can either be beneficial or detrimental to the population at large. For example: the urge to kill is a natural human trait, especially in men.

Many people feel the urge to kill *someone*, at *some* point in time. Laws going far back have been passed to curb this undesirable trait, which has been outlawed by our political system, and our ethical and moral education. It carries a penalty (punishment) if perpetrated.

I don't commit murder, therefore, for a variety of reasons, but the strongest argument is that it carries a severe penalty and is detrimental to society. I deem it wrong because it is harmful. We cannot, however, penalize someone for a behavior without looking at the root cause of that behavior, if we want to change it, in any overall way.

Finding a possible solution to its avoidance should be just as important as meting out, or promising punishment.

All the negative traits – the basic survival mechanisms I carry within myself – have been accounted for and described in great detail for thousands of years.

Any intelligent person who wanted to create a working model of society, had to have internal and external methods of control for it to grow and succeed.

They are the parameters and frames within which the most successful nations can work, since they are the same parameters that help me function in a satisfactory and self-fulfilling manner.

This all sounds like a desire to *manipulate* you, and to a certain degree, *it is*.

However you want to look at it, there is control and self-control, in whatever arena you may consider yourself to be.

As a human being, I have many responsibilities, and I could not take care of these unless I had *self-control*. As a matter of fact, many of the worlds' ills are caused by lack of self-control.

Morbid obesity, beyond being born with an endomorphic body type, can be caused by a lack of control over food consumption. There are however, other mitigating factors. Greed is a lack of control over your desires. Hatred and anger are a lack of control over your negative emotions. Laziness is a lack of control over your will-power. Lust is a lack of control over your sexual appetites.

I am, as a human being, full of fear, anger, hunger, desires, impatience, and a host of other functions that if I don't rein in, make it very difficult to live well in a larger group, let alone in my own body.

It is possible to be out of control and happy.

That requires that I have no empathy for others around me, and that I forget that I am not alone. If I can do that, I'm on my way to becoming another problem for my surroundings. I don't mean that you should be a sheep and follow the herd, either.

If you've read correctly what I've written so far, you know that it's important to be informed and aware of everything around you. If you do not know how to work well with others, though, you will be alone in your endeavours.

Self-control only means, in this case, that you know the limits to which you should act without harming others, that you have control over your emotions and actions, and *not they over you*. Every negative emotion, left unchecked, is a barrier you erect between yourself and the community at large.

One of the greatest and most frustrating barriers I find myself faced with is apathy. Just as society is slowly falling into the hands of the few, the many do not care. They will care, at some point, when they will have lost everything, and their options will have been greatly reduced. For now, we are content with distractions and apathy, because the decisions that are taken seemingly *do not affect us*.

This is one of the reasons why I want you to be awake to the world around you, not just concentrating on your immediate surroundings.

All confrontations are battles, whether fought with words, opinions or weapons. Groups of every nature believe in their intrinsic value, founded on the principles that guide them.

The level of animosity displayed by the various parties involved in the argument reveals the knowledge of the world at large encompassed by their philosophy.

The more violent the argument, the more misguided these values might be. The Aryan Nation, terrorist groups, and Neo-Nazis come to mind in this case (as well as many States or Religions who choose violence as their main *diplomatic* weapon).

Every group battles every other for the minds of followers to their cause, the destruction of those they consider *others*, and the potential resources they might reap.

The emotional strength of their leader's arguments is often what will sway or seduce the people they want in their midst. The knowledge, aspirations, and emotional baggage contained within the individual will determine whether the message resonates with them.

Political groups, religions, businesses, schools of thought, all want to plant within you the seed of knowledge that will make you one of theirs, to swell their ranks, increasing their power.

This is not a bad thing.

This is the way that human populations convince others into following their policies, or, conversely, plant fear about their opposition. The worst thing you can be is neutral, since you are taking yourself out of the fight for one of these groups to win. You, therefore, are helping no one, and are giving the chance for better organized and perhaps less benevolence-inclined groups to take power.

When you add your voice, body, and actions to a group that is against or for something, you are helping it become the dominant idea in a debate, and its power will determine its success in the fight against its opponent.

Your absence in the discourse is then actually a negative.

For example, if there is a group that is spreading lies, and you do or say nothing, then you are letting them get away with lying. How can this be beneficial to anyone?

It is only by calling people out on their dishonesty that they will retract what they have said, or change tactics. Letting them continue to do so is allowing for lies to have the same weight as truth. That's never a good idea in any society.

Since I don't want you to lie to me, I won't lie to you, and I won't lie to anybody else. It goes to reason then, that I shouldn't tolerate anyone else spreading lies.

The same goes for policies that will affect peoples' freedom: if I put myself in the shoes of the people who will bear the brunt of the laws that will be passed, will it put them on an even footing with the rest of society, or take away their freedoms?

No matter what level of society I find myself in, policies that make for a fairer system uplifts the whole of the population, and therefore makes me a part of the beneficiaries of that change. For that, I have to choose my actions and the groups to which I belong, to join in the battle of ideas that is human society.

We (here in North America) are societies of entertainment. Our free time is mostly employed doing things that have nothing to do with the growth of our minds. Meanwhile, the true issues are being discussed behind closed doors by the politicians who are supposedly doing good in our names. They are supposedly elected for the good of the people, yet invariably end up being blinded by the power they have achieved.

They forget the true reason why they had been handed this power. We are more than partially to blame for this state of affairs. We are the ones who give them this power, then turn a blind eye, or blind trust.

If but our knowledge of the character of the human we had put in charge of our welfare had been known, he or she probably would not have received it. If we were to keep an eye on these, our elected representatives, the odds are that they would not feel such impunity in taking advantage of our good natures. But I digress, so it stands.

If I wish to make the pendulum swing in the other direction, I have to be the one who takes the power into *my own* hands. I have to educate myself so that I can no longer be labelled as naive.

You and I live in a day and age where all the knowledge, therefore power, we could ever desire has been placed directly at our fingertips. It is by searching it out and making it our own that we can take control over these, our futures.

An educated populace is a dangerous populace, if only for those who wish to keep everything for themselves. I used to despair that nothing would ever change, but now I know that I no longer accept the status quo, and my desire to make a fairer society has the chance to upset the order that prevails.

Eventually, those who want only power for themselves can be replaced. Those who understand that, only by having a passion for the people they serve, will they elevate everyone. A will to give everyone the desire to learn, and the education they deserve, as well as the spirit to fight, can uplift entire regions, countries, and perhaps even humanity as a whole.

Grandiose claims, of course, but starting with one person (myself), marks the beginning of a different thought process.

I love gaming, watching movies, reading, relaxing, and taking vacations. I won't lie. I think everybody does. I expect you'll love these activities as much as I do. There are a million distractions that exist to make you forget boredom, and they are quite easy to fall into, and very difficult to get out of. I don't think there's anything wrong with any of these things. Taken in the right doses, they are the answer to the weary spirit.

My concern comes from the fact that when I am not working, these things are *all I do*! I am constantly updating my social profile on the internet, or getting into a hot and heavy firing exercise on my gaming machine, or planning and taking my next vacation. I have only two modes: work and play.

As hard as my work is, and as easy as my play is, I think there's room to add one more category to my life that needs to be addressed: the business of life itself. As much as these distractions are great ways to spend lost time, I can't forget that my mind needs a little something to make it happy as well.

That's why I try to introduce some new information into it, every day. Relevant information about what is happening in the world around me, so I don't lose track of the important decisions that will affect my life. Whether or not I like politics and foreign relations, business, and other supposedly boring topics, they directly and indirectly affect me.

Even if I ignore these things, they will not go away, and the more I implicate myself in their unfolding, the better chances I have of getting positive results for myself and all those around me.

It is my job to know what is happening, and my duty to get involved in the processes that shape my reality. Or else I am just existing, and not really living.

Some of the most important decisions I can make are political, since they affect absolutely everybody. Not giving my say in the matter is a betrayal of my principles.

I did not used to think this way. I used to think that since nobody got involved, my vote didn't count either. Then I woke up and realized that it was *because* I didn't vote or get involved that I didn't matter.

I can shape the country I would like to see make its mark on the world scene, to be a bastion of fairness. I want it to be an example to be followed, and an all-around good place to live.

I can also lose hope, stay home, whine about the unfairness and callousness of my government, and watch it go in a direction I can't condone. The decision is mine alone to make, and now I share it with you.

There are many fun things to do in life, but there are many hard choices to make as well, and it's not by shirking my duties that I will have accomplished what I see as a worthy goal.

We'll watch plenty of movies together, and play lots of video games. We'll enjoy trips around the globe to see how other people live, but we'll also try to make our home a better one for all those who want to live there. If we don't, we let others suffer injustice, and that is something I should not accept.

So how do I achieve peace within myself? I try to think of my appetites as things that I need to take care of, but should not control me. As soon as they do, they become obsessions (like I mentioned before), and take over my life. I try to be mindful of the things I do, questioning whether I truly need to spend so much time or expending so much energy toward a particular activity. Remembering that I gave myself a greater purpose makes me put these appetites in their place.

Being able to control the amount of time I spend on my appetites gives me peace of mind. I don't worry about *wasting my time*, because I know I will get right back to giving back to my community, working for a better future, and that to me is more important than any self-absorption.

More Control

The society you will be born in is one that is organized top-down. At the top of the food chain, you will have the industrialists and bankers, as well as the politicians. They will work hand-in-hand to spoon-feed the people on the bottom of the ladder pre-digested fictions in easy to understand formats.

All you are required to do is to agree to all that they propose. Television is the best medium for this, since it requires very little thinking on the part of you, the viewer. The internet is slowly but surely taking over that role. Anyone can say anything and it will be interpreted as *the truth* by just about everybody who is watching.

You might be wondering if I'm kidding at this point. I'm not. What I have just described is one of the main reasons we make such piss-poor decisions. We just don't think.

The majority of people are genetically programmed to believe what sounds like an honest proposition. If I told you that drinking poison or shooting yourself would help you reach another plane of existence, you probably would think twice about it.

That is exactly what happened a few years ago within a <u>few</u> <u>cults</u>, whose members were found dead after signing a suicide pact to go on to the next world. There is a similar <u>cult</u> (without the suicidal aspect) still existing in Canada.

The people who are a part of cults either do not have a "bullshit detector," or have them turned off. How else can I accept that they agreed to the insanity of what was being proposed to them? The reason why more people don't join is that they think to themselves: "Well, that *is* a bit ridiculous."

Except, somehow, alarm bells don't go off when someone tells us that the World will end in 2012. Don't worry, I'm sure someone will tell you the planet will be destroyed in your lifetime as well. It won't happen through divine intervention, whether you repent for your sins or not.

Ditto for when I am told that because my sign is Pisces, this makes me a calm, caring, individual with a penchant for tapioca pudding. Or whatever the inane thought of the day might be.

The idea that stars, millions of light years away from us, command me to be a certain way is ludicrous, on a logical level. Why, in my right mind would I accept it as fact? That's because fact has no bearing on the matter, at all, whatsoever.

I am listening to my emotional brain, my sympathetic desires telling me that this is how I *should* be. And just as if someone else was yawning, I empathize with the *Horoscope of the Day*. To attempt to be like the way I am described.

We all have the ability to be kind and nice and giving, but we are putting the power over the reins of our emotions in the hands of another driver: the journalist in charge of the Horoscope that day.

The world would be a much different place if your Horoscope said: "Be an obnoxious bastard, you deserve it." All of a sudden,

everybody who reads that publication and was born that month would stop being nice for one day. I'm just kidding, of course, but the power of suggestion is a fairly powerful thing.

Such is also the power of hypnosis. The ability to shut down a part of the brain to only use the part that has the desire or ability to do all the things we stop ourselves from doing. That is why it is so amusing.

Logic gives us inhibition. Emotion gives us the drive. Shut down logic and you are left with pure drive and desire, controlled by one another. That other could make you do whatever he felt like, and you would not think twice about it. When we shut down, or have our logical centres shut down, we are ready to believe anything that can be suggested.

Fortunately, most of the time, our logic centres are active, and that is why we can conceive of unicorns, and fairies, and Santa Claus, and the Easter Bunny, but we know for a fact that imaginary creatures only live there, in our imagination.

When a child has an invisible friend, we find it cute, but to the child, even if they know it's not real, it does take on an important role: whether to fend off loneliness, want of someone who understands him/her, to confront fears, anxieties, or to understand their own goals, the imaginary friend is there to help.

We know that when he tells us that "Simon" his invisible friend put baby laxative in the cat bowl, he did it to get attention, and used his invisible friend as a scapegoat.

Some people never outgrow their invisible friends. More so's the pity, since very powerful people would like you to believe that they know what He is saying. And that you should do exactly what they order, for His sake. That is the perfect time to turn on your *bullshit detector*.

Even though we can identify a lot of basic lying, when it becomes embroiled in higher-end and sensible-*sounding* arguments, that is when being aware of all the facts pertaining to a situation becomes crucial.

The business of politics is that of lying and manipulation, to a certain degree.

Yours should be about finding out how much of it and why, and processing it on your own terms.

Why Not Destroy or Overthrow it All?

As you grow up, you'll come into contact with some pretty extreme views, especially in your twenties. You'll be finding out about how things are terrible and unfair, and be filled with righteous anger and the will to do something about it.

Calm down, and breathe deeply. Just keep in mind that that is the peak of your testosterone, and you'll either want to break stuff or have sex, whether you are a man *or* woman. Your desire to foment global revolution is normal, and is shared by just about every angry teen out there who needs to rebel against authority. Been there, done that. Not trying to minimize it.

You should be cautious, though, in the associations that you make and the causes you support. Those who are a bit older and have their own agendas love using that youthful vigor for their own political ambitions. I can sympathize, of course, with the anarchist creed of wanting to destroy every institution and fomenting revolution.

This is a natural part of growing up and wanting to fuck shit up. The inherent problem with that line of thought is that you have to rebuild from the ground up, after you've regained some modicum of control over the situation at hand.

Anarchy is only a passing phase, a transition, like puberty, if you will. What comes out of it is sometimes worse than the system you want to get rid of, if you don't stop to think about what you're doing.

Besides, in general, it's not the *system* that is terrible, it's the *people* running it (I make exception for monarchies, one-party rule, and military dictatorships: they are pretty bad systems).

In any event, your best bet (if you do want to have some sort of influence in the decision-making process) is to participate in the direction your government is taking. Vote, get people to vote, or present yourself for office somewhere, and don't forget your mission.

It's easy to get side-tracked once you're part of the system.

Watch the people who run the place in your name, and make sure they don't get off the message themselves. It's easy for you to get distracted and forget what is really important as well.

Just keep in mind that it should be your duty, among others, to not let yourself or others get abused by your government. If you do lose sight of their actions, you'll be just as responsible for their abuse as they are.

Buck up, it's not that daunting a task to know what is going on around you. You have a voice, you live in a democratic country, and you can be heard, if you so desire. Destruction is rarely the answer, and generally worsens situations more than makes them better.

HOWEVER, and I do add this caveat as a *last resort*: If your government is in the process of, or has taken away people's civil rights and liberties, rule by fear, rip families away from each other, commit murder as a matter of course, and repress all forms of dissent, it is your duty to find ways to sabotage, and implement those actions to counter their ongoing destruction of your country.

Help those who are targeted. Hide them, if need be.

Find the weak points of the regime and destroy them any way you can. Hound them until they lose their minds.

Read *The Art of War*, by Sun Tzu, it will give you pointers as to the best methods of waging war against any sort of enemy.

When the dust has settled, make sure to have those involved judged fairly and sent to prison.

Why Love Matters

Q. You're going to talk about love, right after the part where you tell people they need to revolt and sabotage governments?

A. Yup.

Q. Why? It doesn't make any sense.

A. It does, actually. If you're rebelling, it should be because some minority has decided that there was a part of their population that didn't deserve to live. Classic examples include the Jewish people targeted by the Germans before and during the Second World War in something called the Holocaust, or during the Vietnam War era with the Cambodian genocide. It never starts with mass killings. It starts with denying people their rights, then turning them into an enemy of the State, and *then* carrying out their elimination.

So, if you see a country's agenda moving swiftly along toward that goal, knowing the leader's distaste toward a certain racial minority, you can safely assume that bad things are on the horizon.

Q. What does that have to do with love? Aren't you going against your own creed by getting involved in that way?

A. Not at all. I can love everyone that doesn't want to murder an entire group of people. And I can try to stop or at least hinder the group that wants to harm others. What you mean is non-violence. I can love things intensely, yet still want to defend them. Like I mentioned before, though: that is an extreme situation. Most of your life will probably be lived in very different circumstances.

Love is difficult. When I say love, in this case, I don't mean *being in love*. Being in love is an overpowering feeling that takes you over, and floods you with intense emotional turmoil. That is not what I'm talking about. It's harder to place than that.

You know what it is to fear, to hate, to not care, to be sad, to be happy, even. To live love has to be one of the most pleasurable experiences there is.

It doesn't mean that you can't feel your other emotions. The simplest way I can put it, is that you can live your life any way you want: that is a given.

When you do, there are emotions that will come back more often than others, depending on what it is you are living. Eventually, one of those emotions will be the dominant one. If you are unaware of your feelings, you could very well live anger, or sadness, or bitterness, and just not realize it (you can get used to anything).

Living love is choosing love over the other emotions. To me, it means doing things that I love, as well doing those things with love.

Let love be your driving emotion, essentially.

It is a combination of openness, empathy, acceptance, serenity, logic, and positive outlook. That is my recipe for love.

I chose love as my main emotion, because it means I am open to personal evolution, instead of shutting out the world. It means that when I attempt something, I take satisfaction in its accomplishment, as well as the process that leads to it.

It makes me a kinder person towards myself and others. Yes, I do get angry, like anyone else, but I don't let that anger take over for long, or moult into hatred. I want to go back to love as soon as I can.

Living love reduces my stress. It keeps me calm. It means that I can appreciate my surroundings and those that are a part of it.

It removes all barriers that I might be tempted to create. It is a hard path to take, since it requires me to fight my natural impulses of hatred and fear, at times.

The longer I live it, the easier it becomes, because I starve the neuronal path to fear and hatred, and am left only with love. You will experiment with all your emotions, and you will see which ones you like best. That is what everybody does, and they make their choices consciously or unconsciously, but eventually you will have to live with the emotions that control you, or that you control.

How would you like to feel? Content or frustrated? Sad or serene? Hateful or at peace? Accepting or in denial? The end choice comes down to how you wish to live your reality.

There is an expression that says: "You should live every day like it was your last." I think the author of that little slogan was hoping that those who saw its wisdom would enjoy every day with full zest and vigor.

What seems to be the case, in fact, is people living their lives with reckless abandon, as if tomorrow would never come. This wouldn't be a problem if the world *did* end the next day. So far, it seems to go on no matter what.

The spirit of that thought was that you should enjoy every day. That's what you should do, in fact. Keep in mind, though, that unlike the End of the World scenario that is painted, your life will go on afterwards (unless the stupidity or recklessness of your acts catch up to you).

With that little nugget in mind, it might be to your advantage to live your life as if there *were* consequences to your acts. Love life, and all that is in it. Live it like it was the *first* time you experienced it, and keep your sights on your future, not just what is happening today or at this very moment.

Just like all other emotions that push our actions, love can spread. It influences others. It makes them feel better; makes them feel special, and wanted. Makes them want to be better people. It is the most important emotion because it whispers through the ages, while the other, negative emotions shriek and gnash their teeth. Love wants us to be okay, do well, and elevate us all.

The Corruptibility of Absolutely Everything

When someone, somewhere, comes up with a good idea for all, the odds are that eventually, someone else will take it and corrupt it. Simple as that.

Government for the people? Nope, government for me, now. Love for all? Not a chance. Love me, now. There will always be people who will take advantage of a situation, or a system, to make it about themselves. It is inevitable.

The question after that is: what to do about it? Options are obvious and few: fight for the thing that once was good, or let it consume itself until it is invalidated? The other option is to make the system unattractive to those who would wield it for selfish ends, or somehow only let the right people into the higher echelons of the organization.

Sadly, there is no simple answer, and trying to keep the *bad* out appears to be an exercise in futility. We all start out with good intentions, and then get sidetracked with greed, power-mongering, lust, sloth, and all those things that make life pleasant.

This doesn't mean that we shouldn't strive for the good, however, and keep striving to help others until our usefulness as an organization has run out.

In the past, whenever there was a lack of resources (or a lust for what the neighbor had), or even a surplus of unwanted poor humans, monarchs, religious authorities, tribal leaders, all went to war, hoping to pilfer whatever the other groups had, to fill their stores. As we developed better and better weapons, and better methods of resource collection and growth, business took over the war industry and resource industry.

Now, in developed countries, there is no more need of war, and our methods of waging them are so devastating that causing one would quite possibly destroy most of the earth, demolishing at the same time any resources we could care to cultivate.

This is what is called MAD, or Mutually Assured Destruction. Any fully developed and wealthy country possesses weapons so powerful that the use of them would be suicide for all. That is why weapons industries mostly cater to smaller, underdeveloped countries which are struggling to become something else.

The idea, therefore, for major powers to go to war for resources or population control is no longer a useful option, since most products can be chain-made, and natural resources can be traded for.

This is one of the main reasons that the shift from war economies to business and trade has occurred. The systems involved, though, have not been altered.

We still operate in top-down fashion, with those who desire power at the top, and those who just want to be left alone at the bottom. The trust I place in our elected (or unelected) rulers is one of blind faith, most of the time.

I elect them (or let them rule me) with the idea (or hope) that they will do right by me. I let slip by the quirks (big and small) of these officials, telling myself that a bit of corruption is terrible, but hey, look at those guys in that country *over there*, they have it really bad! Then I put my fears to bed, and tell them a story.

I let them wake up to discover that my liberties and public funds are being taken away from me in draconian fashion, without most of the population being aware of it. How did it come to be so?

As any human system, scum also rises to the top, not just the cream. The less I pay attention to the world around me, the more likely I am to be duped by those who make the decisions for me.

I let them, therefore they can.

In the olden days of the Roman Empire, they would organize games in the Colosseum, with gladiators, and chariot races, and they would even distribute bread to the masses. The mob would love their rulers, and literally let them get away with murder.

Today, no one needs to keep me distracted. I do it to myself. The intake of information – that is not for purely entertainment purposes – is no longer a very important factor in my everyday life, and contributes to the degradation of my society.

How so? It is all a matter of percentages, of course. Let's say only 50 percent of the population go to the voting booths. Since democracies work by representative rule, that means that the ruling party only needs to gather 26 percent of the vote to win a majority. This is when it gets dangerous, obviously.

Let's look at some facts: In Canada, as of May 2nd, 2011, there was a total population of approximately 31.6 million people. On the voter rolls, however, there were 24.25 million people. Of those, only 14.8 million people showed up at the voting booths. That is less than fifty percent of the population. The ruling party won with 39.6 percent of the votes.

That comes to 5.86 million people. In other words, those who control the country do so because of the votes of 18.5 percent of the population. That, to me, does not make any sense whatsoever.

What that demonstrates is:

1. Any thoroughly organized group can easily take over a democratic country; and,

2. When people are too lazy to care about the direction their leaders are taking them, everybody suffers.

When people with self-serving tendencies want to rule, they will, and they will do so through the easiest means possible. If you look at the political landscape today, you see that there are a lot of politicians that are either in the process of working for the benefit of corporations, or will when they retire from politics.

The fact of the matter is, money and profits being the current end-goal of humanity, it is the grease that oils the cogs of *everything*. So in most political systems, there are many fewer idealists than there are opportunists, regardless of the stripes they may be wearing at that particular time. They have every opportunity of attracting the power they so crave to themselves. The willing lackeys of the corporations that desperately want to create a symbiotic and mutually beneficial system with them are in charge of *our* well-being. How quaint.

A part of the blame goes to the death of ideals and values. Government used to be a counterbalance to industry, yet through *fine-tuning*, it has come to work for it.

Government was there to protect people from rapacious behavior, and stop abuses, as well as a ways to control a nation's resources, protect its borders, and its many belief systems. People being people, and infinitely corruptible, it did not take long for those who desire power for its own ends to infiltrate said systems and harness their powers to *their* own ends.

In any event, we return once more to human fallibility. Corruption is the word we use when describing a human behavior that has been overtaken by the desire for something for which it was not intended.

Corruption has existed since the invention of money and greed, and will never go away. How much we tolerate it and accept it, however, is another story altogether. Absolutely every person, knowledge, and thing, is corruptible. No one is immune to it. No matter how *pure* you might think you are, you can be bought off, if you are not careful. Just remember that the short-term gains you might acquire from this behavior are vastly outweighed by the long-term harm you will cause to everyone else *and yourself.*

It all comes down to your views on greed, and how much you truly wish to accomplish.

Justice for All

hat is justice? It means a method of punishment or reward within society to either curb or encourage certain behaviors within certain norms. Taken widely, then, justice is a frame whose borders I must respect, for the good of others and my own.

It is a concept that is there to stop me from acting anti-socially. To take steps in correcting or punishing the acts of individuals who disrespect those rules, as set forth by the people in who power has been invested (or by whom it was taken).

We can therefore surmise that the people who make the laws should fall within their boundaries, since it is by them and for their benefit that said laws were put into place. This is the "perfect world" scenario that I dream of, of course.

Back in the real world, where we live, those who hold the reins of power can pretty much do what they want, until they get caught. Then they get slapped on the wrists, or get someone else to go to prison in their stead for their misdeeds, and everything goes back to how it was before.

There has to be some kind of major catastrophe before sweeping changes happen, unfortunately. Justice is something that happens to poor people, to keep them under control. This should not be, of course, but as the ruling classes perpetrate more and more anti-social acts, how could politicians, in good conscience, punish their brethren and benefactors?

The fact that so many things we could deem as *crimes* go unpunished, perpetrated at the highest levels, seems to confirm it. Does this mean that retribution is in order? No, it just means that the people within the system in place are flawed and corrupt, therefore need replacement.

If the judges are the *property* of the guilty, they themselves should be replaced by others who will do their jobs, and are not afraid of going against their *friends* or *benefactors*.

Very often, the people who must bring the hammer down on those who have committed fraud on a grand scale have received very healthy contributions from these same people. We can easily guess where their interests lie. The *justice* they impart, then, is tainted by the relationship they fomented with those they are to judge. Lady Justice is not so blind in these cases. So what is there to be done?

The severing of the incestuous ties between government and private industry is primordial in taking back power from the few so that they may not take advantage of the many. It remains to be seen who will have the fortitude and incorruptibility to do so. An inching away from money and power as the end-all and be-all of humanity's aims and goals might help as well. Not doing so will have not-so-desirable results. Justice should be the same for all, and not dependent on the income of the individual.

One of my favourite quotes now is: "When the people fear the government, that's tyranny; when the government fears the people, that's freedom." Of course, I think that government should love the people, and vice versa. But when government abuses the people for their own gain? That's a different story. That quote was misattributed to Thomas Jefferson, but is most probably by John Basil Barnhill in a 1914 treatise on socialism.

When the government is corrupt, it is usually out of greed. If corporate interests control the government, it might be a good idea to make those who bankroll them fear the people as well.

There can be no equality in justice when laws are made to benefit the few over the many. When that happens, it is no longer a government of the many, but of the few, and they've lost their legitimacy and can be disposed of.

Ambassadors, Diplomats, Teachers

In everything that I do, with everyone I meet, I am a representative of all that I am. Every concept I describe as being my belief is a description of what is at my core. Every act that I perpetrate is a definition of my being. What I do, how I do it, what I mean, how I act, are all me. I am my own ambassador, and I act accordingly.

Every aspect of my personality, everything I show, or refuse to show, dictates how people will react to me, as a human being. That said, the more varied ways I know of being, and the more positive, the better my interactions with others can go. It all depends on my mood, thoughts, goals and attitude.

I represent who I am by the clothing I wear, which symbolize the status I convey upon *myself*.

I extend myself to my surroundings by the objects which I purchase, or create, and adorn myself or my personal space with.

I am a physical representation of my mind.

I consider myself an ambassador of everything I think. Since I want to be respected for these thoughts, I respect others for theirs. When I say that I am an ambassador, I don't mean that I feel pompous and self-important. That's not what an ambassador is.

An ambassador is aware of what he represents, and acts in a manner that will not embarrass or offend those with whom he interacts.

This is said to be acting diplomatically. An ambassador is aware that he is not limited to being one person, but a representation of all the lenses that others can see him through.

Diplomats

I am a diplomat because I want to create a favourable impression in the minds of those with whom I interact. Not in any self-serving way, but to strengthen bonds between people. To show that trustworthiness is a worthwhile trait that should be explored. Suspicion and hatred sometimes being the more prevalent traits, I find it better to pursue the opposite, because I have it within me to do so.

Teachers

A teacher can be absolutely anything we can conceive of which has affected our lives in any way, shape or form. Teachers are the most important people, events, and things you will encounter in your life.

They are what will allow you to grow beyond what you know. The best ones are those that will teach you the most fundamental truths, and leave you a better person for it.

In human form, their knowledge and beliefs are tinted with their own biases, emotions, goals, and attitudes. Our human teachers either instill the desire to learn more about a subject, or make us despair at even having to suffer through the lesson.

If knowledge is power, the teacher holds all the power, and imparts it in bite-sized pieces so that the student can receive it, conceive it, and hopefully retain it to live it. The best of teachers will be those who light the flame of desire to learn within the heart of their students.

We have millions of teachers in our lives. Some are people, some are situations, some are places.

Whatever external input affects our lives are teachers. If you live in the ghetto, the crack dealer on the corner with a nine in his back pocket is as much a teacher as your mom working two jobs trying to make enough to keep the house and feed you, as your father who may or may not be there for you, as the street you live on. All of the information these people and the situations they bring, teach you *something*.

The same goes for the man who owns a company and wants to make enough money to buy a new jet and spend his vacation in Dubai, who went to Harvard Law and would like to head into politics.

Everything that surrounds him tells him something. The fact that both are part of two different socio-economic contexts, and that they both have two different world-views and goals, changes nothing about the fact that they are both trying to live, survive, propagate, thrive, in their own way.

No, they are *not* the same people, and they do *not* have the same problems, but both live according to what they know, and what they are expected to aspire to.

If they learn something from their environment, that is what they will carry with them to the next generation. The boy or girl who lives in the 'hood might try to reproduce what he sees, or try to escape it entirely. He may also attempt to alter his environment to better it.

The wealthy man has exactly the *same choices*, even though they are not within the same socio-economic spheres, and have vastly different *opportunities*. Both people will love others and hate still others, and both will not know why they do the things they do unless they question themselves.

The teachers we have are the single most important things we will encounter in our lives. The ways in which we will react to them will dictate our chances of survival. If we encounter so much negativity, it is because we either had problems with our teachers or we reacted badly to them.

We are often predisposed, genetically, to react in certain ways to our environment. For certain people who were dealt wild-cards in their genetic makeup, a difficult environment will activate the dormant genes within them, which will help them to better survive.

All in all, the information one can possess to overcome any particular situation seems to be the main controllable factor that comes into play.

You have no control over your genes, you have very little control over what other people do *to* you, or where you were born. Therefore your primary weapons in this world are your body, your mind, and the knowledge *you* pursue.

You cannot expect anybody to act well all the time. The only person over which you have any measure of control, is yourself. Your reactions to any given situation say a lot about you, and how you were raised, and how much you questioned yourself and your environment.

In physics, they say that for every action, there is an equal and opposite reaction. It is true also for humanity, for every individual to react according to his or her own genetic background and upbringing.

If you realize why you react a certain way, it is because you are conscious of your reaction, therefore that you have reflected upon your own actions. By questioning your actions, you need not necessarily react in the way you usually do. You can pause, and reflect, and analyze why you do the things you do, why you hate or love the things you do.

You may not come to any clear conclusions unless you open your psychology toolkit, but you will at least begin to walk down the path of a person who is interested not only in him or herself, but in humanity as a whole.

This is a very funny, sad, happy, exciting, dangerous, corny, preposterous, mad path indeed, but if there is one thing it is not, is boring. Once you begin to question, you will realize that there is always another question afterwards.

When you begin answering those questions with proven facts, you begin to understand the watch for its gears, or the car for its engine.

You become a student.

You are no longer satisfied with "because it is so," since you will realize that that answer is kind of a copout by those who have stopped looking and want you to do the same (Leave your brain at the door, please, we have all the answers!).

The truth is that no one has all the answers, and the fun in life is to not only find them, but find new tools to look for them. Our teachers are there for that, or should be. If they have passion, and drive, and knowledge of what they teach, they infect us with that joy.

We return to them that sympathetic *yawn* of happiness in teaching, · by learning what they have to offer. Truly, all we are doing is opening the door to our minds to let in knowledge that we could have acquired in any way we wanted. Except that this is the occasion we chose to get it.

"He's an awesome Prof! Really knows his stuff!" "Cool, I have him this semester!" How often does that happen? A lot! When we realize that the professor (or whatever teacher you can dream of) is the middleman of knowledge, we still need him or her, because he or she has the skills we require to acquire the tools we need to solve even more problems.

In turn, the problems we solve become tools as well. A problem always becomes a tool after it has been solved. Sometimes we don't know what for, but then we use it and find it a use. The Teachers are there from our birth to help us surmount our problems, and give us some of their own, and it is then our task to solve these problems.

If we do not realize that most things are solvable, we stay at the level of: "I give up!" and nothing changes within us that could give us the tools we needed to solve the problem. We could have been happy, but we were too frustrated, lazy, annoyed, disenchanted, or afraid to even try. So there we stand.

For me to be a good teacher, I have to light the fire of interest in the heart and mind of my students, with my enthusiasm and knowledge. For me to be a good student, I have to pay attention to, and respect, my teacher. For you, I want to be that teacher, since you are my children.

Maybe if I do a good job, you will respect and learn from myself and your other teachers. Perhaps that will make you want to be that kind of person when you are older, as well. If I am imparted the passions of the teacher, I may feel its contagion, and wish to emulate them.

When you are going to school, you are going to *people*. A brick building won't teach you much, or an empty room either. It is the person who will be giving you his or her knowledge that you go to.

School can be fun, just as it can be extremely boring, depending on the motivation of your teacher, your openness to the ideas he or she wants you to take in, your attention-span, and a plethora of other details that you will see once you are there.

Now, even though you might not like some of the subject matter, or think it will be irrelevant to your life in the future, their purpose is to open the doors of your mind to all the various possibilities in the human spectrum of thought.

They are there to express their existence, and your acknowledgement of their *being* makes for the further study of one of these areas the *possible* goals of your life. They are the baby-steps that bring you to someday sprinting headlong. Yes, another method of thought direction, but one that opens the doors of your mind.

Always remember that there are many different ways of thinking, and the ones that bring you to thinking less, are usually the ones that are the most wrongheaded.

Thought control would be an apt name for those systems that try to make you to *stop thinking*.

Even though the public school system has its limitations, it is still one the most valuable assets any State has developed to encourage the mental growth of its entire population.

One of the common threads that has made countries great and powerful has been the uplifting of its citizenry through its education.

If it is said that 'Knowledge is Power,' the converse is also true, and certain governments seem loathe to allow their *common people* to achieve more than a cursory education, either through an artificial lack of funding or to keep a tight rein on the power they have achieved.

It seems strange to me that States would want to curb the intelligence of its citizenry, since it is through their education that nations become innovators, augmenting their net worth on the world scene. I can understand the threat certain leaders feel from the loss of power that would result in their citizens making educated choices based on logic. Then again, if I was to think only of myself and certain special interests, and not for the good of my entire country, I wouldn't be a very good politician, or human being.

Be a good and patient student, and when the time comes, try to be a good and patient teacher, as we should all try to be.

Citizen of the World

You can be many things. You are a child, you grow older and become a teenager, an adult, then, an elder. You are a student, a worker, an artist, a businessperson, or you might be unemployed. You are a man or a woman, somewhere in between, or none of the above. You might be religious or not. You are straight, gay, or something along the spectrum. You are the inhabitant of your Region, Province, State, Prefecture, Country, Continent, and Planet, depending on what suits the situation.

Most of all, you are a Citizen of the World.

We are all together on a pretty small rock covered in land and water. Learning to accept this and your neighbours is an intrinsic fact of life. You can bury your head in the sand, but nothing will change this simple piece of information. However special you may believe you are, or which the group you belong to believes it is, you are just as special as the seven billion other people (and growing) that the human population includes.

You are no less of an individual. You are still unique. You are just not *special* (but your mom and I think you are) in the Grand Scheme of Things. Whatever artificial classifications you introduce into your life, nothing changes the fact that you are human, and so is everybody else.

Being a Gentleman or Lady of the World, is nothing short of accepting the unique nature of the Human Being. This means that you extend the courtesy you reserve for your in-groups to any other person, whether they require your assistance or not. That you also respect others for the positive attributes they may possess. That you have the self-control to resist the urge to violence unless attacked.

Sometimes it is impossible to deal with a bully with words when forced into a corner, but every situation should be gauged carefully before an action is taken.

Self-defense should be your greatest use of force towards any kind of overt violence. The neutralization of an aggressor should be your goal, no matter who that aggressor is, if you truly aspire to a peaceful neighbourhood.

As a Citizen of the World, you owe it to your extended family to give them all the regards you have for your immediate family. You owe it to everyone to not pose a danger to those around you.

It is your Human duty to be the best person you can, no matter what other people might think of that notion. The most elevated label you should possess is Human, for that is you, at your core, however you define yourself in other terms, or *decorate* your existence.

Mental and Physical Self Defense

gnorance is bliss. That was either said by someone who discovered something they wished they hadn't found out, or by someone trying to convince others of the validity of that statement.

In any event, both reasons are wrong. Not knowing one thing does not preclude that I will not learn something else that will bother me. It is by learning to adapt to any information that I am better equipped to deal with any uncomfortable tidbit that comes my way.

Once again, I do not live in a vacuum. Things happen. People who are truly *ignorant* do not have the *capacity* to learn more. Therefore, is it truly better to be ignorant, if my capacity to do so is not restricted in this way?

Do I really wish to live in a bubble, avoiding any discomfort, or would it not be better for me to develop the antibodies that make it so that no knowledge could harm me? If I spend my time avoiding uncomfortable information, I think I'll be wasting a whole lot of time.

If I make the conscious decision that ideas are harmless until implemented, I have effectively rendered them harmless. I can, in this way, at least let the ideas reach me, where I can judge them for their validity, and reject or accept them based on my own criteria.

When we refuse to face our problems, we try to live that old adage. What needs to be done is to find ways to either A) deflect the harm, or B) neutralize the harm, without doing what we are best at doing: Ignoring the harm.

Whenever a fact is not to our liking, we are pre-programmed to push it aside and look for the flaws in the argument. Even if the argument is sound, we would rather it not be so.

We can do something else, though. We can face the facts. This is also something that requires self-knowledge. It takes fortitude to admit that we may be wrong, but if someone has a strong argument that what we may be doing is harmful, either to ourselves or to others, would it not be in our own interest to at least listen to the facts presented instead of plugging our ears and ignoring what is being said?

This doesn't only apply to personal problems, but to social ones as well. If a thing is known, and proven to be harmful (Global Warming, say.), isn't it somewhat childish to say that the proof is inconclusive when there is so much proof to be had? Clouding the issues by manufacturing dissent under the guise of *Free Speech* is the last bastion of the greedy and amoral.

There is truth to be had, and you should root it out so that you do not become the willing puppet of those who have no regard for it.

Fear of Knowledge

Another trap I've encountered in learning, is that of information rejection. I did this with any information that I found uncomfortable or unpalatable. As soon as I began reading something I disagreed with, I would put it down and repudiate it as *wrong*. I think it was my minds' way of protecting itself from *parasitic* thoughts.

Thoughts that might alter my world-view, therefore challenging me to think differently, were dangerous to me, or so I thought. I think that that is the reason why certain books, words, or thoughts *are* banned.

The thought is that if they were free to circulate, they would negatively affect the people they encountered, like viruses being planted in fertile hosts. How else could we see the harm in reading books like Hitler's *Mein Kampf*?

It is the *ideas* inside which are considered dangerous, even seditious. To a certain degree, I have to agree. To a mind that is still looking for answers, or unsure of itself, or even looking for someone to hate, it very well could be. The possibility exists that we may find those answers we are looking for in the proscribed books. Whose fault is that? The books, or the reader? Both schools of thought (Freedom of Speech versus

Censorship) vie for control, but wouldn't have to if the education process involved critical thinking.

I know that no two thoughts are of the same value, because I can judge them for their merits and base in truth. If I am of the opinion that all thoughts have the same intrinsic value, then none are better than the other, and therefore, there is no point in pursuing any more lines of questioning.

I can settle for whatever answer is given to me without bothering to figure out if said knowledge has any worth. This is why people want books to be banned. If my mind is weak, any thought can compromise it, it is therefore cause for distrust or alarm.

If I know, though, how to properly protect my mind, I have no reason to fear information. Call it my *bullshit detector*, but information that I can properly analyze, has no power over me unless I let it. It is not dangerous, because its effects are nullified by my ability to discern truth from bullshit. So don't be afraid of information itself, just be weary of false information. Once again, knowledge is power. No subject should be taboo, or banned.

Knowing Too Much?

We also say that it's not good to know too much. Why, if knowledge is how you derive pleasure, then wouldn't knowing too much drown you in pleasure?

The thing is, when we know too much, it is usually associated with a negative connotation, and we are stuck with this image that knowledge will destroy us, and that it is up to someone else to use this dangerous knowledge to extricate us from danger, when the first people who should be trying to figure stuff out should be we ourselves.

Why leave it to the experts when we ourselves should be semi-proficient? That's what they say: Leave it to the experts. Why aren't I an expert again? Right, because knowledge is dangerous. So why does that person have the knowledge if it's so dangerous?

Knowledge is not fissile material: it can't hurt you if you don't let it, and it's not dangerous unless you use it to hurt people, so having it should never pose a problem, unless your intention is to use it to harm others.

Which, unfortunately, is usually the use some people reserve for it.

So, as the circular argument goes, why should you not have knowledge to protect yourself from those who would try to use it against you?

The goal is not to be bullet-proof, in an intellectual sense. It is to realize that there is no bullet.

There are occasions in your life where you will be physically attacked. I sincerely hope that these will be very few. You should, of course, never go looking for a fight, but people being people, fights can come to you.

There is no reason you should become a victim of violence. You should learn to defend yourself to the best of your abilities, in whatever self-defence method you choose, so that those who might want to hurt you do not have the opportunity to do so.

Your goal should never be one of revenge, or to seek out people to victimize. You should be able to preserve your physical body from harm, to defend those who cannot do so themselves, and this, always as a last resort.

I thought long and hard about the use of violence, its consequences on all people concerned, and I believe that there is no way to avoid it happening, sometimes. There are only methods of minimizing its use, and the contexts in which it is justified.

There should always be another way of dealing with a problem, if at all possible. If worst comes to worst, though, self-defence is the best option. No one should have the right to aggress you physically.

The End of Thinking Small

don't say this about many people, but Ayn Rand was a divisive enabler. Strong words coming from your father, I know. After everything I've written, it's clear that I have a penchant for a more social approach to human interaction.

Ayn Rand was an author who proned the opposite. She thought that the achievements of the individual were infinitely more important than that of the group.

She thought that greed and pride were the pinnacle of human qualities. To be fair, her feelings on the subject are understandable, since her parents' store was seized during her formative years by the Bolsheviks in the 1917 revolution.

I am surprised, though, that she never realized the irony of her philosophy: a system of thought (Randian) that was brought about as a means of revenge towards the movement (Bolshevism) that was fighting what could be construed as the pinnacle of her thought process (the Russian Monarchy).

Then again, she was probably too close to the subject to look at it objectively. In any event, since words have power and influence, that little thought experiment went out into the world (especially in the United States), and is slowly bringing a once great nation to its knees.

The germ of an idea she has sown, was planted deeply into the psyches of those who needed an excuse to let loose their baser instincts. It has been driving a wedge deeper and deeper into society, with some truly astonishing effect.

The ideological sons and daughters of a selfish and bitter woman have been spreading their bile and child-like petulance for quite some time now, quoting their guru as if she were something to be proud of. The institution which, of old, helped free the slaves is now there solely for the profit of the few.

Don't get me wrong, it has always been so to a certain degree, but in this case, it became endemic, unbridled, and legalized. Unless the education of the people who desire to seize power is altered, brought off the Randian road to destruction and its false sense of entitlement, no amount of course correction will redirect the giant elephant from its destiny with a tall cliff.

In any society where there is incredible inequality and lack of solidarity, bloodshed and misery will be the rule of law, always.

As much as individual pursuits are laudable and should be recognized for their greatness, most human endeavours require the support of the many to succeed.

Any architect worth their salt can design incredible structures. Let them try *building* them alone.

Any business-person with talent can control a company. Let them try without *employees*.

Any politician worth anything can gain political office. Let he or she try without garnering any *voters*. The whole of society works better when everyone is in it together, *period*.

Try driving a car while two people are vying for control of the steering wheel and you have very good chances of finding yourself in a ditch. Some might argue that only in times of great crises or disaster can people come together to do the right thing. Events in the past seem to indicate that this might be the case. Yet if the underlying social philosophy is that of the individualist, then only can they do so *in extremis*, and not to keep the ship of state away from the icebergs in the *first* place.

Being an individual does not preclude my participation in the projects of my country, or humanity, for that matter. Great people are needed to lead, and great people are needed to *participate* for their ideas to come to fruition. Everybody has a part to play, and every individual makes the whole greater for having done his or her part. It doesn't matter which end of the equation you decide you want to be a part of, as long as you participate. Let the mistakes of others help drive you in the other direction.

Social behavior is complex. I can only figure things out with what means I have at my disposal. I am filled with emotions and logic, I filter them through my body to accomplish what I want to, or can.

Depending on the goal I set for myself, I need to figure out how best to achieve it. Figuring things out is one of the things we as humans do best. We know how to make cars, we know how to build bridges, we know how to navigate the globe in ships, and we have sent probes to other planets, to name but a few.

All of the things that we figure out how to do, and build, are made up of complex parts. We had to invent tools to make these things, and fix them.

Imagine for a moment that I asked you to fix your car with only a screwdriver. If you know anything about cars, you might say that's impossible.

What about a beautiful painting? Paint me an incredible picture, with rainbows, as well as varied and complex scenery, while only using one colour. Same result.

Create a symphony, using one instrument, producing two notes. Ditto.

We cannot do very complex things using the single-purpose instruments, and in such a limited way as we have and as we do, so why is it possible to reduce humanity to: Good and Bad, or Good and Evil, or even the most ridiculous thought of all: "I did it all by myself!" If everything else in life is complex, how is it even conceivable that we could attempt to oversimplify human behaviour or our environment into such specific and unsatisfying groups?

It would be like saying that the Empire State Building is comprised of a *top* and a *bottom*, but that's it, nothing else. We, as a species, are able to adapt to almost anything, because we are made for survival. The tools we are given, which we have evolved, are neither Good, nor Bad, they just *are*. A tool is a tool until you use it, and the purpose you give it. Then you see what the results are. If you know nothing about cars and you decide to try to fix it yourself, the results may vary, but invariably, the odds are that you will fail.

The same thing goes for everything else around you. If you have not learned the most you can, or even the least bit possible about a certain subject, you cannot consider yourself an expert. You will therefore probably not accomplish very much good by attempting something with very little knowledge.

This is why knowledge is so important. All emotions and attitudes are important for our survival, that much is clear. As we grow into larger and larger societies, though, there are certain human traits that are more damaging than beneficial. They obviously served a purpose, or we would not possess them.

Even though we are unique individuals, we are now part of mega-structures we call societies. We are no longer groups of cave-dwellers, living ten to twenty in one tribe, and so much the better. We still have many of their individualistic, aggressive, and overly selfish traits, though. Those are traits which, if they become too commonplace in large societies, cause massive breakdown to the machine.

A society needs *all* of its members to work *together*, and not just for themselves, if it is to survive. By this I don't mean that everybody needs to be the same. Communism is a failure and a sham. Those who refuse to participate in the project called a Nation, though, either by laziness, hatred, greed, or any other reason they can conjure up, are the problems.

If you refuse to work even though you can, you're a problem.

If you don't want to pay your fair share of taxes, you're a problem.

If you hate all your neighbours because they are different from you, you're a problem.

If your prime motivator is money over people, you're a problem.

If you think you are somehow superior to all others, you are definitely a problem.

If you think lying and cheating your way to the top is okay, you are one of the biggest problems there are. So don't be a problem.

Be a solution.

Having positive, open traits helps perpetuate goodwill and honesty in a society. If you care about where you and your society are going, you will set the example. If you start seeing society as a type of eco-system, in which all its different members have a role to perform and a duty to one another, you have the ability to expand your influence and involvement.

Even though social interaction itself is complex, the tools you can adapt to simplify it will make it so that you can dedicate your time to other projects. Viewing the world in its many hues and tones and intricate variety is a part of that. The next big hurdle is to unite the world. Then to go beyond it. That's the end of thinking small.

Many Over Few

Every single person is unique. Through upbringing, surroundings, and even the genes that made us who we are, we're all different. Neither should anybody want to be the same. Imagine having conversations with millions of copies of yourself, all making the same conclusions and decisions! How terribly boring would that be (or potentially dangerous)?

Of course, as the joke goes, unique does not necessarily mean useful. Who says, though, that humans have a use? Only those who want to use them, of course. Your purpose, even within a group, should be your own – and when you will have found a direction that appeals to you, you will have found your purpose.

There are many different ways of pursuing goals, some negative, and some positive (depending on the criteria you use). I have the choice to promote myself over others. I can decide that the group takes precedent. I can be a selfish animal, or I can be an altruistic human being (that's how I see it, anyway).

If I choose to be altruistic, I promote the survival of my entire species. If I am selfish, I take what I can for myself, with no thought for the future and what my destructive actions entail. Eventually, it is not my actions alone that will define the fate of all mankind, but how many others decided to follow one path over the other.

Just like one cigarette won't kill you, but the two packs a day for twenty years just might. If everybody decides they, in their uniqueness, are better than the entire group and would benefit more from selfish acts that altruistic ones, they in effect decide to null and void the social covenant.

Like climbing a tower by removing the bricks that make its foundations along the way, I make it to the top in time to have it all fall down. My being unique has a ripple effect around me, in all that I do. Other unique individuals feel validated in their uniqueness when I am with them. How I behave will influence the manner in which they express their character.

The fact that I can promote the values of a group over an individual takes nothing away from the individual. If anything, when all individuals work together on a project, more people have the opportunity of seeing it accomplished than if they went it alone.

They are still free to decide how they want to be. Everybody is. The core never changes: I am a single person among millions of individuals. I can bring about sweeping evolution in thought, but only if others see the good in it. I can promote the individual as well as the group, since one is directly affected by the other.

I know that you are not just a purchaser of goods. You are a biological machine that feels and intuits, and needs validation in what you do. You need a sense of purpose, and challenges, to feed your mind and to lead a satisfying life.

For that you need to fight for it. To fight you can't go it alone. It basically comes down to that. Your independence depends on the help of others, as paradoxical as that sounds. To have a passion for life, you have to have the freedom to enjoy it. To have freedom you have to go beyond survival.

You might not be at that point, but others around you are, and as long as they are, they are not enjoying life for what it could be. If you are not fighting for the freedom you are enjoying, you should fight for the freedom others *could be* enjoying. That is what makes for a more equal society.

Music, the arts, sciences, philosophies, all come from the most unlikely sources. The more a person can go beyond basic survival to achieve a plateau of comfort, the better their chances are for adding to the human store of knowledge and competences. Leaving people behind to struggle for their lives is like throwing human potential to the trash can, and allowing misery to be a trifling matter.

It is an unconscionable act on my part to allow it to go on. Lifting any individual from the hell they are living should be one of my highest priorities, if I myself have the means to do so. If I consider myself human at all, I cannot stand idly by while the country I love lets its citizens slip through the cracks as if they were so much human garbage.

The resulting net effect would be that of having the disenfranchised join in the project that is the country, making them a positive addition to the group. I can't do that if I close my eyes to the world. I can't do that if my priority is what kind of stereo, computer, TV, or phone I will purchase next. I certainly can't do that if I care about myself, and no one else.

Why Learn?

You have needs, like any person. If you are not careful, though, you will do like most people and try to fulfill them with a veritable cornucopia of things that bring you nothing tangible. By tangible, I mean useful mental abilities.

As great as material possessions are, if you don't have a brain to back you up, there's not much you can enjoy in and of itself. The development of your mind will fuel your passions. If you wish to be a part of something, you *should* do so because it is your passion.

Realistically, there are things you'll have to do that are not enjoyable. These things, though, shouldn't be the main focus of your life. They should be the incidentals along the way. Everything you will do will have a certain amount of frustration involved.

The happiness you derive from that frustration will dictate whether or not you are doing what you enjoy.

For instance, your mother and I are raising you. I'm pretty sure it won't be a party every day, but all in all, the joy we will have in raising you will make up for all the less savory aspects we'll have to put up with.

Most importantly, the things which are most worthwhile to achieve, require hard work to get. It's all a matter of positive over negative perspective. If the balance is in the positive, you're good to go.

There are people out there who excel at their jobs, since they found that they were great at what they did, and enjoyed them to the fullest. The opposite is also true, and they do not love what they do, therefore have no motivation, therefore do a very poor job of it.

The things you will do because you have to, will not have the same flavour as the things you will do because you love to do them. It is a matter of attitude, to a certain degree. Another problem is, if I hate the process of learning something, I can't see that the end result is worthwhile. The process is just as important as the ends itself, since it is what will dictate how well I will perform the subject later on. I might hate the process because it is a chore I did not choose, or is difficult, or boring. If it is something I truly wish to know, I will take it upon myself to make it more fun to learn, since that is the best way for it to stick.

Learning Methods

sometimes forget that the learning process is a means to an end, and if I hadn't honed my patience, I might have given up entirely on a lot of things. Patience is one of the most important basic emotion-control methods you will have to learn. Without patience, I would spend all my money on *stuff* as soon as I had some, instead of waiting, saving, and buying more important things.

Without patience, I wouldn't even attempt to learn a language, or an instrument, or to get to know someone. I would only be searching for instant gratification, in all possible fields. I would miss out on some of the most wonderful things that I could do as a human.

All of these things are controlled by my brain, and my brain has almost infinite potential. If you say you have no patience, it is true. That does not preclude the fact that you could.

It is just an aspect of your mind you have a hard time exploring. If you say you cannot do something, that is also true. You do not have the tools yet to comprehend how you can do that thing. That by no means mean that you can never achieve those tools, it just means you have to work for them.

When I say: "I give up!" I close the door on a subject, and do not want to broach it again. I am tapping into my frustration and giving it a negative outlet because I find a subject too difficult. What I lack are the tools I need to comprehend the matter, therefore I abandon the whole project. Whereas it would be easy to go back and reanalyze the tools that I need to solve the problem so that I may understand it, I decide to close the lid on the whole affair as impossible.

I have done this many times, with many different subjects, and I now realize that the root of my thoughts were wrong. The basic thought pattern I was operating under was severely limiting my ability to learn. What I needed mostly was patience. The patience to try again and again until I understood what it was I needed to do, or how to do it better. Mostly, I lacked perseverance. As soon as something looked too tough, I gave up. Lastly, my laziness is what finished off what my lack of perseverance started. I was so good at procrastinating that I could avoid doing anything worthwhile.

These three traits are your worst enemy when you are attempting to learn something. They are inherent in everybody, and will ruin any learning experience.

Work hard on your patience, because it will keep you calm when all you want to do is throw your lessons to the wall.

Persevere, because giving up is for losers. You can't achieve anything if you give up. One of the more important aspects I neglected was love. By loving what you are doing, you are turning whatever it is into worthwhile and enjoyable endeavour.

Lastly, and very importantly, force yourself to do those things you have to do to achieve something. It is incredibly easy to waste your time, since that is what is expected of you from our leisure society, but it's a trap.

There is nothing wrong with taking a break and enjoying life. There is something wrong with thinking that any time not spent working is just a very long break. If you want to grow, you have to know. This learning process means that at some point in time, you will produce something of your own, not just enjoy the products of others.

Influence of Parents

Bad news for you, kiddos, you will grow up to be like your parents. Oh the horror! It is the inordinate fear of every child to be like their mom and dad (I think it's that whole prospect of not being a truly unique individual).

For good or ill, we will be your first examples of society at large. The microcosm of our family unit will prepare you for the larger world outside. I'm already giddy at the prospect of corrupting your fragile minds. It'll be payback for 2:00 AM feedings and diaper changes, as well as borrowing the car until all hours of the night.

For example, and this will be your case, as a child you will be naturally curious, exploring every possible thing your body will be able to do. We're ready for it. Bring it on. My parents understood my basic humanity, underlying my incredible lack of knowledge (we do too, don't worry).

I did things that no grown person would do, but would not do so for very long, since they weaned me from that behaviour. When I coloured on the walls, my mother made me wash them. I never did that again. Her reaction to my action was calm, composed, and made me realize that to my acts there were consequences.

My father's reaction to just about every misdemeanor was a smack to the butt with a wooden spoon. His reaction of frustration was externalized in a physical way in a method he was sure would create a desired result, according to his upbringing. I'm not sure what that may have done, psychologically, to me, but I do know that for a long time, people thought I was the most adorable and obedient child that there ever was.

Until I hit my teens and did absolutely the worst things I could, to catch up for lost time. On the one hand you have a measured response that teaches responsibility for one's actions, on the other you have physical violence to alter a behavior, inducing a fear response to every possible course of action, making me fearful of action, or even the thought of action.

Perhaps that could be one of the root causes of adolescent rebellion. Not having been educated in proper behavior through explanation may bring back all undesirable behavior at a later date, since much experimenting was not able to take place at a much younger time? Just a theory. I'm not saying either one is right or wrong, but we have to consider what we want from ourselves and what we want you to be.

Do we want you to obey in fear, or understand with peace?

We, as future parents, must decide what reaction will be most beneficial in the long run in counterpart to your behavior. They say you are the future, but you might as well be the past if nothing changes in our actions. As much as I love my parents (your grandparents), I want what is best for you. That's why I won't be reproducing every single behavior they manifested (if I can help it).

Before you let out a sigh of relief, keep in mind that it is hard *not* to reproduce the same patterns as our genitors. We are an image of them, and as our first teachers, they are our role-models, and forever after we unconsciously reproduce the family we had, for good or ill.

We don't choose a person, we choose characteristics. Our mate might not look at all like our mother or father, but they will have a similar mind, and we try to find that as much as we can, in the others we seek. In the end, we are a mind with a physical envelope, making its way through life and trying to profit the most we can from it before spreading the seed of our knowledge, our genes, our art, to the next generation and eternity.

It is our way of living forever. The methods we will use to raise you will affect you in positive and negative ways, and how you will react will dictate the methods you will wish to use to raise your own children, and live your own life.

Life in Short

was reading a book recently, and the question asked was: "Is man good?" I thought what would have been a better question would have been: "What is a human?"

Here is my own answer to this riddle, since answers seem to vary wildly from person to person: A Human is adaptable, following the flow, rethinking his options when his flow is blocked. That, to me, is the basis of humanity.

Everything else that follows comes from that basic thought. Let me tell you a story, and you can decide whether it sounds right or not.

You wake up, one morning, and find that you have been born. For the first little while, you look around, and see that the world you have been thrust into is under the control of those who have you in their care.

You are alone, defenceless, and depend solely on the mercy of those who will take care of you. You have needs, and express them in the ways that you can. As you develop, you devise new methods to acquire the attention and love of those people who care for you.

You realize, one day, that you are in a boat. It is a small boat, following the current of a large river. Your caregivers follow the flow of the river, directing the boat, paddling when they have to course correct, and you take in their methods very intently. It is the only thing you can do, at this point.

Sometimes, other people join your family in your boat, and their interactions with you give you different perspectives on the flow of the river. Inevitably, the boat hits rapids, or rocky patches in the river, and your parents are there to guide the boat around or through those trouble spots. You start noticing that there are other boats on the river as well, and that it is much wider than you first believed.

With this new information, you begin to ponder about the nature of the inhabitants of the other boats. They accost yours, and the children from the other boats join you on yours, and you get to play with them, discovering new people.

As time goes by, you get to leave the boat on your own, and join other kids on a bigger one, where adults feed you information. The information you receive helps you understand the possibilities and nature of the river you are all on, drifting sometimes quickly, sometimes slowly, but always forward.

Eventually, you reach your teens, and the information you've been getting from your parents and the orders you have been getting about the navigation of the river seem oppressive. You are eager to jump in your own boat. You know that you are ready to go out onto that river and face those rapids, and rocks all by yourself.

You see that there are millions of different boats on this river, and that it is not really a river at all, but an ocean, where all the boats are of different shapes, and sizes, and have all sorts of captains.

Each captain has different crews, depending on what association they make with each other. Some band together as nations, and have immense boats, some are banded together as religious beliefs. There are business boats, there are pleasure boats, there are boats where the crew are frightfully angry at the world around them.

Fights break out on the boats, sometimes, when the captain and his mates decide that they deserve much more than what the crew are getting. After all, aren't they the ones guiding the boat? Sometimes they decide to take too much, and the crews suffer, and rebel against their captains.

They are then removed from the post they were entrusted with, since they are no longer doing what their intended job was. It is always to lead their crew down the river, unharmed. This small fact is often forgotten, by the crews, and by the captains.

Once in a while, some mutineers come up with interesting ideas about the nature of the body of water that drives them forward. They give it attributes, names, feelings, and desires. They speculate as to what comes after the river. Is it a dark hole? Is it an infinite body of water?

They write down and communicate their speculations to their fellow travellers. Some finding them interesting ways of contemplating the water, take what has been said as proof, or truth, about the nature of the flow.

They add their own addendums and modifications to the stories they have received. They ask: who turned on the water in the first place? Is he or she good? Since it is such a wonderful flow, with amazing things to see along the way, the creator of this river must be great indeed.

They band together and build beautiful boats to contain the worshippers who adore the flow of water. Others contemplate the water and see a completely different creator. When they argue with others who are passengers of the other boats, they are ready to kill (and often do), those who do not believe in their origins of the creator of the flow.

Humans on boats have been killing each other for millennia, since they have a hard time understanding each other. They do so because they do not want to get on the other peoples' boats and see their points of view, preferring to stay ignorant of the beliefs of the other crews and captains.

They come along on the river and capsize the weaker boats, or enslave those aboard them to do their hard work, so they can enjoy the flow of the river more easily, in more comfort.

Once in a while, captains create giant battleships and go about destroying other boats that surround them, to control them, gain the resources on the boats, and live more comfortable lives themselves.

The surrounding boats retaliate by building their own armadas and defending their own fragile ships as best they can. All this time, their main goal is to understand the flow, and to travel it more easily, with the skills they have.

There are more and more people born, and the giant ships get quicker and better. There are often catastrophes on the boats, where everyone gets into arguments over who is right, and who is wrong in the direction the boat is going.

They will try to turn the boat around and attempt to paddle in the opposite direction of the flow. This makes the ship wobble and weave, and makes it vulnerable to attack from the other ships, or the flow itself.

That is usually when they pounce, and destroy the crew, taking what they want. Great ships can sometimes hit great rocks, or too strong rapids, and the entire boat itself is almost smashed to smithereens.

The survivors have to think long and hard as to how they will overcome the terrible things they have to face. Some decide to leave the giant ship, build a raft and go off on their own, seeking more hospitable waters.

The remainder sometimes see that it is only through their cooperation that they will be able to rebuild their once great ship. They keep the good lessons they learned from the past, and get rid of the ones that made them so vulnerable in the first place, and build a better ship.

They understand that on an inhospitable ocean, the best thing they could possibly do is to share their resources and work together. They must find good captains who will not abuse their power, and steer the ship in the direction of the flow, anticipating what will come next.

They develop good relations with the other boats around them, so that whatever storm may come, or hardship befalls them, they will have a friend who will be able to help them out, just as they would them.

They must be wary of the greedy captains who control massive ships, but have no choice but to contend with them.

At some point in the past, crew-members of different ships began to analyze the waters they were in. They analyzed the skies at night. They tinkered with substances they would find along the way, and began to posit different questions than the ones that had been asked before.

They started showing these discoveries to those who were directing the ships. At first they were thought to be mad, and burned for their heresy (a tricky thing to do on a boat). Eventually, enough crewmembers were able to prove the same things as those who were killed for their blasphemy and the captains had to somewhat begrudgingly admit that they were right.

At some point, a great many of these crewmembers developed their own branches of collected knowledge, and helped the other crewmembers build better boats, and everybody's lives improved.

Those who refused to admit that those scientists were right, had a stake in the status quo. They could not freely admit that science was any better than faith, since that would be tantamount to admitting that they were, in fact, wrong.

Even though the improvements that were brought about through the analysis of the flow were all around them, they could not bring themselves to see it that way. Why should this be so? The answer is as easy as it is strange.

Age takes precedence over truth. What I mean is that, the Faith boat had been around for so long, that it was made more reliable for having stood the test of time.

Another harsh reality is that everything is a battle of ideas. It is not the right ideas that win, but those that garner the most followers. This continues even today, with certain scientists duking it out in their research papers over supremacy of an idea.

Here are the basic mechanics of humanity, as I see them, after this beautiful story: Humanity is not Good and it is not Bad. It has an appetite for selfishness and altruism which, depending on how they are fed, will make it into an adult that will be more or less responsible for its environment (and by environment, I mean everything around it).

As genes play a major role as well in the human development, the interpretation it has of its reality will be strongly influenced by its basic building blocks. I sincerely think, though, that the nature and direction we attribute to the flow of life determines how we treat each other and our reality.

The most potent genetic defect we may have inherited was our ability to work as a group, and it is that which, combined with our ego, our emotions, and our logic, create the dynamics that we employ to better maneuver the flow of life and time.

We choose, as a group, where we will go. We allow captains to drive the ships of states and nations for our benefits, so that we can follow the flow more comfortably, and more easily.

We choose the path of least resistance, and when we hit rocks in our lives, we take stock, look around us, and figure out what we have to do to get back into the flow. If we keep hitting the same rocks, we are simply paddling backwards, and the current keeps bringing us back to those same obstacles.

The quicker we realize this, the easier it is to get over them. There are navigation maps, called *knowledge*, that we acquire while we go down that river, and the more we get, the better the ride is, and the bumps smooth out more quickly.

When we don't, we just keep hitting those same rocks, over and over and over again, until we either figure out what we have to accomplish to overcome them, or our boat capsizes and we are lost.

Not quite, perhaps, but you get the idea. The bigger the boat, the more interests are at play, and those who carry more influence with the captains will have their wills done, even though that may not be the best solution for the crew.

But as long as the crew says nothing and suffers in silence without taking action, they are not taking the power into their own hands. They are not changing the course of the boat on their flow, or their captain. We can therefore be captains, and have the care of our crew, or be the crew, and help the captain, but each is dependent on the attentiveness of the other, and as soon as one is not pulling his weight, or abusing what has been entrusted to him, the whole ship suffers, and may be lost.

Yet the flow will not stop for them, because it does not care at all for the ships that skim its surface.

I am a bundle of emotions and thoughts, all dancing together, some stronger, some lighter, depending on my moods, my thoughts, my desires. They are a mixture of chemicals within my body which are released depending on my thoughts and moods. Think of different air-freshener scents being released in your house depending on your how you feel. If you are happy, it smells like spring. If you are angry, it smells like burnt toast. If you are afraid, it smells like dust.

They are not smells, but actual emotions in chemical form, all emanating from your mind. Some are controllable, some are simple reaction, but each one can be identified, if I take it upon myself to do so. My mind is arranged in such a way as to be pliable and elastic.

When you say: "I changed my mind." You absolutely did. A connection of thoughts, attached to one another was let go of, and you put another connection in place. You do it consciously and unconsciously, but you do it nonetheless.

When I become used to thinking a certain way, I reinforce the pathways that are travelled the most, and make them wider, somewhat like building a highway over a secondary road, which used to be a dirt track.

This can lead to interesting problems later on in life, especially if, as a child, I was not taught empathy, respect, kindness, honesty, or any one of the things I consider positive traits in us. I require very little positive traits to function *correctly* in a society, but I require more and more for that society to function optimally.

Consider the problems you might encounter in a developing society which believes in respect, but does not place a very high mark on honesty. You might get a society riddled with corruption.

In any event, all the positive traits are usually what I call outward-facing ego traits, or open. The negative traits are inward-facing ego traits, or closed. Take altruism, for example. It is an outward-facing ego trait, because you are taking from yourself, to give to others, and it is the act of giving that gives you the tiny jolt of pleasure in your mind.

Theft is the opposite: You get the jolt of pleasure by taking from others. So, I consider positive traits the ones that are open to others, and create pleasure in us because they create pleasure in others, or gratitude, or some form of positive reinforcement.

The inward-facing ego needs not cause any pleasure in others, but is its own reward. So, knowing this, you can think of every possible *positive* trait we have as being mostly outward-facing ego, or open type emotions. These are the traits that helped us start to develop larger and larger societies, through better communication, altruism, honesty, justice, loyalty, kindness, positive reinforcement, non-violence (self-control), equality, and respect. As well as a host of other positive traits that we see in the societies that thrive the most in the world.

As no man (or woman) is an island, it is through the positive, constructive help we have given each other through the centuries that we have come to be who we are today. Imagine where we would be if we had not been so busy trying to destroy each other?

I digress. There will always be those who will try to take advantage of others, and do everything they can to sabotage progress. They should be identified, and not allowed to pursue their agendas, for they are the ones who, through their selfish and destructive acts, tear down society.

We let them do this because we are not informed, or think that kindness means not taking action to stop the destructive nature of others. They are our aggressive opponents, and they should not be given the reins of power, or industry. They should not have power over us, and our trust. If we know how to recognize them, we are one step closer to stopping war or abuse of power.

It is within our power to stop them, and if we know for what we fight, we can and should use force as a legitimate tool to disrupt or stop oppression and aggression.

Drugs

W hen I say that I am "set in my ways," I have let the system of my mind become a rigid and unchangeable tool, and have decided to do so of my own free will. "Nothing will make me change my mind" is true, since I have decided that those connections will stay the way they are.

Sometimes I come across an idea so powerful that all the relays in my mind are in a tizzy, and the sparks fly, as when I may be high on drugs, or drunk, or make a life-changing realization.

All reactions within the mind being chemical, I may sometimes drown myself in substances to activate parts of my mind for pleasure, or some sort of sensory overload.

Magic mushrooms or psylocibin are a poison that can be taken in small doses which have the properties of inducing visual hallucinations, sometimes of a geometric variety. They have been used in the past by religious figures to attain *oneness with the Universe.*

I have no clue as to their success, but it has been scientifically proven to reduce brain activity and improve receptivity towards the oneness I may feel about my reality. Marijuana makes you peaceful. Alcohol is a depressant, so at first it will calm you down. Too much, and it will make you agitated. Taken in too high doses for a long enough time, and it may cause permanent brain damage.

Everything you do has an effect on you (and those around you, as well), great or small. Sometimes you can get addicted to the effect, most of the time because it is almost instantly felt, and creates a dependence to it within your body.

I gave up on all those things just because of my dependence. I don't think most drugs are good or bad *in and of themselves*, but the use you make of them, and the effect they have on your body, are.

There are words to describe every chemical release, in every combination possible, which your body produces. Oxytocin is involved in orgasm, pair bonding (love), helping during and after childbirth, as well as breast-feeding. A release of serotonin causes sleepiness, regulates mood, as well as appetite. Dopamine is related to the reward-system of the brain.

There are many more chemicals in your body, and every possible way you react will unleash a chemical reaction inside you, and this is normal. This is how your body reacts to *everything*.

Depending on socially accepted norms, we sometimes seek out the substances that will activate the pleasure centres that we have a hard time unlocking on our own.

We use alcohol to lower inhibitions in a sociable setting because we have forgotten that, as a child, we were less shy and could make friends just by saying: "Do you want to play with me?" The fear of rejection stops us from being that open, but alcohol lowers our embarrassment levels and our fear levels, and we can be more open.

Marijuana is a crutch for relaxation and deep thought. Even if it is purely silly deep thought, it makes people access parts of their creative minds that they have difficulty accessing without it. This is one of the reasons artists often use it.

Cocaine makes people fearless and driven, so you often see it in business settings, where money managers must make tough and quick decisions as well as the fact it's extremely expensive. Overdosing can kill you.

Peyote is the button of a cactus plant that is found in the Southern United States and Mexico that is said to bring people on spiritual journeys.

The interesting aspect about all mind-altering substances is that all they do is overload the brain with chemical reactions we cannot induce on our own.

What if you knew your body well enough to do it yourself, without damaging drugs to ruin your pocketbook and your health (as well as the legal aspect, of course)?

What if, instead of drinking an energy drink, all you had to do was access a part of your brain and you could turn on the adrenaline for a little while.

Even though I myself cannot do it to the extent that I am entirely stoned, I can induce a nice buzz. It has been done by others, and more as well. The only thing that makes the experience less attractive is that it takes a bit longer to master than rolling and lighting a spliff or opening a bottle.

You might wonder then what the attraction might be. Well, for one thing, doing it without outer forms of chemicals means it's free. It also means that it is not illegal, unless someone wants to make thinking illegal.

You can snap out of it instantly, whereas you have to wait for other substances to leave your body on their own, after a few hours. The best part, though, is that it causes no physical damage to you, like illicit substances invariably will.

Granted, my developing these thoughts was because I too like to escape from reality once in a while, but I don't become anti-social, or violent, harm myself or others, and I end up feeling even better afterwards.

Learning to do these things on your own will help you avoid a lot of unpleasantness later on. My purpose in telling you about drugs is not for you to go out and try all of them at once.

Even though the feelings they induce are incredible, the damage they can do can be as well. Although some, taken in small doses can be very pleasant, many are highly addictive and dangerous.

Some can take you on incredible journeys of inner discovery, but the vast majority are taken to perform a task of social integration and instant gratification you could do yourself without their help.

In the long run, any mind-altering drug, whether it be cigarettes, alcohol, coffee, or any of the illicit kind, only hurt your body more than help it. If I had read what I am about to write several years ago, I would have laughed at myself for my straight-lacedness. Whether it is through my conscious realization about my abuse of some of these, or never doing them at all, they are not and should never be *necessary* for your happiness.

I can tell you though, other things you can do to feel well. These are a few things I do, to feel great:

I let go of my hate. Every once in a while, anger or frustration builds up inside me. I can't help it, I'm human. The mental chemicals involved with hatred are a pretty bad buzz, and they exist whether you are thinking about them or not.

When I realized that I didn't hate the people around me, that I actually only carried hate inside me, it changed my outlook. When I learned that I couldn't change anyone but me, it changed the way I viewed others, and when I accepted all this as fact, not just knowledge, I became at peace.

You cannot change, improve, or alter a single person for the better but yourself. You might ask, then, why I am explaining this to you, if I do not want to change you. I don't. I want to tell you how I evolved myself. I expect nothing of you. I can only care for myself and the people around me, and you are one of those people.

You can only do what you can do. What or how you decide to do it is entirely out of my hands, and I fully accept it. All I can do is try to be a better person, according to what I know, and leave the rest in the hands of those who are dealing with their own reality.

Through it all, though, I love you, and you should remember that. There will come a time, as well, when you will consider using drugs and alcohol. We will have those talks when you are ripe for them. As I said, there are not many things that are inherently bad, but what you do with them.

There are, however, reactions to every action, and those you can have under the influence of narcotics or mind-altering substances can be fairly extreme. Please take the time to question your mom and I about the effects of all these substances *before* indulging in them.

Forgiveness

Two of the most important things that you can do in your life are to forgive others, and to forgive yourself. The third is to actually go out and tell those you may have hurt or offended that you are sorry for the harm you have done.

This does not guarantee forgiveness. It may not do anything at all. What *they* do with that information thereafter is out of your hands, but you at least took the steps to show them your emotions.

Every little anger bubble we create within our minds is a little wasp's nest that buzzes at its own intensity and rhythm. If you have a lot of anger, you have a bunch of these little bastards in different areas of your mind. They are inevitable.

Life being what it is, there is always frustration, and it leads to hate. The hatred gets associated with events, people, and places, and then you have it stuck in your mind. You go back to it sometimes, and you poke the wasps nest with a stick.

Sure enough, it buzzes angrily, and if you poke it long enough, it takes over your entire brain, until you stop poking it with your thoughts.

There are many things you can do about these little buggers. You can leave them alone, but they won't go away. You can poke at them, but that only brings out your hatred and negative emotions. Unless you're a sucker for punishment, that is also a bad option. My last offering is the most difficult choice you have, but truly the most satisfying.

Why is it the most difficult? Because it asks you to swallow your pride and let go of your hate. I love my hate. I carry it around like a medal. I won that hate fair and square. Why would I ever want to give it up? It is eating your brain, that's why.

297

The more time you spend with your hate, the more you think that that is what life is all about. Remember, we are what we think, and we project our reality around us. The same can be said for fear, or lust, or gluttony, or material possessions. Anger, though, is the most destructive.

It's the emotion that controls our impulse to kill, to hurt, to destroy. Every time I let my hate take over, very bad things happen to either myself or people around me. That qualifies it for a nice big leash. Patience is the leash that tempers anger, but forgiveness is its destroyer. When I forgive my enemies (I've had some, and so will you, no matter how wrong that thought is), I put my mind to rest.

When I commit an act that I myself reprove, I will regret it all the time, until I let it go. When I ask for forgiveness, I show that I feel sorry for my actions, and that wasps nest that I had been holding for however long goes dark and no longer bothers me. Every time I do this, a weight is lifted off my shoulders. I very much do feel lighter, and yes, I get a mental buzz from it.

All these problems related to anger and what I held inside me were problems that I had created and blindly refused to fix, so they stayed there, obstinately, and refused to go away. When I faced them, instead of ignoring them or making them stronger, I made those *problems* go away.

The events are still there, but the emotions attached to them no longer are. Yes, others will appear to take their place, but it doesn't matter, since I now know how to deal with them. Every negative emotion or action I take, either against myself or others has an opposite action I can take to remedy the situation.

Those are the basic tenets of religions, they are what have brought people together for the past several thousand years, and helped them understand their problems, and solve them in the best way they could. The *appetites* that we have, either physical or mental, can very often get out of hand. It was those early philosophers, trying to build larger coalitions of people, in an age where population and organization were beginning to become a factor in the success or failure of their group, that posited solutions to our natural tendencies. Most early organized religions preach more or less the same basic tools for societal integration.

The fact that we now call them *ethics* instead of *morals* changes nothing about their origins or natures. Whether we attribute them to a Maker or to man, the end result is the same: we need an emotional education to help us deal with life's natural tendencies of making us selfish, ignorant, piggish, lustful, hateful, spiteful, base, unethical creatures.

Yes, we got all those positive social attributes from the desire to *become* like prophets and deities ourselves. Shouldn't we hold onto them as being positive social traits to value, instead of throwing them out as being as outdated as the institutions that birthed them?

I am not a proponent of organized religion, but I do give a respectful nod to the philosophies that eventually became those institutions.

People have been trying to push one philosophy or another on others from the beginning of thought and speech. People have come to self-realization through various means in the past, and have tried to teach them in the way they thought was appropriate. Pure ideas have been hijacked by selfish people for their own ends since before Jesus was crucified, and yet it remains that we pursue an ideal.

One of unity, by any means necessary. I have given up on the idea of unity at *any* cost. It is never ever worth dying for any ideal. It is only worth living for one.

Once you realize that no ideal is worth dying for, that you can't bring forth positive from negative, ever, you change how you think about everything, and your mind goes haywire, because you have never been able to accept everything. You have never been able to love yourself entirely.

Once this step is achieved, you can do anything. Why do I say anything? Because you can only fully enjoy doing what you love. If you love everything, as you accept and love yourself, then that means you can easily learn and accept everything.

Don't expect to sleep for a few days, because the realizations keep coming in waves. It is a trip you would not believe. A conscious body and mind elation of pure positive emotions. It is very difficult to hate afterwards, because you accept everything as possible, and hating feels like going back to being a person you no longer are. Therefore everyone has changed, since you have.

You have serenity.

As I mentioned before, every time you remove a wound from your mind, by apologizing to the people you may have harmed, you physically feel yourself getting lighter and lighter. You then no longer want to add wounds, since that would bring you back down. Why destroy all the hard work, right?

It is thereafter very hard *not* to want to help people, or somehow slip them a nugget of positive information that could help them in a dilemma.

Imagine for a moment you had been a battery that had both a positive and negative charge, and depending on the situation, you would discharge either negative or positive energy. What if by doing so, you transferred the charge to someone else. You give someone positive energy every time you do something positive, and negative energy in the other case.

What if you realized that you could be always positively charged, and only transfer positive energy, wouldn't that be great? Here is the kicker, though. You might think: "What if I transfer all my positive energy? What's left?" That's not how it works. You're not really a battery at all. When you give your positive energy, a lot of the time, it comes back in the form of positive energy from others as well.

That is at the heart of it, what getting in touch with your mind entails. You can be anybody you want, if you want to be. You can have any *charge* you want. You can spread any *charge* you want. But if you had the choice, and you knew that by harming others all you did was harm yourself with your negative charge, and that on the opposite end, if you only had a positive charge you only spread positive energy, and that you gained energy every time you did so, what would you choose?

The only real difference is that the pursuit of the positive takes time and effort, and will possibly make you content in your life. Allowing yourself to naturally fall into the negative is easy and requires no effort, but will allow you to be unsatisfied, and will grant you no complete peace for as long as you live.

Here I am not talking about *happiness.*

Happiness is an emotion we feel when joy is triggered by a reaction. It is a chemical that is spread through your body in times of elation. It cannot be a continuous state of being, or you would be exhausted all the time. You can, however, be constantly satisfied, content, at peace, and accepting. These are not neutral feelings. Neutrality means absolutely no feeling whatsoever, and borders on complacency. What you might feel is a desire to do good, or positive to others.

When I was a kid, my parents taught me a language. At first, I was not very good at it. Eventually, with practise, trial and error, I got to know a few words. As time went by, I began to fill my mind with the languages that surrounded me, as I tried to comprehend and be understood by my surrounding. Eventually, it was as if a floodgate had been opened, and all the knowledge I could want about that language was as easily acquired as I breathed.

The same process is inherent in absolutely every undertaking. Everything is difficult at first, but then, as the pieces begin to fall into place, you are able to intuit the mechanisms that underpin the machine you are trying to discover, whether it is the controls of a video game, or riding a bike, or any activity whatsoever.

What should make learning something enjoyable is the fun you get out of the process. What further enhances the process is the things you can do *after* you have mastered the art and begin to show our own mastery within the medium.

Who can honestly say, that even without knowing the art of skateboarding, they are not impressed by the likes of Tony Hawk? Or maybe I do not know much about music, but I can still be awed by the mastery of certain musicians, like Jimi Hendrix or John Frusciante. Whatever the medium may be, there are people who are willing to give their all to acquire the skills necessary to leave their mark, and it is extraordinary to think that we, with no doubt whatsoever, could do the very same things if we applied ourselves.

All it takes is a first step.

Then a second.

The daunting mountain of achievement that you see before you will only get smaller as you progress. The fear is caused by seeing only the peak. If you only concentrated on every step of the journey, and took comfort in every little step you took along the way, you would not see the impossibility of the task. Eventually, you will get to the peak of the mountain you choose to climb. You will plant your flag in its craggy top, and wonder: "What's next?" The most satisfying answer I can give you is: more mountains to climb and best.

The Body

The last, and most important part that you should look after is your body. For better or for worse, it is the only thing that you will truly possess until the day you die. How you treat it will determine how well you will live your life.

There are things you will have no control over, that will damage you. It is the things you have control over that you should care about. What you eat, and how much of it, how you exercise, what stimulus you give it, what poisons you put in it, all these things will determine your success at every stage of your life.

Of course, you should push your limits. Of course, you should see what you are capable of. Your body can take a lot of abuse, and keep on ticking. The question is, for how long will you be able to enjoy it until it becomes sick and seriously harms you?

If you do things that interrupt its natural healing capabilities often enough, this may happen pretty quickly. There is nothing wrong with indulging in sugary or greasy foods once in a while, but if these are the main staples of your diet, you won't be able to enjoy your bodies' litheness for very long.

Watching television and playing videogames is great! Doing it *all the time* means that you do very little working out, though. That may result in your feeling sluggish, and subject to a weak immune system.

Smoking cigarettes and marijuana *feel* awesome! They give you a killer buzz. Unfortunately, one has also been proven to cause cancer, the other increases the risk of schizophrenia in youth.

Drinking also gives you a great feeling. Too much and for too long, and you might get cirrhosis of the liver, brain damage, or help you do things you might regret.

Staying up all night is great for partying. The downside is that you feel tired all the time. There are any number of ways to enjoy your life. The really fun ones, when abused, have detrimental effects on your body and mind.

I won't try to discourage you from doing things (except for smoking cigarettes or doing hard drugs), since you have to live your life. Not everything is a huge downer that should be avoided, BUT! Just remember that the choices you make today will affect the person you will become tomorrow, or not.

It is said that your body is a temple. Try treating it that way and it will house you in good health for the rest of your life. No slight deviance will destroy your temple, only repeated unrelenting assaults. Be kind to yourself and your self will be kind in return.

Meditate, exercise, do yoga, feed yourself healthy foods, rest well, do regular medical checkups, these are simple things you can do to ensure that you will have proper use of your body for the rest of your life. Respect your body and the bodies of others. No single person is the same as another. Don't judge other people's bodies, and concentrate on what you wish to do with yours. Love the one you have, and do with it what you can.

Fact Versus Faith, and Beyond

know this is a lot to take in, and you might even find better ways of doing things that I did. To this I say: Awesome! You should try to be better than your old man. I'm here to make you ready for life. You have to live it, in the best possible way you can. Your mom and I promise you this, though: We will always be there for you, in *spirit*, if not in body. We will always listen to what you have to say. If we don't know the answer to a question, we will go find the answer together. We swear to never abuse your body or your mind, or let others do harm to you either. We swear to raise you right, and let you become the person you want to be, with as many advantages as we can manage to give you. We will support you in all your positive endeavours, and try to talk you out of some of the shadier or dumber things you will consider doing. One thing we know for a fact, is that through all that you will experience, we will love you, with all our hearts, unequivocally, and without restraint, for as long as you live, because that's what being human is all about.

For the past two thousand years, Western civilization has lived within the moral confines of Faith, as the directing line of all its activities. The belief in a higher power both gave purpose to those who believed, and used the fear of terrible retribution if those who did strayed from the very clear path that was set out for them.

The structure of religious doctrine, though, could not bear the advent of questioning minds unsatisfied with the official lines of the church. Being a closed system, there was no room within its structures for answers other than: "God did it," or, "That is God's will."

Nevertheless, curiosity won over the strict edicts of Church pronouncements, and we came into an age of discovery and research into the unknown. Superstition, the belief in magical powers and miracles, seemed to be leaving us.

Here is the big problem, though. Superstition is still with us. The only thing that we got rid of, when we killed God, was a clear direction for humanity.

You see, the scientific method, or, empirical research, is only a method. It is a means to clarify what is unknown to us. It only provides answers, not direction.

Religion, as falsely based as it was, provided direction, but no real answers.

So we come to a quandary: Which do you choose, as your directing line? Do you want answers, with no direction, or the opposite? That was, and is, for many, the trouble of leaving the Faith. Why leave comfort and a false sense of Truth, when I can imagine I've got all the answers in one book, no matter how false?

So now we have these great debates being had is the arguments of Fact versus Faith. The trouble lies with the false equivalency of faith having as much *value* as Fact, as if it were just another type of *belief*. It's not even in the same ball park. Even though Fact is a belief to a certain degree, it is one in something that is testable and provable, over and over. That is why, to me, and to a great segment of the human population, science is held to have more Truth than Faith, at least in the arena of human *knowledge*.

Thinking logically on the subject, you can see that science keeps making new discoveries about the world around us, pinpointing new details about the mechanics of the Universe. If Faith had the capabilities of doing these things for us, but Science had tried to hold us back, we would have put our faiths in... Faith. But like I said, Faith is not about Truth, but about being sheltered from it. Its main positive side is giving people *purpose*, and a handbook for living well in large groups, not Truth in any tangible sense.

Science is helping us discover what lies hidden, and brings us closer to verifiable, empirical Fact. For that, I hold it in higher regards than I do other methods of *discovering truth*. This doesn't mean that Faith or Belief is *wrong*, in a universal sense. It only means that those who put their Faith in an all-encompassing belief in areas that are provably false holds them back, even though they have *some* very good values by which to live. It is the premise that an omnipotent being created and commands them which enslaves them. You can't search for answers with a blindfold on.

Human methods of analysis keep evolving through time. It is just as important to have good values by which we live our lives, as logical methods to seek out the deeper truths of our reality. You can live your life with pure logic, which has no ethical direction, or with pure belief, which ignores facts, as many do. But, it is much better to both have a good purpose, using ethics as your guiding light, within the framework of scientific discovery.

Here's the problem: there are no clearly defined guides to existence for the Atheist. What we have is the leftovers from the Judeo-Christian era (which, I have to admit, have some good to them), and the scientific method. What Atheists lack is purpose, since, avowedly, existence has none inherent to it.

Whereas before, God was all-powerful and commanded us, his creations, we have now been left to deify whatever our *appetites* command.

What the Judeo-Christian faiths defined as Sins, those terrible things we weren't ever supposed to do if we didn't want to end up in Hell, (the horrible place you supposedly went to if you did wrong), are in fact natural human appetites gone out of control. Let's see what they are, shall we? There were, in order: Lust, Gluttony, Greed, Sloth, Wrath, Envy, and Pride. These were considered the worst of the worst things you could do in Christian religion. They practically guaranteed an eternal stay in Hell, a place where you would get tortured on a daily basis, forever and ever.

We've known for a while that we weren't created out of whole cloth in a day. The evidence against this simplistic view is overwhelming. Only people who live in a fantasy world in their heads believe this anymore.

So what are we? We are an evolved form of something that preceded us. We are animals. The difference between us and other animals on the planet is that we've developed tools that have brought us a kind of supremacy over the planet.

What, then, are sins, if they aren't edicts against horrible acts from a benevolent and terrifying omnipotent being? They are our natural appetites gone too far.

Philosophers have been around for a very long time. They noticed what they thought were positive and negative traits in humanity. The starting point that they took into consideration was society, the gathering of more than one tribe within city walls. It was important to have everyone get along and be healthy, so that the whole could thrive. After all, there were other societies happening elsewhere, and it was important for them to survive in the face of competition.

You have to remember that these societies lived without science, therefore, a lot of survival depended on self-restraint. They were the obsessions that turned you away from your true purpose of worshipping God.

Take Lust, for example. If you gave in to your sexual impulses, there was a high chance of fathering numerous unwanted children, causing havoc within society. The other negative trait was the spreading of disease. With contraceptives today, we have solved part of the problem.

Gluttony meant that you ate more than you should, potentially making you obese, therefore less productive. This was catastrophic in agrarian societies which needed able-bodied men and women to take care of the fields. The main downside of this trait today is the general lack of health of the individual and the strain it causes on the health system.

Greed is the taking of more than your fair share. This caused widespread poverty and the loss of vigor within society, since most people were struggling to eat. When a few take the lion's share, there isn't much left for the masses. This hasn't changed much, except that now we worship this trait in the form of unbridled capitalism.

Sloth, generalized laziness, is closely related to gluttony. When people don't do their share of the work, it's up to others to pick up the slack. This, too, hasn't changed much. There are still people who believe that they do not need to work to receive money from the government. This is much different from those who absolutely can't work, who deserve to receive money for their survival. Until we have a system where people can survive without having to work, we have no choice but to do our best with what we have now.

Wrath, or, getting furiously angry, can lead to terrible acts, and is frowned upon as antisocial behavior. This, too, hasn't changed much over time. It can lead to any number of crimes of passion, including murder, which can engender retribution, starting a potential never-ending cycle of violence.

Envy, when you want what others have, means that you can't ever appreciate what you *do* have. You're constantly trying to compete with others to have what they do, and therefore can never know true satisfaction.

Pride, crowing about your won achievements, is frowned upon because it makes others jealous and angry. It swells your head and makes you believe you are invulnerable. You then make mistakes that make you realize there wasn't much to be proud of in the first place.

So, all in all, these are methods of control, pure and simple. Thing is, I believe they are still valid, since we do live in society, and we should try to get along, as much as possible. Those things that I listed before in a previous section are the opposites of these Deadly Sins – what we call virtues. They were created as a counterpoint to the natural inclinations of human nature toward self or other destructive tendencies, to help us live in large groups.

We might think that having laws in place can keep us honest and on the right path. The thing is, laws were created for those who absolutely refused to live within the social contract. The basis is yours, mine, and everybody else's behavior. For that we have to have a generalized agreement on how we should act. For now we live on the fumes of Judeo-Christian self-restraining laws. We need to strengthen those pacts with society to ensure that there is not further breakdown.

What we need is *purpose* for our society, not just inner or overt laws to govern how we live on a day to day basis. We don't need more police to keep us in check. We need to check ourselves.

It is as if we go to work every day and put a brick over another, until the end of the day. We return the next day and see that all the bricks have been taken away, and we have to start again.

Before, life was a lot simpler, albeit false: You were simply trying to make your way into Heaven. You worked every day to become worthy of entering the Pearly Gates. Not so anymore. Now we have let those appetites become our new goals, and we bathe in them like virtues. We really do need goals more lofty than stuffing our faces, making the most money, and having sex on a daily basis.

There *has to be* more.

Let's start with the basics: Society. Society hasn't changed that much in millennia: we still want to have decent jobs that pay well, have kids, and grow old, and not fall into the gutter and die penniless.

Why don't we work on a plan to: eliminate poverty, increase education, limit environmental destruction, and once that is done, promote space exploration and planetary colonization?

Don't laugh, they used to say flight was impossible. Besides, with a growing population and degrading environment, we should consider whatever lies beyond our little blue marble.

We have the means to do it, or can develop them. What we need is the political will to put it into motion. This should be our struggle, our battle.

We should provide the services necessary to everyone to bring them out of hardship, as well as take away the tools of those who promote war and destruction.

This might seem like a naïve plan, but it is one we *should* believe in as a people who wants to go beyond the rut we've been living for the past several hundred years.

Everything begins as a seed, and can grow into a tree, if it is watered and cared for well enough.

This, what I'm proposing, is a battle. A real one. It is for the soul of humanity.

How long can we go on with our dwindling resources? How long can we survive each other if all we do is sell weapons to, and use on each other? What choice, do we have, really?

Like all political action, we have three choices: Be against this, and continue as we have. Do nothing, and be just as bad as those who are against; or, my favourite, have a concerted action that will lead to the results that we want?

And remember, like everything, it's just a thought. But thought leads us to do everything, doesn't it?

Finally: How Do We Get There?

spoke a lot of the mental aspect of things, which, of course, are the main ways in which we will follow with actions. If any of this is of interest to you, you might want to pursue with your own ideas and ameliorations, which would be brilliant. Like I said, these are my general guidelines *for myself*, not so much a set of concrete rules. Here's how I do it: I write stories. Others might create memes, or songs, movies, graphic novels, or any other sort of creative endeavour.

I realize that reading a philosophy book only appeals to a very small portion of the world population. That's why different media are so important.

But there is also the concrete aspect of things: We need scientists, and environmentalists, and engineers, who want to build this future, and aren't afraid to do so.

We require industrialists who will put the money into these endeavours, regardless of the status quo.

The spreading of a set of ideals can be done in many different ways, and it is through joyfulness and enthusiasm that it should be carried on the wind to new destinations, to be planted in the brains of likeminded individuals. When the purpose is to lift burdens, why not? When the result is the uplifting of the individual, why refuse?

The thing is, since it is based on a state of mind, everything that you do, physically, will have this philosophy reflected within it. So all you need to do is live this, and you will be doing what is necessary to improve yourself, and by extension, the lives of others. That's it.

I understand most people's reticence. It sounds like hard work. To a certain degree, it is. But as I mentioned before, the amount of work you put into something will be remitted to you in satisfaction a-hundred-fold, and belongs to you the rest of your life. In short, you get back a lot more than you put in. When the action is performed by more than one person, the return is exponential.

About that last bit: Exploring possibilities on other Planets

We need to go to space because all we do is fight for diminishing resources, and for the sake of fighting. The purpose of our militaries is no longer to defend our countries, but to engage in never ending wars against vague enemies we, ourselves, create. We use jingoistic nationalist sentiment to pursue these pointless adventures that only cause untold misery for people who never did anything to us, finance the very people who attack us, give them weapons, and wait until they attack so that we may continue the circle of violence. All this to feed the military industrial complex, our main sources of revenue.

We need to go to space because we are burning through our resources at an unsustainable rate, and our population growth, even if it were to be checked, would eventually ensure our running out of the things we need, causing the extinction of the human race and/or of this planet.

We need to go to space, because we are ready. Philosophers might say that we are far from so, but we need to be confronted with the next frontier. This doesn't absolve us of our responsibilities toward our citizens of lesser means, or that we are abandoning this planet for others. Only that there are other things on which to focus than what we are fighting over now.

We need to go to space because when the technological revolution has reached its peak with AI, many of the jobs we have will be gone forever, worse still than the jobless rate we have at the moment.

We need to go to space so that those who remain at a tribalistic/religion-based system can keep doing so to their heart's content without interference. It is not our place to decide which direction a nation takes: it is theirs. Our constant meddling only antagonizes them and attracts their ire. We need to change our attention to worthy pursuits.

We need to go to space so that if ever some large celestial body comes crashing into this planet, our race will go on elsewhere.

We *need* to go to space because we are an expansionary race, and we have run out of room to expand. The economic wheels we are spinning produce nothing of great worth to the future of the human race. It has been shown that even with the relatively small budget the space programs receive, they have done much.

As well, the only nation kept out of the arms race, Japan, has been extremely successful in producing goods unrelated to weaponry. Even though this was forced upon them, and not a choice, it shows what incredible things can be achieved when the focus of our lives is not solely to produce and distribute weaponry.

This part, to me, is the most important: we need to go to space because we've lost our directing line. Beyond consumption, beyond sex, beyond feeding ourselves to excess, or being better, smarter, faster, stronger, beyond being the most violent, we absolutely, positively cannot survive without a common goal that unites us. This goal has to be other than fear or anger or greed. We've turned in on ourselves, and we must force ourselves to look outward. Where once we thought we were something else's creatures, we now know we are the product of evolution.

It behooves us to evolve even further and go beyond the confines of our birthplace to seek out new questions, and new answers. We need to do so in the spirit of exploration, not conquest. We need to do so with cooperation in mind, because it is only through openness and cooperation that we will succeed. Not as individual nations, but as a planet, and a species. The small-minded, secretive games we play against each other hold us back, and show, truly, how petty humans behave. Let us go beyond that. Let us be open, and *create*.

For that we need politicians with vision, who can set fire and purpose to the hearts of the populace. The first will be ridiculed, laughed at. They will be the pioneers. When everyone jumps on the bandwagon, they will be heralded as the heroes of the new age of truly sapient, or wise, humanity.

We need our armies to be trained in *new ways*, to be the finest officers in our fleets. Not so that we become invaders, but so that we are ready for anything. We have fine military institutions, and we will need well-trained men and women to add structure within the exploratory nature of our endeavour.

We need our moneyed classes to stop thinking in such small-minded ways when there is a lot more to be gained out there than on this planet, who are ready to help finance this human mission so that they become the heroes instead of the villains we now have.

We need our weapons manufacturers to put their R&D into space worthy weapons, defenses, and materials, so that we may be able to defend ourselves and survive come what may.

We need engineers, scientists, actors, janitors, artists, teachers, programmers, linguists, chemists, and biologists; in short, we need *everybody* for this to work. We need them for the planning stages, we need them for the construction phase, we need them to go forth into the unknown and discover for those of us who will stay behind, using the technology developed along the way to change the Earth back to a cleaner, more sustainable place. We need them because they all have a part to play. WE all have a part to play.

On top of all the jobs that we already have, there will be adjunct industries created, things we haven't even thought of, which will appear out of need, with time. New industries to employ people in areas we aren't even aware of yet.

We need individualists and adventurers, fearless people willing to go into the unknown to discover what it may hold.

We need to develop terraforming techniques to make those worlds we find uninhabitable, livable.

We have to realize this is all possible, because we once thought flying was impossible.

We have to realize this is necessary, unless the survival of our species is unnecessary.

In short, *we need to go to space.*

Coupled with the need for a better philosophy of life, I believe that the human race will be stronger and more ready for a future beyond the borders we pig-headedly cling to. Like I said, this is not just some science-fiction fantasy, but a very real need the whole of humanity must grapple with as a means to our survival.

We can do all these things, but we must start working now, and we must start working together. Not as enemies, but as allies, toward one, constructive, common goal.

I have started my journey.

I extend my hand to you in joining me, if such is what you desire.

Love is my engine and source of energy, Science is my steering wheel.

May we create the future that will carry our species, and all Earth's species into it.

Universal Wisdom

About the Author

Benoit Chartier is an author of sci-fi, fantasy, speculative fiction, short stories, a children's book, a podcast collaboration, and whatever goes through his mind. He likes to spend his days slaving over a hot computer to bring interesting thoughts coated in fiction to his readers. He shares his time between his home country of Canada and that of his spouse: Japan. He is father to two young children.

Universal Wisdom

"So we shall let the reader answer this question for himself: who is the happier man, he who has braved the storm of life and lived or he who has stayed securely on shore and merely existed?"

Hunter S. Thompson

"Most problems of teaching are not problems of growth but helping cultivate growth. As far as I know, and this is only from personal experience in teaching, I think about ninety percent of the problem in teaching, or maybe ninety-eight percent, is just to help the students get interested. Or what it usually amounts to is to not prevent them from being interested. Typically they come in interested, and the process of education is a way of driving that defect out of their minds. But if children['s] ... normal interest is maintained or even aroused, they can do all kinds of things in ways we don't understand."

Noam Chomsky

CPSIA information can be obtained
at www.ICGtesting.com
Printed in the USA
FSHW012146060122
87450FS